PRACTICAL MANX

Practical Manx

Jennifer Kewley Draskau

LIVERPOOL UNIVERSITY PRESS

First published 2008 by
Liverpool University Press
4 Cambridge Street
Liverpool L69 7ZU

British Library Cataloguing-in-Publication data
A British Library CIP record is available

ISBN 978-1-84631-131-4

Designed and typeset by Carnegie Book Production, Lancaster
Printed and bound in the European Union
by Bell and Bain Ltd, Glasgow

Contents

Preface and acknowledgements   xix
Abbreviations   xxiii

1   Initial sound change   1

                        Part 1: Lenition

1.1   Lenition in nouns   1
1.1.1   Feminine singular nouns   1
1.1.2   After possessives   2
1.1.3   After ordinal numbers   2
1.1.4   Vocatives   3
1.1.5   Genitive singular of proper nouns   3
1.1.6   After *dy*   3
1.1.7   After a preposition in fixed expressions   3
1.1.8   In compound nouns   4
1.1.9   After *dy chooilley*   5

1.2   Lenition in verbs   5
1.2.1   Inflected past, independent conditional and future relative 5
1.2.2   Verbnoun in perfect tenses   6
1.2.3   After pronouns in 'stative' constructions   6
1.2.4   After *dy*, 'in order to'   7
1.2.5   Verbnouns after prefixes   7
1.2.6   After *ry-*, *dy*, *y*   7
1.2.7   A simple table showing sound change in verb tenses   7

1.3   Lenition in adjectives   7
1.3.1   With feminine singular nouns   7
1.3.2   Vocatives   8
1.3.3   Plurals   8
1.3.4   After *feer, ro*   8
1.3.5   After prefixes   8
1.3.6   After adverbs   9

1.4	Variable lenition in nouns	9
1.4.1	Masculine genitive singular nouns after the article	9
1.4.2	Singular nouns after a preposition followed by the article	9
1.4.3	Compound nouns	10
1.4.4	Genitive of proper nouns	10
1.5	Variable lenition in adjectives	10

Part 2: Nasalisation

1.6	Regular nasalisation	11
1.6.1	After *nyn*	11
1.6.2	After *dyn*	12
1.6.3	After *cha, nagh*	12
1.7	Variable nasalisation	12
1.7.1	Voiceless consonants after *cha, dy, nagh, mannagh, my*	12
1.7.2	Present dependent of *ve*	12
1.7.3	Future dependent	12
1.7.4	Conditional dependent	13
1.7.5	Dependent in interrogatives and negatives	13
1.7.6	Verbnouns after plural object	13
1.7.7	After *er*	13
1.7.8	After genitive plural of article	14

Part 3: prefixed *h-, n-, g-*

1.8	Prefixed *h-*	14
1.8.1	After unstressed words ending in a vowel	14
1.8.2	After *ny*	15
1.8.3	Verbnouns after *dy*	15
1.8.4	Adjectives after *dy*	16
1.9	Prefixed *n-*	16
1.9.1	After *ny* in genitive plurals	16
1.9.2	In copula phrases after *cha, dy, nagh*	16
1.9.3	In future and conditional of regular verbs	16
1.9.4	After *er* in perfect tenses	16
1.10	Prefixed *g-*	16
1.10.1	With verbnoun in participial function	16
1.10.2	With *foddym, jannoo, ve*	16
	Table of mutations	18
	List of circumstances triggering mutation	19

2	Nouns	23
2.1	Gender	23
2.1.1	Feminine nouns	23
2.1.2	Masculine nouns	24
2.1.3	The default gender	25
2.1.4	Pronouns used to refer to nouns	25
2.2	Forming the plural of nouns	25
2.2.1	Adding the suffix *-yn*	25
2.2.2	Internal vowel change	25
2.2.3	Adding *-ee,* or changing *-agh* to *-ee*	26
2.2.4	Changing final *-agh* to (*-ee + yn*) = *-eeyn*	26
2.2.5	Other pluralising suffixes + *yn*	26
2.2.6	Changing *-ee, -y, -ey, -gh* to *-agh + yn*	26
2.2.7	Adding the suffix *-aghyn*	26
2.2.8	Irregular plurals	27
2.3	Collective nouns	27
2.3.1	+ singular article	27
2.3.2	+ plural adjective	27
2.3.3	+ plural pronoun	27
2.4	The declension of nouns	28
2.4.1	Nominative	28
2.4.2	Vocative	28
2.4.3	Genitive	28
2.4.4	Dative	29
2.5	Nouns formed with affixes	29
2.5.1	Nouns formed from adjectives	29
2.5.2	Forming actor-nouns	30
2.5.3	Forming nouns denoting females	30
2.5.4	Forming nouns denoting males	31
2.6	Compound nouns	32
2.7	Diminutives	32
2.8	Nouns expressing a state	33
2.8.1	*Lomarcan*	33
2.8.2	Nouns expressing a permanent state or quality	33
2.9	The verbnoun	33
2.9.1	The verbnoun as gerund	33
2.9.2	The verbnoun in nominal constructions	34
2.10	Avoidance of abstract nouns	34

3	Pronouns	35
3.1	Personal pronouns	35
3.1.1	Familiar and 'polite' forms of 'you'	35
3.1.2	Word order when both subject and object are pronouns	36
3.2	Possessive pronouns/particles	36
3.2.1	Ownership or possession	36
3.2.2	Possessives used with 'state' verbs	36
3.2.3	Possessives used with nouns to describe a state	36
3.3	Alternative construction when the object is a pronoun	37
3.4	Emphatic forms	38
3.4.1	Reinforced forms	38
3.4.2	*-hene* and *-pene*	40
3.4.3	*Hene* and possessives	41
3.5	Indefinite pronouns	41
3.6	Interrogative pronouns	41
4	Prepositions	43
4.1	Pronoun-prepositions	43
4.1.1	*ass*	43
4.1.2	*ayns*	44
4.1.3	*da*	45
4.1.4	*ec*	46
4.1.5	*er*	47
4.1.6	*fo*	48
4.1.7	*gollrish*	49
4.1.8	*gys, dys, hug*	49
4.1.9	*harrish*	50
4.1.10	*jeh*	50
4.1.11	*lesh*	51
4.1.12	*marish*	51
4.1.13	*mysh*	52
4.1.14	*rish*	53
4.1.15	*roish*	54
4.1.16	*shaghey*	54
4.1.17	*veih, voish*	55
4.2	Emphatics	55
4.3	Phrasal prepositions	55
4.3.1	'Fixed' prepositional phrases with preposition + article/ possessive particle	55

4.3.2	Possessive particle + preposition	56
4.4	'Fixed' prepositional phrases with *lesh*	60
4.4.1	*lesh* agrees with the subject	60
4.4.2	*lesh* with copula expressing 'liking'	61
4.4.3	*lesh* expressing ownership	62
5	The article	63
5.1	The singular definite article	63
5.1.1	*yn* shortened to *y*	63
5.1.2	The *y* of the article may be dropped	64
5.2	Feminine genitive singular *ny*	64
5.3	Plural definite article *ny*	64
5.4	Mutation after the article	65
5.4.1	Feminine nouns	65
5.4.2	Feminine nouns beginning with dentals	65
5.4.3	Masculine nouns in vocative and genitive	65
5.4.4	Singular nouns after preposition + article	65
5.5	Uses of the definite article	65
5.5.1	Before abstract nouns	65
5.5.2	In questions	65
5.5.3	Before noun + demonstrative	66
5.5.4	Before established compound nouns	66
5.5.5	After *lheid* and *veg*	66
5.6	The article expressing 'of' or possession	66
5.6.1	Possession expressed with article + *ec*	66
5.6.2	'of' expressed with article and two nouns	67
5.6.3	'of' in compound nouns	67
5.6.4	The article replaces a possessive	67
5.7	The article with collective nouns	68
6	Adjectives and adverbs	69
6.1	The formation of adjectives	69
6.1.1	The form of Manx adjectives	69
6.1.2	Adjectives with separate plural	70
6.1.3	Adjectives with collective noun	70
6.1.4	Adjectives with duals	70
6.1.5	Adjectives with feminine noun	70

6.2	Predicative adjectives	70
6.2.1	Subject complement	71
6.2.2	Object complement	71
6.3	Changing the meaning of an adjective through prefixes	71
6.3.1	Prefixes meaning the contrary	71
6.3.2	Prefixes changing meaning	71
6.4	The verbal or participial adjective	72
6.4.1	Uses of the participial adjective	72
6.5	Nominalised adjectives	73
6.6	Mutation after adjectives	73
6.6.1	Preceding adjectives	73
6.6.2	Possessives	74
6.7	Adverbs	75
6.7.1	Forming adverbs in Manx	75
6.7.2	Position of adverbs	75
6.7.3	Omission of the adverbial particle *dy*	76
6.7.4	Permanently lenited adverbs	77
6.8	Adverbs of direction	77
6.8.1	With *h-*, at rest	77
6.8.2	With *n-*, towards	77
6.8.3	With *s-*, away from	78
6.8.4	Compass points	78
6.8.5	Other adverbs of direction	79
6.9	Adverbial clauses	79
6.9.1	Time clauses	79
6.9.2	Place clauses	80
6.9.3	Causal clauses	80
6.9.4	Clauses of purpose and result	81
6.9.5	Clauses of concession	81
6.9.6	Clauses of condition	81
6.9.7	Clauses of comparison	83
6.10	Preceding adverbs: mutation	83
6.11	Intensifiers without *dy*	83
6.12	Prominence	83
6.13	'About to'	84
6.14	Adverbs with *ry*	84
6.14.1	*ry-hoi*	84
6.14.2	*ry-lhiattee*	84
6.14.3	*ry-cheilley*	84

6.15	Indefinite adverbs	85
6.15.1	*erbee*	85
6.15.2	*ennagh*	85
6.15.3	*erbee* (negative)	85
6.15.4	*rieau, dy bragh, çhioee*	85
6.15.5	*sheer*	86
6.16	Interrogative adverbs	86
6.17	Comparison of adjectives and adverbs	86
6.17.1	*-y* with attentuated vowel	87
6.17.2	*smoo, sloo*	87
6.17.3	Attributive comparison	87
6.17.4	Predicative adjectival comparative/superlatives	88
6.17.5	Adverbial comparative/superlatives	88
6.18	Changes in adjectives in the comparative/superlative	89
6.18.1	Monosyllabic adjectives	89
6.18.2	Stem changes	90
6.18.3	*-agh* to *-ee*	90
6.19	Irregular comparative/superlative	90
6.20	Equative comparisons	91
6.21	Comparative constructions	91
6.21.1	*chammah*, etc.	91
6.21.2	Concessive comparison	93
6.21.3	Inversion	93
7	Conjunctions	95
7.1	Co-ordinating conjunctions	95
7.1.1	*as*	95
7.1.2	*agh*	95
7.1.3	*ny*	95
7.1.4	Co-ordinating conjunctions in modern use	96
7.2	Subordinating conjunctions	96
7.2.1	*chamoo*	96
7.2.2	*choud, choud's*	96
7.2.3	*derrey*	96
7.2.4	*dy*	97
7.2.5	*fakin dy/nagh*	98
7.2.6	*ny-yeih*	98
7.2.7	*ga*	98
7.2.8	*er-y-fa, er-yn-oyr*	99
7.2.9	*dyn, gyn*	100

7.2.10	*myr*	100
7.2.11	*son*	100
7.2.12	*tra*	101
7.3	Conditions	101
7.3.1	*dy*	101
7.3.2	*my*	101
7.3.3	*my* used instead of *dy*	102
7.3.4	*erbe, er-be*	103
7.3.5	*mannagh*	103
7.3.6	*myr*	103
7.3.7	*ny slooid*	104
7.4	Conjunctions used with *dy* or *nagh*	104
8	Numerals	105
8.1	Cardinal numbers	105
8.1.1	0–20 without noun	105
8.1.2	21–30 without noun	106
8.1.3	31–39 without noun	106
8.1.4	40–59 without noun	106
8.1.5	60–100	107
8.1.6	Cardinal numbers greater than 100	107
8.1.7	Counting in scores	107
8.1.8	A modern counting system	107
8.2	Cardinal numbers with noun	108
8.2.1	Lenition after *un, daa,* etc.	108
8.2.2	Singular noun after numerals	108
8.3	Duals	108
8.3.1	Singular article	108
8.3.2	Plural adjective	108
8.3.3	*ghaa* when no noun directly follows	108
8.3.4	*jees* used instead of *daa*	109
8.4	Nouns of measure after numeral	109
8.5	Numerals preceding nouns	109
8.6	Nouns embedded in compounds	109
8.7	Numerals with *dy*	109
8.7.1	*feed* and *keead*	109
8.7.2	Plural nouns preceded by *dy*	109
8.8	Numerals used as nouns	110

8.9	Ordinal numbers	110
8.9.1	'first', 'second', third'	110
8.9.2	Other ordinals	110
8.9.3	Lenition after ordinals	111
8.9.4	Compound ordinals with a noun	111
8.10	Fractions	111
8.10.1	*lieh*	111
8.10.2	*kerroo*	112
8.11	Telling the time	112
8.11.1	Whole hours	112
8.11.2	Half past, quarter past	112
8.11.3	Minutes past the hour	112
8.11.4	Minutes and quarter to the hour	112
8.11.5	Seconds	112
8.11.6	Days	113
8.12	Mathematical terms	113
8.12.1	Geometrical figures	113
8.12.2	Decimals	113
8.12.3	Other mathematical expressions	113
9	Verbs	115
9.1	The regular verb: inflected tenses and imperative	115
9.1.1	Future	115
9.1.2	Conditional	117
9.1.3	Preterite	118
9.1.4	Future relative	119
9.1.5	Subjunctive	120
9.1.6	Past subjunctive	120
9.1.7	Imperative	120
9.1.8	Optative and jussive	121
9.1.9	Negative imperative and optative	122
9.2	Periphrastic past tenses	122
9.3	The verbnoun	123
9.4	*ve* (to be), verb and auxiliary verb	124
9.4.1	Present	124
9.4.2	Preterite	125
9.4.3	Future	126
9.4.4	Conditional	127
9.4.5	Perfect	128
9.4.6	Future perfect	129

9.4.7	Pluperfect	129
9.4.8	Imperative	131
9.5	*jannoo* (to do), verb and auxiliary verb	131
9.5.1	Present	131
9.5.2	Preterite	131
9.5.3	Future	131
9.5.4	Conditional	132
9.5.5	Imperative	132
9.5.6	Past participle	132
9.5.7	Pluperfect	132
9.6	Irregular verbs	133
9.6.1	*çheet*	133
9.6.2	*clashtyn*	133
9.6.3	*coyrt, cur*	134
9.6.4	*fakin*	134
9.6.5	*geddyn, feddyn*	135
9.6.6	*goll*	135
9.6.7	*gra*	136
9.6.8	*goaill*	136
9.7	The copula	137
9.7.1	Position of the copula	137
9.7.2	Tense of the copula	138
9.7.3	The copula in comparatives and exclamations	138
9.7.4	The copula used for emphasis	138
9.7.5	The copula in use	139
9.7.6	Omission of the copula	139
9.7.7	The 'zero' copula	140
9.7.8	The copula with preposition: *saillym, baillym*	140
9.7.9	Necessity: copula + *egin*	141
9.7.10	*Shione, bione* (know)	142
9.7.11	The copula + *lesh*: liking and preferring	143
9.7.12	Other expressions with copula + *lesh, da*	144
9.7.13	The copula + *shimmey, nhimmey*	146
9.8	Defective verbs	147
9.8.1	*foddym*	147
9.8.2	*lhisagh*	148
9.8.3	*hioll, hiollee, dobbyr*	148
9.8.4	*strooys, stroo-hene*	148
9.9	Impersonal verbs	148

9.10	The past participle	149
9.10.1	The usual formation of the past participle	149
9.10.2	Verbnouns in *-aghey*, verbs in *-ee*	150
9.10.3	Doubling of consonants	150
9.10.4	When only *-t* is added	150
9.10.5	After removal of suffix	150
9.11	The passive	151
9.11.1	*ve* + past participle	151
9.11.2	*ve* + *er* + possessive + verbnoun	151
9.11.3	*goll* + *er* + verbnoun	152
9.11.4	*ve* + *dy* + infinitive	152
9.11.5	The passive infinitive	153
10	Phrasal verbs	155
10.1	With *çheet*	155
10.2	With *cur*	156
10.3	With *geddyn*	158
10.4	With *goaill*	158
10.5	With *goll*	161
10.6	With *jannoo*	161
11	The verb in use	163
11.1	Uses of the tenses	163
11.1.1	Future and future perfect	163
11.1.2	Future relative	164
11.1.3	The past tenses: the preterite	166
11.1.4	Past tenses: periphrastic or compound past tenses	166
11.1.5	Aspect in past tenses	166
11.2	'State' verbs	169
11.3	Infinitives with *dy, y, ry-*	170
11.3.1	*dy* of purpose	170
11.3.2	*y* before *ve*	171
11.3.3	Verb with *y* functioning as a noun	172
11.3.4	*y* embedded in a phrasal verb	172
11.3.5	Infinitives formed with *ry* and verbnoun	172
11.3.6	Negative infinitives	173
11.4	Verbs requiring prepositions	174

11.5	Manx equivalents for English '-ing' forms	176
11.5.1	Gerunds	176
11.5.2	Present participles	177
11.5.3	With verbal force	179
11.4	Emphatic forms of the verb	181
11.5	English verbs expressed as phrases in Manx	181
11.5.1	'have'	181
11.5.2	'own'	182
11.5.3	'know'	182
11.5.4	'need'	183
11.5.5	'think'	183
11.5.6	'owe'	184
11.5.7	'meet'	184
11.5.8	'help' ('can't help doing something')	185
11.5.9	'be able'	185
12	Word order and sentence structure; word building	187
12.1	Sentence structure	187
12.2	Omission of the relative pronoun	188
12.3	The usual order of elements	188
12.4	Position of the object	189
12.5	The older order of elements	189
12.6	Negative, conjunctive or interrogative particles precede the verb	189
12.7	Interrogative elements precede the verb	190
12.8	Conjunctions with the conditional	190
12.9	Avoidance of the subjunctive	191
12.10	Periphrastic constructions	191
12.11	Word order in copula sentences	192
12.12	Statements of existence	192
12.13	Subordinate clauses	193
12.13.1	Reported speech, and verbs of asking, fearing, thinking	193
12.13.2	Verbs of requesting, advising, commanding	193
12.13.3	Relative clauses	193
12.14	Nominal phrases	196

12.15	Verbal phrases	197
12.15.1	Simple verbal phrases	197
12.15.2	Complex verbal phrases	198
12.15.3	Position of adverbial elements	199
12.16	Word building with affixes	199
12.16.1	*aa-*	199
12.16.2	*co-*	200
12.16.3	*lieh-*	200
12.16.4	*myn-*	200
12.16.5	*ooilley-*	200
12.16.6	*do-* and *so-*	200
12.16.7	*ym-, yl-*	200
12.16.8	*yn-*	201
12.16.9	Negatives	201
13	Dates and seasons	203
13.1	Seasons	203
13.2	Months	203
13.3	Days of the week	204
13.4	Expressions about days and nights	204
13.5	Times of day	205
13.6	Periods of time	205
13.7	Festivals	205
14	Emphasis	207
14.1	Word order	207
14.2	Copula	208
14.3	Emphatic elements may be added	208
14.3.1	Personal pronouns	208
14.3.2	Verbal inflections	209
14.3.3	Emphatic pronoun-prepositions	209
14.3.4	Emphatic adverbs	210
14.4	Emphatic personal pronouns	210
14.4.1	For emphasis	210
14.4.2	For contrast	211
14.4.3	As the antecedent of a relative clause	211
14.4.4	Emphatic imperative	211

15	Spelling and pronunciation	213
15.1	The spelling system	213
15.2	Pronunciation: regional variation	214
15.2.1	Vowels: general	214
15.2.2	Pronouncing vowels and diphthongs	216
15.2.3	Writing vowels and diphthongs	220
15.3	Consonants	223
15.3.1	Broad and slender consonants	223
15.3.2	Pronouncing consonants	224
15.3.3	'Intrusive' consonants	228
15.4	Stress	228
15.4.1	In numbers	229
15.4.2	In diminutives	229
15.5	Elision	229
15.6	Intonation	230
Gist English translations of recorded Manx conversations		231
Glossary		255
Select bibliography		293

Preface and acknowledgements

Manx, like Scottish Gaelic and Irish, is a Goidelic language. Other authorities have provided overviews of the Celtic languages, detailed accounts of their phonology, bilingual dictionaries, histories of Manx, creative writing in Manx, course-books and primers. This is not the place for any of that. Interested readers are advised to consult Cregeen, Goodwin, Kelly, Kneen, Pilgrim, Stowell, Thomson, and other authorities featured in the bibliography.

For various reasons, its present spelling system differs radically from traditional Goidelic spelling, but in other respects Manx displays many similarities with related languages and is to some degree intelligible to speakers of Irish and Scots Gaelic, once they have recovered from the initial shock of its orthography. The system itself is riddled with exceptions and some inconsistencies. Hyphenation is variable in Manx as in most languages. The hyphens and apostrophes used throughout this book represent one option, perhaps the most current at time of writing, but it is not the intention to present a prescriptive system.

It will be noted that the examples in this book are taken from as broad a spectrum as possible, from both spoken and written modes, and from the various chronological stages of Manx: from the earliest known texts and from Classical written Manx to twenty-first-century writers and poets, from the recorded speech of the so-called 'Late Manx' native speakers to that of today's fluent speakers. Initials after the examples refer to four speakers recorded in spontaneous Manx conversation while this book was being written. Their conversations feature on the accompanying website: http://www.practicalmanx.com. The speakers recorded are:

B	Mr Bernard Caine
W	the late Mr Walter Clarke RBV[1]
J	Mr Juan Crellin RBV
L	the late Mr Leslie Quirk RBV

[1] RBV: Reih Bleeaney Vanannan award for outstanding contribution to Manx culture.

Leslie Quirk died at the age of 90 before the recordings were complete. Walter Clarke died the year after their completion. All honour to them, keepers of the flame, and to the thriving new generation of speakers. If this book serves to demonstrate one thing, it is the stubborn resilience of the Manx language and the language community despite the many setbacks (many people outside the Isle of Man still think Manx is dead, others remain bitterly affronted by its revival!).

Manx is a rich and expressive language: while its lexicon is being replenished through the efforts of translators and revivalists, its syntax has long offered speakers a wide array of options and nuances of expression. The aim of this book is to include as many of these syntactic options as possible, with authentic examples of their use, taken from as many different stages in the language's development as possible.

Technically, the focus is on the fundamental principles of Manx grammar (syntax and morphology): however, the object is to combine and consolidate existing work, and to provide useful and accessible insights for the language user, rather than to reinvent the wheel or to produce yet another prescriptive textbook. For readers curious about the way Manx grammar functions, in some places literal transcriptions ('parsing') are provided under the examples. These may safely be ignored by readers who regard grammar with fear and loathing.

As well as a bibliography, at the end of the book there is a glossary of the terms used, with definitions. The various sections are cross-referred to by number.

To vindicate and promote the resurgence of Manx, the language must be kept alive through use. It must be spoken, written, sung, exploited to the full for the communication of concepts and the expression of ideas. The sole aim of this endeavour has been to provide support and encouragement for those who wish to do just that.

The enterprise was undertaken with the generous support of the Manx Heritage Foundation. The knowledgeable advice of MHF's Charles Guard was invaluable.

Many other dedicated people helped in the preparation of this book: Adrian Cain, *Yn Greinneyder*; Dr P. J. Davey, former Director, Centre for Manx Studies; Mrs Rosemary Derbyshire, Manx Language Officer; Hon. Philip Gawne, MHK, Minister for Agriculture; Andrew Hamer and Dr Breesha Maddrell, University of Liverpool; Dr Brian Stowell, crusader, author, teacher, translator, broadcaster, and pioneering first Manx Language Officer, in more ways than one *primus inter pares*. Above all, the debt to Adrian Pilgrim, whose knowledge is as profound as his generosity is boundless, is quite irreparable. *Bannaghtyn*, Adrian!

On the other hand, I myself may with a clear conscience lay claim to any omissions or errors which remain. Like the Rev. Philip Moore, whose proficiency greatly exceeded my own, 'I do not pretend to a profundity of skill in our language, but am only a plain Manxman' (Rev. Philip Moore to Bishop Hildesley, 21 January 1764).

Jennifer Kewley Draskau

2008

Abbreviations

The following abbreviations are used in some places in this book (for instance in Chapters 12 and 14):

ART	article
CON	conjunction
COP	copula
DEP	dependent form of the verb
EMPH	emphatic
FUT	future
INTER	interrogative
NEG	negative
PART	particle
PREP	preposition
PRES	present tense
REL	relative

For full definitions of these terms, see the Glossary.

1   Initial sound change
Caghlaa sheeanyn ec toshiaght goan

In Manx, as in all Celtic languages, the beginnings of words may undergo changes. These are of two kinds: mutation, and the prefixing of a consonant.

a) Mutation occurs in two forms

Lenition (sometimes called 'aspiration')
Nasalisation (sometimes called 'eclipsis')

b) The prefixed consonants *h-*, *n-* and *g-*

At the end of this chapter you will find a reference table of lenition and nasalisation, and a list of the circumstances that trigger them. The different 'triggers' affect a small number of consonants in different ways: for this reason, the table divides lenition into three types, nasalisation into two, depending on the different changes that occur in this handful of consonants. The numerals in brackets (1), (2), (3) identify the type of lenition or nasalisation shown on the mutation table at the end of this section.

1 Part 1: Lenition

Lenition or aspiration is the 'softening' of the first consonant of a word in certain circumstances. It is of two types: regular and variable. The base form is shown in brackets after the example.

1.1   Regular lenition in common and proper nouns: (for verbnouns, see 1.2)

1.1.1   (2) In feminine singular nouns after the definite article *y*, *yn* (see 5)

y ven (ben)   the woman

Initial *s-* mutates as follows:

> *s-* followed by a vowel → *t-*
> yn tooill (*sooill*)   the eye
>
> *sh-* followed by a vowel → *çh-*
> y çhuyr (*shuyr*)   the sister
>
> *sl-* → *cl-*
> yn clat (*slat*)   the rod
>
> *str-* → *tr-*
> y traid (*straid*)   the street

Exceptions:

a) In some cases the 'dentals' *çh-, d-, j-, t-* do not lenite

> y çhibbyr   the well
> y duillag   the leaf

b) *f-* does not always lenite and is often retained where, according to the rules of lenition, you might expect it to disappear

> y frough   the mist
> y fuill   the blood

1.1.2   (1) After possessives
Lenition occurs after the possessives (see 3.2.1) *my, my; dty,* your singular; *e* (m) his, its:

> my hie (*thie*) my house (*thie*)   my charrey (*carrey*) my friend
> dty hie   your (sg) (thy) house dty voddey   your dog
> e hie   his house   e ven   his wife

1.1.3   After numbers
Lenition (1) occurs after all the ordinal numbers ending in *-oo* (see 8.9.2, 8.9.3) and also after any cardinal numbers which include *daa* (two):

> daa ghooinney   two men
> daa ghooinney yeig   twelve men

Exception: Lenition type (2) occurs in ordinal numbers after the article *y(n)*:

> Elam yn wheiggoo (*queig*)   Elam the fifth
> Jehohanan yn çheyoo (*shey*)   Jehohanan the sixth
> Elioenai yn çhiaghtoo (*shiaght*)   Elioenai the seventh

Exception: Lenition type (3), where initial *t-*, *d-*, and also *s-*, *çh-* and *j-* do not change, occurs after *un* (one) or *chied* (first). Very occasionally this also applies to *trass*, third.

un vac (*mac*)	one son
un charrey (*carrey*)	one friend
but *un dooinney*	one man
daa vac, daa charrey, daa ghooinney	two sons, two friends, two men
jean-jee eh yn trass cheayrt	do it the third time
	[I Kings xviii.34]
yn trass persoon	the third person
	[Fargher 1979: 774]

1.1.4   (1) In vocatives
Lenition occurs in vocatives (see 2.4.2) both singular and plural:

Ghooinney! (*dooinney*)	Man!
Yuan! (*Juan*)	John!
Yee! (*Jee*)	God!
Chaarjyn! (*caarjyn*)	Friends!

1.1.5   (1) In the genitive singular of proper nouns
Lenition occurs in the genitive singular of all proper nouns:

thie Yuan (*Juan*)	John's house
mac Voirrey (*Moirrey*)	Mary's son

The genitive shows ownership or possession (see 2.4.3)
Exceptions: Most foreign names, except for certain Biblical ones, are not usually lenited at all. Sometimes the names of males do not lenite, either, in modern Manx.

1.1.6   (1) After the preposition *dy*

lane dy vree (*bree*)	full of life, energy
punt dy hoo (*soo*)	a pound of jam
palchey dy vess (*mess*)	plenty of fruit
goll dy valley (*balley*)	going (to) home

1.1.7   (1) After a preposition in certain fixed expressions

gyn vree (*bree*)	without energy
gyn yss (*fys*) *da*	unaware (without knowledge) of
fo halloo (*thalloo*)	underground
fo harey (*sarey*)	under orders
fo lieau (*slieau*)	under (at the foot of) a mountain

paart dy gheiney (deiney)	some men
ry-chosh (cass)	by the foot, on foot

but *fo boayrd*   under a table

gyn shugyr   without sugar

1.1.8   In compound nouns
The second element of compound nouns usually lenites:

a) (1) After the prefixes *aa-, co-, lhiass-, lieh-, mee-, neu-*

aa-hilley (shilley)	second sight
aa-chlashtyn (clashtyn)	rehearsal
co-haglym (çhaglym)	congress, meeting
co-chruinnaght (cruinnaght)	gathering
lieh-chiarkyl (kiarkyl)	semi-circle
lhiass-vac, lhiass-voir (mac, moir)	step-son, step-mother
mee-chredjue (credjue)	disbelief
mee-chairys (cairys)	injustice
neu-hickyrys (shickyrys)	uncertainty

Sometimes *f-* may be retained:

aafilley	evolution	
co-fendeilagh	co-defendant	
meefollanid	unhealthiness (of climate)	
lieh-faill	half pay	[Kelly 1991]

b) (1) In a genitive noun after another noun which is feminine singular

ooh-chirkey (kiark f)	hen's egg
meinn-chorkey (corkey m)	oat-meal

Again, initial *f-* is sometimes retained:

meinn-flooyr	breadstuffs	[Kelly 1991]

c) After a prefixed adjective
Certain adjectives which, unlike most Manx adjectives, normally precede
the noun, cause it to lenite, also in compounds:
drogh, bad (1):

drogh vraane (mraane)	bad women
drogh-chooilleen (cooilleen)	revenge
drogh-haghyrt (taghyrt)	accident

(Type 3): *çh-, d-, j-, s-, t-* do not lenite after prefixed adjectives ending in *-d, -n*:
ard-, high:

ard-çhiarn	sovereign lord
ard-saggyrt	high priest
ard-valley (balley)	city, capital
ard-ghoo (goo)	fame, renown

shenn, old:

shenn ven (ben)	old woman, crone, ancestress
shenn warree (mwarree)	grandmother
shenn sidoor	veteran, old soldier

1.1.9   (1) After *dy chooilley*

dy chooilley pheiagh (peiagh)	every person
dy chooilley ghooinney (dooinney)	every man

However, *gagh, dagh*, which also mean 'each', 'every', do not cause lenition (in spite of an indication to the contrary in Wood's dictionary of 1950):

dagh peiagh, dagh dooinney	each person, each man

1.2   (1) Regular lenition in regular verbs

1.2.1   In the inflected past, independent conditional and future relative
coayl (to lose):

Past:	*chaill mee, chaill oo*	I lost, you lost, etc.

Conditional independent:
chaillin, chaillagh oo	I would lose, you would lose, etc.

Future relative: *my chaillym*, etc.   if I shall (will) lose, etc.
yn argid chaillym   the money (which) I shall/will lose

troggal (to lift/build):

Past:	*hrog eh*	he lifted

Conditional independent:
hroggagh ad	they would lift

Future relative: *my hroggys eh*   if he will lift
y thie hroggys eh   the house (which) he will build

1.2.2   (1) Lenition in the verbnoun in perfect tenses
Lenition occurs in the verbnoun after *er, er ny*, in the perfect, pluperfect and past conditional tenses:

a) In the perfect tenses

Perfect: *cha nel shiu er ghra (gra)*   you have not said

Pluperfect: *v'ee er chur* (or *choyrt*) *(cur)*   she had given

Past conditional: *veagh eh er chlashtyn (clashtyn)* he would have heard

It is now more usual in cases like these to find lenition rather than nasalisation, but some common verbs still seem to prefer nasalisation, especially those beginning with a dental consonant:

> *Vel ee er vakin? (fakin)*   Did she see?

b) With first, second or third person (masculine only) singular pronoun object (*my, dty,* and *ny*)

> *V'ad er my* (or *m'*) *akin*   *(fakin)*   They had seen me
> *T'eh er dty chlashtyn*   *(clashtyn)*   He has heard you

c) When the subject is a singular pronoun in a literary sentence in the passive

> *V'eh er ny chlashtyn*   He was heard
> *T'eh er ny akin (fakin)*   It is seen
> *Row uss er dty ghreimmey? (greimmey)*   Were you bitten?

Note: lenition in these cases occurs after the third person singular only in the masculine and not after third person singular feminine.

> *T'ee er ny fakin*   She is seen

1.2.3   (1) After pronouns in stative constructions
Lenition occurs after pronouns *my, dty, ny* in the special 'stative' constructions, where the verb expresses an ongoing situation or semi-permanent state, rather than an action or event (see 3.2.2 and 11.2):

> *Ta mee my hassoo (shassoo)*   I am standing
> *V'ou dty chadley (cadley)*   You were sleeping (asleep)
> *V'eh ny chadley (cadley)*   He was sleeping

and

> *T'eh ny ghaaue (gaaue)*   He is a blacksmith
> *V'eh ny er-ynsee (fer-ynsee)*   He was a teacher

1.2.4   (1) After *dy* (in order) to

ta mee goll dy chur shilley orroo	I am going to visit (put a sight on) them
aarloo dy gholl ersooyl	ready to go away

1.2.5   (1) In verbnouns after prefixes *aa-, co-, mee-, neu-*

aa-hroggal (*troggal*)	rebuild
co-akin (*fakin*) (to see)	interview
mee-chredjal (*credjal*)	disbelieve
neu-chassey (*cass*)	untwist, unwind

[Fargher 1979: 830]

1.2.6   (1) After *ry-, dy* and *y*

Bee yn thie er ny chreck (*creck*)		The house will be sold
ry-akin	(*fakin*)	to be seen
ry-gheddyn	(*geddyn*)	to be got, had
ry-chreck	(*creck*)	to be bought, for sale
ry-heshaght	(*çheshaght*)	in company

1.2.7   A simple table showing initial sound change in verb tenses

Tense	Independent	Dependent	Interrogative	Vowels prefix
Regular Preterite:	lenition	lenition	lenition	*d-*
Conditional:	lenition	restricted nasalisation	restricted nasalisation	*n-*
Future:		restricted nasalisation	restricted nasalisation	*n-*

1.3   Regular lenition in adjectives

1.3.1   With feminine singular nouns

a) (1) After feminine singular nouns in the nominative and accusative (see 2)

y ven vooar (*mooar*)	the large woman
ben verçhagh (*berçhagh*)	a rich woman
awin ghowin (*dowin*)	a deep river
eddin waagh (*bwaagh*)	a pretty face

b) (2) In adjectives which follow the article before a feminine singular noun

shenn ven	old woman
yn çhenn ven	the old woman
shenn lioar	an old book
yn çhenn lioar	the old book

1.3.2   (1) In most vocatives, both singular and plural

Ghooinney choar!	Dear man!
Chaarjyn veen!	Dear friends!

Note: *Vraane as gheiney seyrey!*   Ladies and gentlemen!

1.3.3   (1) Plural adjectives lenite after

a) a singular noun lenited by *daa*

daa inneen veggey	two little girls

b) a collective noun

mooinjer veggey	little people

1.3.4   After *feer*, **ro**

a) (1) After *ro*, too

ro vooar (mooar)	too large

b) (3) After *feer*, very, and *lane*, quite, completely, the 'dentals' *t-*, *d-*, *çh-*, *j-*, and *s-* do not lenite

feer trome	very heavy	
feer jymmoosagh	very wrathful	[Esther i.12]

Y dooinney ta feer seyr as jesheenagh ny-vud eu
The man that is tender among you, and very delicate
                                    [Deuteronomy xxviii.54]

T'ou lane keoie	You're completely mad	[WC]

1.3.5   (1) After the prefixes *aa-*, *an-*, *co-*, *mee-*, *neu-*, *ree-*

aa-chlashtynagh (clashtyn)	appealable
anghowin (dowin)	shallow
co-gherrey (derrey)	equidistant
mee-hreisht (treisht)	distrustful, despairing
neu-ghooie (dooie)	unkind, barren

ree-veg	tiny, extra small, infinitesimal
ree-vie	excellent
ree-vooar	outsize

and some compound adjectives:

trome-chadlagh (cadlagh)	sleepy

1.3.6 (1) Adjectives and adverbs are lenited after preceding adverbs Adverbs which precede the adjective or adverb they intensify, or otherwise modify, cause lenition, changing the first sound of the following word

braew	extremely (literally: 'fine')
braew vie	very good, well (*mie*, good)
ro	too, excessively
ro vooar	too large
mie	good, well
mie chiune	well calm

(*kiune*, calm) (compare English 'well good', 'nice and calm')

Exception: (3) words beginning with *s-, sh-, d-, t-, j-, çh-* do not change after:

feer	very	*feer vie*	very good
lane	quite	*lane vie*	quite good
feer dree		very tedious	
feer çheh		very hot	
lane jymmoosagh		very angrily	

1.4   Variable lenition in nouns

1.4.1   (2) In masculine nouns after the article in the genitive singular

carrey yn vac (mac)	friend of the son
mac yn er (fer)	the man's son

(Type 2) *t-, d-, f-, çh-, j-* do not lenite in this position:
   ushag y juys   goldcrest (*juys*, fir)

1.4.2   (2) Singular nouns after a preposition followed by the article, *y (yn)*

car y touree (souree)	over the summer
da'n taggyrt (saggyrt)	to the priest
ayns y çhirveish (shirveish)	in the service

gys y clieau (slieau)   to the mountain
fo'n treean (streean)   under the bridle

(Type 2) *çh-, d-, j-, t-* are not affected:

laa yn Çhiarn   the Lord's Day

1.4.3   (1) In the second noun of compound nouns

a) When the first part of the compound noun is a prefixed adjective

ard-chloie (cloie)   star turn, high jinks
ooilley-Cheltiaghys (Celtiaghys)   pan-Celticism

b) When the first part of the compound noun is a noun
In Manx, when compound nouns are made up from two nouns, the second noun (like the first noun of similarly-formed compound nouns in English) really functions like an adjective and tells us more specifically 'what kind of':

boalley cloaie   stone wall (a wall made from stone)
lioar-skeeal   story book (a book of stories)
pabyr-naight   newspaper (a paper containing news)
blein vishee   leap year (*bishee*, of increase)
ben-varrey   mermaid (sea-wife, woman of the sea)
                    (*marrey*, of the sea)

These examples contain feminine nouns in the genitive singular. Exception: *t, d, çh, j,* and in this case also *n, l, s, sh,* do not mutate. Initial *f* is sometimes retained:

fer-fysseree   astrologer
guilley-faaie   groundsman   [Kelly 1991]

1.4.4   (1) In the genitive of proper nouns
Names in the genitive usually lenite:

Co-chorp Ghoolish   Douglas Corporation

(although this particular form has been avoided on their vans!)

1.5   Variable lenition in adjectives
Adjectives may lenite:
(1) After plural nouns where the plural is formed

a) by vowel change alone

tuill ghoo (sg towl)   black holes

b) by changing -*agh* to -*ee*

peccee hreih (sg *peccagh*)	miserable sinners
kellee rangagh (sg *frangagh*)	turkeys
loaytree heear (sg *sheear*)	western speakers

Exception: Where a word ends in -*d*, -*l*, -*n*, -*sh*, -*s*, -*r*, and the following word begins with *çh*-, *d*-, *j*-, *s*-, *sh*-, lenition may not occur:

ben-çhiarn	lady
feer sheeoil	very peaceful

Adjectives in *çh*-, *s*-, *sh*-, and *t*- are often not lenited after prefixes:

anshickyr	insecure
co-soylagh	similar

1 Part 2: Nasalisation

The changes caused by nasalisation are shown in the Table of Mutations at the end of this section, divided into two types, depending on whether or not *b*, *d*, *g*, and *j* are affected.

1.6   (1) Regular nasalisation

1.6.1   After *nyn* (our/your (pl) their)

a) in nouns

nyn gaarjyn (*caarjyn*)	our/your/their friends
nyn goamrey (*coamrey*)	clothing, our/your/their clothing
shinyn nyn beccee hreih (*peccee*)	we miserable sinners

b) In verbnouns in 'stative' constructions

T'ad nyn gadley (*cadley*)	They are asleep, sleeping
T'ad nyn daaue (*taaue*)	They are idling

c) After *er nyn* with a preceding plural object in passive constructions

Va ymmodee eabbaghyn er nyn yannoo (*jannoo*)
Many attempts were made

T'ad er nyn goayl (*coayl*)
They are lost (= have been lost)

V'ad er nyn vakin er y traid (*fakin*)
They were seen in the street

1.6.2   (1) Regular nasalisation occurs after *dyn* with a plural pronoun object (us/you plural them) in literary constructions

T'eh dyn vakin (fakin)
He sees us/you (pl)/them

Ta mish dyn goyrt shiu magh (coyrt)	I send you out
T'eh dyn vaagail (shin) (= t'eh faagail shin)	He is leaving us

1.6.3   (2) Regular nasalisation occurs after *cha, nagh* in copula verbal phrases and interrogatives

Nagh gooin lesh? (cooinaghtyn)	Doesn't he remember?
Cha gooin lesh (cooinaghtyn)	He doesn't remember
Cha dreih lhiam (treih)	I'm not sorry

1.7   Variable nasalisation
In the following cases nasalisation is now variable:

1.7.1   (2) In the voiceless consonants only (*p, t, th, c, k, qu, çh, ch, f*) after *cha* (not), *dy* (that), *nagh* (that not), *mannagh* (if not, unless), *my* (before) (conditional and future only)

cha n'aagym (faagail)	I shall not leave
dy drog eh (troggal)	that he will lift
nagh gionnee ad (kionnaghey)	that they will not buy
mannagh gooinee shiu (cooinaghtyn)	if you do not remember
dy gaillin (coayl)	if I were to lose
(roish) my jyndaa oo (çhyndaa)	(before) you return

1.7.2   In the present dependent of *ve* (to be)

Vel oo fakin nagh vel ad goll?   Do you see that they are not going?

1.7.3   In the future dependent of other verbs

Cha greidym y lheid shen (credjal)   I will not believe such a thing
[John xx:25]

Ta treisht aym dy vaikmayd oo reesht (fakin)
I hope we shall see you again

dy drog eh (troggal)	that he will lift
nagh gionnee ad (kionnaghey)	that they will not buy
(roish) my jyndaa oo (çhyndaa)	(before) you return

1.7.4   In the conditional dependent

Cha greidin shen (credjal)
I should (would) not believe that

Va aggle orrym dy duittagh eh (tuittym)	I was afraid he would fall
Saillym dy greckagh eh eh (creck)	I wish he would sell it
Mannagh gooineeagh shiu (cooinaghtyn)	If you did not remember
Dy gaillin (coayl)	If I were to lose

1.7.5   (2) In the dependent form used for interrogatives and negatives

Gionnee oo? (kionnaghey)	Will you buy?
Gionneeagh oo? (kionnaghey)	Would you buy?
Cha dannee eh (tannaghtyn)	He will not wait
Cha danneeagh eh (tannaghtyn)	He would not wait

1.7.6   (1) In verbnouns after a plural object which is preceded by *er* or *dy*

T'eh dyn dilgey ad 'syn aile   He is throwing them in the fire

(In this example, *dy + nyn = dyn*):

1.7.7   (1) Sometimes nasalisation occurs after *er* (after), in the perfect tense of (mainly) irregular verbs, although usually it is lenition that occurs rather than nasalisation

Cha row shin er vakin (fakin)	We had not seen
T'eh er n'gholl (goll)	He has gone
Cha beagh shiu er n'gheddyn (geddyn)	You would not have got
Veagh oo er jeet (çheet)	You would have come
Vel ad er jeet dy valley? (çheet)	Have they come home?

* Note: *'n'* is prefixed to an initial vowel:

T'eh er n'aase (aase)   He has grown

The mutation of *'f'* + vowel varies between *n'* and *v*:

Ta shin er vakin /er n'akin yn ard-valley (fakin)
We have seen the city

1.7.8   (1) In nouns, nasalisation is still sometimes found after the genitive plural of the article *ny*. Usually nowadays this is found only in set phrases and place names

Close ny Gabbil	Enclosure of the Horses
Bwoaillee ny Mayr	Fold of the Roads
Bwoaillee nyn Giark	Hens' fold
shooyl ny dhieyn	walking the houses*

* which presumably means begging, although it was a proud traditional boast that begging was unknown in the Island

1 Part 3: prefixed *h-*, *n-*, *g-*

In addition to the two kinds of mutation, another change may occur in Manx at the beginning of words. A consonant may be prefixed to an initial vowel.

This consonant is usually *h-* or *n-*, but is sometimes *g-*. *g-* is prefixed to verbnouns for grammatical reasons but has been included here because it affects the initial sound of words.

1.8   *h-* is prefixed to the initial vowel of a stressed word in these circumstances:

1.8.1   After unstressed words ending in a vowel
This sounds more complicated that it is; the examples should clarify the situation. In a stressed word which starts with a vowel and follows a connected but unstressed word which ends in a vowel, in cases where, if the stressed word had begun with a consonant instead of a vowel, neither lenition nor nasalisation would have been required or appropriate, *h-* may be prefixed to the initial vowel of the stressed word: typically these preceding unstressed words will be:

a) a possessive such as *e* (her)

e haght	her skill	*e haegid*	her youth	*e heam*	her cry
e hidd	her hats	*e hobbal*	her denial	*e huillin*	her elbow

hug ee graih e hannym da   she conceived a passion for him
(literally: she gave the love of her soul to him (*annym*, soul))

b) the particle *dy*

Ghow eh dy holk eh   He took it badly (*olk*, bad)

Note: Prefixed '*h-*' was not always written, but it was usually pronounced. At other times, even in very early texts, it was written:

Ghow ad dy holk (olk) rish   They were very sorry

[Matthew xviii.31, 1745]

1.8.2   In nouns with an initial vowel after the article *ny*

a) *Ny* may refer to a feminine singular subject

T'ee ny hAlbinagh	She is a Scotswoman
V'ee ny hinneen veg vitçhooragh	She was a naughty little girl
Ta Maria ny hIddaalagh	Maria is Italian

b) *Ny* may precede a genitive feminine singular noun

Ayraghyn ny hAgglish	Fathers of the Church (*agglish*, church)
eeanlee ny h-aer	birds of the air (*aer*, air)
Purt ny hInshey	Peel ('Port of the Island' (*innis, innys*, island))
ny heayst	of the moon (*eayst*, moon)
arrey ny hoie	the night watch (*oie*, night)

c) *Ny* may precede a plural noun

ny hooillyn	the eyes
blass ny hooylyn	taste of the apples
Jannoo ny hOstyllyn	the Acts of the Apostles

d) *Ny* may be used in a passive sentence where the subject is feminine

V'ee er ny haarlaghey	It was prepared
Va'n cheyrrey er ny hoanluckey	The sheep was buried

In the following examples the prefixed '*h*' is pronounced but not always written:

ny (h)arraneyn	the songs
ny (h)ushagyn	the birds

1.8.3   Verbnouns after *dy* representing a feminine object in written Manx

T'ad dy himman	They drive her (*imman*, drive)

1.8.4   Adjectives after the adverbial particle *dy* prefix *h-*
Many adverbs in Manx are formed by placing the particle *dy* in front
of the adjective (see 6.7).

The *h-* prefixed to adjectives with an initial vowel after *dy* is heard
but very rarely written:

dy holk	(*olk*)	badly, wickedly
dy houryssagh	(*ouryssagh*)	suspiciously
dy himneagh	(*imneagh*)	anxiously
dy harryltagh	(*arryltagh*)	willingly

1.9   *n-* is sometimes prefixed to initial vowels

1.9.1   After *ny* in genitive plurals
This happens chiefly in place names such as *Lough ny Nedd*.

1.9.2   In copula phrases after *cha, dy, nagh*

Cha naillym   I shall not wish
Nagh ninsh eh?   Will he not tell?

1.9.3   In regular dependent forms, in the future and conditional
tenses, of verbs beginning with a vowel

Cha niuin shen (*iu*, drink)   I sh/would not drink that

Nagh neeagh oo dty yinnair? (*ee*, eat)
Wouldn't you eat your dinner?

1.9.4   After *er* in perfect tenses of verbnouns beginning with a vowel

T'eh er nynsaghey Gaelg (*ynsaghey*, learn)
He has learned Manx

1.10   *g-* may be prefixed to a verbnoun beginning with a vowel for
grammatical reasons

1.10.1   When the verbnoun is functioning as a present participle

As honnick eh ad geiyrt er (*eiyr*, follow, drive)
And he saw them following him   [John i.39]

1.10.2   With *foddym, jannoo* and *ve*, even where the verbnoun is
functioning as a verbnoun rather than as a present participle
(see 9)

Cha vel eh lowal dhyt gymmyrkey dty lhiabbee (*ymmyrkey*, bear, carry)
It is not lawful for thee to carry thy bed   [John v.10]

Here the traditional construction would be:

Cha vel eh lowal dhyt dty lhiabbee y ymmyrkey

Exception: *ooashlaghey*, worship, never seems to prefix *g-*. It doesn't seem to form inflected tenses either:

Dy jarroo, t'ad ooashlaghey   In truth, they worship

[Isaiah xlvi.6]

Ren ny ayraghyn ain ooashlaghey Jee er y clieau shoh
Our fathers worshipped God on this mountain   [John iv.20]

Chamoo t'ou er ooashlaghey mish lesh dty hebballyn
Neither hast thou honoured me with thy sacrifices

[Isaiah xliii.23]

Table of mutations

Note: This table is intended as a guide and for quick reference, so it doesn't include many definitions or examples. At first sight it may look fairly daunting: however, in reality, many modern speakers at times muddle or omit mutations and this does not appear to impede communication to any appreciable degree. The best speakers make allowances for new speakers who are getting used to the system (and even the experts sometimes make mistakes themselves), and all languages change all the time. So if at first mutation takes some getting used to, the main thing is not to be discouraged but to aim to get as much practice as possible in speaking and listening to Manx. Learners of German and Russian, for example, start by finding the case systems of these languages extremely challenging but with practice these things become much easier, if not quite second nature.

Table of mutations

The 'radical' is the first letter of the word as given in most dictionaries and word lists (except Cregeen, who often lists the mutated initial letters as well, helpfully giving the radical in the margin).
'n.c.' means the radical does not change, or mutate.

Lenition (Aspiration)		Nasalisation (Eclipsis)	
Radical	**Types 1, 2 and 3**	**Radical**	**Types 1 and 2**
b	v	c	g
bw, boo	v *or* w	çh	j
c	ch	f	v
f	disappears	k	g
g	gh	p	b
gi	ghi *or* yi	t	d
k	ch		
m	v		
mw, moo	v *or* w		
p	ph		
qu	wh		

	Type 1	Type 2	Type 3		Type 1	Type 2
s	h	t	n.c.	b	m	n.c.
sh	h	çh	n.c.	d	n*	n.c.
sl	l	cl *or* tl†	n.c.	g	ng *or* n'gh	n.c.
shl	l	n.c.	n.c.	j	n'y *or* y	n.c.
sn	n	tn†	n.c.			
str	hr	tr	n.c.			
çh	h	n.c.	n.c.			
d, dh	gh	n.c.	n.c.			
j	y	n.c.	n.c.			
t, th	h.	n.c.	n.c			

* often written gh
† rare

These changes to the initial letter(s) of a word are found:
(V indicates where the occurrence of the mutation is variable)

Lenition type 1

1.   after the numeral *daa*

2.   after all ordinal numerals ending in *-oo*; after *dy chooilley* (every)

3.   in the vocative case of singular and plural nouns and adjectives

4.   after the possessive adjectives *my*, *dty* and *e* (= his)

5.   in the genitive case of names (V for names of males)

6.   after the prefixes *aa-*, *mee-*, *neu-* (but *f-* often remains)

7.   after a preceding prefixed adjective, e.g. *drogh-* (but see also 24 below)

8.   in a noun following a preposition in certain set phrases, e.g. *fo halloo*, *gyn vree*

9.   in the second element of a compound noun after a feminine singular

10.   in an adjective after a feminine singular noun

11.   in an adjective following a collective noun preceded by *y(n)* (V)

12.   in an adjective after a masculine singular noun in the genitive case (V)

13.   in an adjective after a noun where the plural ends in *-ee* or is formed by internal vowel change, e.g. *kiyt*, *dew* (V)

14.   in an adjective or adverb after the adverbs *ro*, *ree-*, *mie*, *kiune*

15.   after *by* (nasalisation is often incorrectly found here)

16.   in verbnouns after *my*, *dty*, *ny* (masc. only), *ry-*, *dy* and *y*

17.   in the preterite, independent conditional and relative form of regular, and most irregular, verbs

18.   in the regular verb-noun after *er* in the perfect tense (V with nasalisation)

Lenition type 2

19.   in feminine singular nouns after *y(n)*

20. in masculine singular nouns in the genitive case after *y(n)* (V)

21. in singular nouns after a preposition and *y(n)* (V)

22. in ordinal numerals after *y(n)*

Lenition type 3

23. after the numerals *un* and *chied*

24. after *feer* and *lane*

25. after a preceding prefixed adjective ending in -*d*, -*n*, e.g. *ard, shenn*

Nasalisation type 1†

26. after *nyn*

27. after *dyn* when this represents a preceding plural pronoun object

28. after *er* in the perfect tense of (mainly) irregular verbs (V)

29. after the genitive plural article *ny* in set phrases and place-names (V)

Nasalisation type 2†

30. in the interrogative and after *cha, dy, nagh* in the future and conditional tenses of regular verbs.

* An initial *d-* is prefixed to a vowel (often *j-* when the vowel is *ee*).
† In a position where nasalisation would take place in a consonant an initial vowel is prefixed by *n*.

2   Nouns
   Enmyn

Manx has proper nouns, common nouns and the verbnoun (2.9, 9.3).
Common nouns include:

> Abstract nouns (2.1.2c, 2.10)
> Collective nouns (2.3)
> Actor-nouns (2.1.2, 2.5.2)
> Compound nouns (2.4.3e, 2.5.3, 2.6)

Manx nouns are either feminine or masculine, singular or plural and
may be declined. They may be formed in a variety of ways. The verbnoun
is in many respects the cornerstone of Manx syntax.

2.1   Gender
Every Manx noun is assigned to one of two genders: masculine and
feminine. In Manx, grammatical gender is unstable, and often unrelated
to sex/gender, although nouns referring to females are usually feminine,
and those referring to males are usually masculine.
   The following offers a rough guide to the way grammatical gender
is allocated in Manx. There are many exceptions.

2.1.1   Feminine nouns
Feminine nouns refer to most females, and also to some groups of inanimates, such as cities, countries, rivers, trees, languages and parts of the
body.

a) Words of more than one syllable ending in *-ag*, *-age*, *-aght*, *-eig*, *-id*,
-oge, and a few in *-ys*, are often feminine

ushag	bird
creenaght	wisdom
trimmid	weight

Note: *aalid*, beauty, and *doilleeid*, difficulty, are sometimes listed as
       masculine

b) Nouns ending in one or two consonants preceded by a 'slender' vowel (-*i*-, -*e*-) are feminine

çheer	country
sooill	eye
keeill	church

Note: There are a few exceptions, including diminutives in -*in*, -*een*, most of which are masculine. *Caillin*, a girl, is now usually classed as feminine.

c) Verbnouns (2.9, 9.3) are generally thought of as feminine, especially those which end in -*eil* or -*ail*. This only really matters in cases where the verbnoun is functioning as a noun and has an adjective with it, because then the adjective will need to be lenited when the verbnoun is feminine

goaill kiarail vie jeh   take good care of (*mie*, good)

2.1.2   Masculine nouns
The following classes of nouns are usually masculine.

a) Actor-nouns
Nouns denoting professions, occupations, etc. (2.5.2) especially when these denote male occupations and/or end in -*agh*, -*ee*, -*er*, -*erey*, -*oon*, -*oor*:

greasee	cobbler
wardoon	warden
fidder	weaver
dunver	murderer
bard	poet
scrudeyr	writer
Frangagh	Frenchman
coagerey	cook, chef
ree	king

b) Diminutives ending in -*an*, -*ane*

crongan	hillock
carnane	barrow, monument

c) Most abstract nouns ending in -*ys*

yindys	wonder

d) Nouns ending in one or two consonants preceded by a broad vowel

boayl	place
leagh	price
croan	mast

e) Nouns ending in -*oo*, -*ey*

jalloo	image
eggey	web

Note: There are numerous exceptions, including: *linney*, line; *eoylley*, dung; *fainey*, ring; *lurgey*, leg; *keyrrey*, sheep.

2.1.3   The default gender
Masculine is the 'default gender', the 'unmarked' form: so, when in doubt, it is safest to assume that a noun will be masculine.

**2.1.4   The use of masculine and feminine pronouns to refer to
            nouns**
The pronouns *eh* (he, him) and *ee* (she, her) are used to refer to animate nouns denoting living beings, but for inanimate objects many people now use the masculine *eh* to mean 'it' for both genders.

2.2   Forming the plural of nouns
There are eight principal ways in which Manx nouns form the plural:

2.2.1   Adding the suffix -*yn* to the noun stem, or base form

dreeym, dreeymyn (m) (in 'Late Manx')	back or ridge
lioar, lioaryn (f)	book
mess, messyn (m)	fruit

2.2.2   Internal vowel change

mac, mec (m)	son
mair, meir (f)	finger
dooinney, deiney (m)	man
kayt, kiyt (m)	cat
towl, tuill (m)	hole
stott, stitt (m)	bullock/steer
lhiannoo, lhiennoo (m)	infant/child

Note: These nouns are mostly monosyllabics.

2.2.3   Adding -ee, or changing -agh to -ee

kimmagh, kimmee (m)	criminal
lheiy, lheiyee (m, f)	calf
ollay, ollee (f)	swan
lugh, lughee (m)	mouse
kellagh, kellee (m)	cockerel
mwaagh, mwaaee (m)	hare
ynseydagh, ynseydee (m)	learner, pupil, student
Yernagh, Yernee (m)	Irishman

2.2.4   Changing final -agh to (-ee + yn) = -eeyn

mullagh, mulleeyn (m)	roof, summit
keynnagh, keynneeyn (f)	moss

2.2.5   Other pluralising suffixes + -yn

Plurals may be formed by adding other suffixes, often only one consonant, followed by *-yn*:

lheiney, lheintyn (f)	shirt
geaylin, geayltyn (f)	shoulder
briw, briwnyn (m)	judge
keyll, keylljyn (f)	thicket or wood
uillin, uiljyn (f)	elbow
glion, glionteeyn, glionteenyn (f)	glen
lair, laaireeyn (f)	mare
oe, oeghyn (m, f)	grandchild
oaie, oaieghyn (f)	grave

2.2.6   Changing -ee, -y, -ey, -gh, etc., to -agh + yn

lhiabbee, lhiabbaghyn (f)	bed
lhiattee, lhiattaghyn (or *lhiatteeyn*) (f)	side
lurgey, lurgaghyn (f)	leg
ushtey, ushtaghyn (m)	water
tushtey, tushtaghyn (m)	understanding
stuggey, stuggaghyn (m)	lad
sniaghtey, sniaghtaghyn (m)	snow

2.2.7   Adding the suffix -aghyn

ayr, ayraghyn (m)	father
leigh, leighaghyn (f)	law
ree, reeaghyn (m)	king
roih, roihaghyn (f)	arm

2.2.8   Irregular plurals
Some common nouns form irregular plurals:

ben→mraane (f)	woman
slieau→sleityn (m)	mountain
keyrrey→kirree (f)	sheep
lheeannee→lheeantyn (f)	meadow
seyr→seyir (m)	carpenter

2.3   Collective nouns
A few nouns are singular in form but plural in meaning:

ollagh	cattle
sleih	people
mooinjer	people, family (= relations)
cloan	children (compare Eng. 'offspring')
*feallagh**	people

* Exception: *feallagh*, ones, folk, people, is also found in the plural *feallee*, persons, people, ones:

Ta'n feallee runt ny share The round ones are better
[John Kneen, 'The Gaaue' (c. 1852–1958)]

2.3.1   Collective nouns take a singular article

hooar eh ayns y chiamble … y vooinjer va caghlaa argid
and found in the temple … the changers of money [John ii.14]
(literally: the people who were changing money)

* *Mooinjer* is feminine singular in form, hence the lenition of *m* to *v* after the singular article *y*.

2.3.2   Collective nouns take a plural adjective where possible* (6.1.3)
* Only monosyllabic adjectives ending in a consonant have plurals.

sleih/feallagh aegey	young people
mooinjer veggey	little people

2.3.3   Collective nouns are referred to by plural pronouns

As y vooinjer va caghlaa argid nyn soie … as deiyr eh ad ooilley ass y chiamble
And the changers of money sitting … and he drove them all out
of the temple [John ii.14–15]

2.4   The declension of nouns
There are only three cases still used in modern Manx for most nouns: nominative, vocative and genitive. In older written Manx and in fixed expressions the dative is sometimes found.

2.4.1   Nominative
The nominative is the case of the grammatical subject of the sentence and is the 'base form' given in dictionaries and lists.

2.4.2   Vocative
When addressing someone the first letter of their name, or that of the common noun, is lenited:

'*Voirrey!*' (*Moirrey*)	'Mary!'
'*Y charrey!*'	'(o) friend!' (*carrey*, friend)
(This is found in more recent Manx.)	
'*O Yee (Jee)!*'	'God!'

Lenition occurs in both singular and plural nouns in the vocative:

'*Chaarjyn!*' (*Caarjyn*)   'Friends!'

Note: Foreign names do not usually lenite. (For the pattern of sounds and the changes caused by lenition see 1.)

2.4.3   Genitive
The genitive case shows ownership, possession, belonging.

a) Masculine genitive singular nouns are lenited after the article *y*, *yn*

Er laa yn chaggey (*caggey*)   On the day of the battle

b) Proper nouns of both genders are lenited in the genitive

Mac Voirrey   Mary's son

c) A few nouns, mostly feminine, have retained a distinctive form for the genitive singular

laa ny banshey (*bannish* f)	the day of the wedding
car ny bleeaney (*blein* f)	all year round
	(literally: 'a turn of the year')
bun ny coshey (*cass* f)	sole of the foot

Note: Feminine nouns very often follow the classical rule for masculine nouns in the genitive singular:

kione y ven	the woman's head
ree yn çheer/ree yn çheerey	king of the country

d) Distinctive genitive singular forms also survive in fixed phrases

> *folt e ching (kione* m)   the hair of his head
> *eaghtyr y thallooin (thalloo* m)   the surface of the earth
> or *ny hooirey (ooir* f)

Note: The only Manx noun to have retained a distinct genitive plural
form is *keyrragh*, 'of sheep'. The usual form of the plural is
kirree.

e) Verbnouns, especially those ending in *-(agh)ey*, may generate a
genitive form in *-ee* which is used to form compound nouns
These compounds are often well-established, possibly hyphenated, and
may correspond to a single term in English. The article may precede
compound nouns of this type:

> *sheshaght-chaggee* (f) *yn çheshaght-chaggee*   army (*caggey*, fight)
> (literally: 'company of fighting')
>
> *dooinney-poosee* (m)   bridegroom (*poosey*, marry)

2.4.4   Dative
Traces of the Manx dative survive in fixed phrases:

> *ry-chosh*   afoot, on foot
> *çheu-my-veealloo (beeal* (m) mouth)   in front of me

2.5   Nouns formed with affixes
Manx, like other languages, can build nouns from other word-classes
by adding either suffixes or prefixes:

2.5.1   Nouns formed from adjectives
To convert adjectives into abstract nouns, Manx uses the suffixes *-aght,
-ys, -id*:

foasley	false	*foalsaght* (f)	falsehood
creeney	wise	*creenaght* (f)	wisdom
foddey	far/far away	*foddeeaght, foddiaght* (f)	longing
firrinagh	true	*firrinys* (m)	truth
mie	good	*mieys* (m)	goodness
trome	heavy	*trimmid* (m)	weight
aeg	young	*aegid* (f)	youth
aalin	beautiful	*aalid* (m)	beauty
graney	ugly	*granid* (m)	ugliness

2.5.2   Forming actor-nouns (2.1.2)

Actor-nouns may be formed from other nouns or verbs by means of prefixes or suffixes:

a) Actor-nouns formed with suffixes
-agh, -dagh, -tagh:

fendeil	to defend	*fendeilagh*	defender
ynsaghey	to learn or teach	*ynseydagh*	pupil
sauail	save	*saualtagh*	saviour

-eyr, -deyr, -teyr:

shelg	a hunt, to hunt	*shelgey*	hunter
screeu	to write	*scrudeyr, screeudeyr*	writer, secretary
shiaulley	to sail	*shiolteyr, shiaulteyr*	sailor

-der:

iu	to drink	*iuder*	drinker
leigh (f)	law	*leighder*	lawyer
bwoalley	to strike	*bwoalleyder*	striker

-ee:

buinn	to reap	*beaynee*	reaper
obbraghey	to work	*obbree*	workman

b) Actor-nouns formed with prefixes *ben, mraane* (woman, women), or *fer, fir* (man, men)

ben-ynsee (pl) *mraane ynsee*	female teacher(s)	(*ynsaghey* teach)
ben whaalee		
(pl) *mraane whaalee*	seamstress(es)	(*whaaley* sew)
fer-arrey	watchman	(*arrey* a watch, vigil)
fer-aitt	comedian	(*aitt* comical, odd)
fer-lhee	doctor	(*lheihys* (m) a cure)
fer-oik	official	(*oik* (m) an office)

2.5.3   Forming nouns denoting females

a) Female nouns may be formed from nouns denoting males by prefixing *ben* (woman)

Benainshter	Mistress, Mrs
ben-çhiarn	lady
ben-jee (pl) *mraane-jee*	goddess

benainshtyr phost (pl) *mraane-ainshtyr post*   postmistress
benainshtyr clienney (pl) *mraane-ainshtyr clienney* governess
ben-çhiarn Injinagh (pl) *mraane-çhiarn Injinagh* ranee
ben-çhiarn thallooin (pl) *mraane-çhiarn thallooin* landlady

b) Sometimes there is a special term for the female of a species

booa (pl) *booaghyn*   cow
minjagh (pl) *minjaghyn*   nanny-goat
lair (pl) *laaireeyn*   mare
laair-assyl (pl) *laair-assylyn* she-donkey

c) Where there is no specific form denoting a female of a species, the adjective *bwoirrin, bwoirryn* (female), is added to the male term

l(e)ion bwoirrin   lioness
moddey-bwoirryn (pl) *moddee woirryn* bitch
drean-bwoirrin   jenny-wren
gimmagh-bwoirrin   hen-lobster

d) The prefix *moir*, mother, occurs in compound nouns

moir-abb   abbess
moir ny shellanyn   queen bee

This prefix is used to form inanimates too

moir-heer   mother country
moir-reill   matriarchy
moir-ushtey   water source
moir-awin   river source
moir ny hushtaghyn   catchment, river basin
moir-chreg   parent rock
moir y sterrym   eye of the storm
moir-oyr   root cause

2.5.4   Forming nouns denoting males

a) To form nouns denoting males, where the unmarked or 'default' form is female, the suffix *fyrryn* (male), may be added

assyl fyrryn   jackass
conning fyrryn (pl) *conneeyn fyrryn*   buck rabbit

b) For male birds *kellagh* (cock-bird) is used

kellagh thunnag (pl) *kellee hunnag*   drake
(*thunnag* (f) *thunnagyn* duck)

c) *Bock* (buck) is used for many male animals

bock	gelding (horse)
bock goayr (pl) *buick ghoayr*	
or *goayr fyrryn* (pl) *goayr 'yrryn*	billy-goat

2.6   Compound nouns

In compound noun formation, the noun or other element acting adjectivally follows the more general noun:

shirragh ny giark (m)	hen harrier
ooh-chirkey (f)	hen's egg
paal-chirkey (f)	hen-coop
connagh ny giark (f)	henbane
giarreyder-cloaie (m)	stone cutter
seyir-cloaie (m)	stone mason
quarral-cloaie (m)	stone quarry
boalley-cloaie (m)	stone wall
skeaban-braagey (m)	shoe brush
buggyl-braagey (m)	shoe buckle
key-braaghey (m)	shoe cream
laatçhey-braagey (m)	shoe lace

2.7   Diminutives

Manx has three sets of suffixes which form diminutives:

-in/-een;   *-an/-ane;*   *-ag/-age*

a) Words formed with the first of each pair (i.e., *-in, -an, -ag*) have the accent on the first syllable

blebbin	simpleton	(*bleb* fool)
treoghan	orphan	(*treogh* widowed)
broddag	bodkin	(*brod* prick or stab)

b) Words formed with the second of each pair (*-een, -ane, -age*) have the accent on the suffix

dooinneen	pygmy	(*dooinney* man)
creggeen	little rock	(*creg* rock)
croagane	hook	(*croag* claw)
cuilleig	nook	(*cuill/cooill* corner)

Note: Many words which started out as diminutives in Manx are now regarded as ordinary words:

buighan	the yolk of an egg
strooan	stream

2.8   Nouns expressing a state

2.8.1   *Lomarcan*
The noun *lomarcan* (loneliness) is used with a possessive in a similar construction to that of stative verbs, that is, verbs which describe a state or ongoing situation rather than an event or action:

Ta	*mee*	*my*	*lomarcan*
Am	I	in-my	state of loneliness
I am alone			

Veih	*Jee*	*ny-*	*lomarcan*	
From	God	in-His	state of loneliness	
from God alone				[John v.44]

smooinee	*mee*	*dy*	*row*	*eh*	*dy kinjagh*	*ny*	*lomarcan*
thinking	I	that	was	he	still	in-his	state of loneliness
I thought he was still single							

2.8.2   A permanent state characteristic or quality may be expressed with noun + substantive verb *ve* + personal particle

T'	*eh*	*ny*	*ghooinney*	*mie*
Is	he	in-his	man	good
He is a good man				

Tra	*va*	*mish*	*my*	*ghuilley*	
When	BE+ Past	myself	in-my	state-of boy	
When I was a boy					[WC]

2.9   The verbnoun

2.9.1   The Manx verbnoun can function, without any change in its form, as a noun rather than a verb in gerund constructions where English would need to add the suffix '-ing' to a verb. It is able to fulfil all the grammatical functions of a noun within a sentence, as subject, object, governing a preposition, etc.

Ta giu feeyn taitnyssagh	Drinking wine is enjoyable
V'eh er goll er yn eeastagh	He had gone to the fishing
	[Mrs Eleanor Karran (1870–1953)]

2.9.2   Manx often avoids using the verbnoun as a noun in nominal constructions

a) by introducing a finite verb

> *Agh veagh gaue ayn **dy beagh** rouyr sheshaghtyn **ayn** eisht*
> But then there would be a danger **of having** too many societies
> [Brian Stowell, *Dooraght*, 16 December 1999]
>
> (literally: 'but then there would be a danger that there **would** be too many societies')

b) or a prepositional phrase

> *Va imnea imraait dy beagh Radio Vannin sluggey seose argid Ving Ymskeaylley Gaelgagh **lesh** y chlaare noa shoh.*
> Concern was expressed that the Gaelic Broadcasting Committee's money would be swallowed up by Manx Radio in **putting** on this new programme.
> (literally: '... Manx Radio would swallow up money **with** this new programme')

2.10   Avoidance of abstract nouns

Manx is less willing than English to use abstract nouns such as 'absence', and tries to avoid them by an alternative construction.

Rather than apologising for his absence, for example, a Manx speaker would say that he apologised because 'he was not there':

> *as   mish   ersooyl*
> and   me   away
> in my absence

> *Yeearreeyn share ort as uss dty haaue*
> Best wishes on your retirement

> *Moylley dhyt as uss yrjit*
> Congratulations on your promotion

3   Pronouns
Farenmyn

3.1   Personal pronouns
In Manx the personal pronouns are:

		Singular		Plural	
first person	*mee*	I, me	*shin*	we, us
second person	*oo*	you, thou (familiar)	*shiu*	you (plural or formal)
third person (m)	*eh*	he, him	*ad*	they, them
third person (f)	*ee*	she, her		

The nominative and accusative forms are identical:

> *honnick **eh mee***   he saw me
> *honnick **mee eh***   I saw him

Note: In spoken Manx, the '*eh*' is often pronounced 'a'.

3.1.1   Familiar and 'polite' forms of 'you'
For modern English 'you', Manx distinguishes between the familiar pronoun '*oo*', used when addressing one relative, close friend, child, animal, or God (compare English 'thou'), and '*shiu*', used when addressing more than one individual, or adult strangers. The use of '*shiu*' when addressing an individual may indicate formality or politeness. Many 21st century Manx speakers would use the familiar singular form automatically when addressing another individual Manx speaker, because the limitations of the speech community mean that there is a considerable degree of solidarity and common interest.

The second person singular pronoun 'you' is *oo*, except in the elided forms *t'ou, v'ou, r'ou*. Forms such as *yiow, vow* (future independent and future dependent of *geddyn*, get, find, and *gow*, future dependent of *goaill*, take, may also contain an elided form of the second person singular personal pronoun.

3.1.2   Word order when both subject and object are personal
pronouns

When both the subject and the object are personal pronouns, the subject
comes first: as it usually does in English, too:

> *Er-y-fa dy dooyrt mee rhyt, dy vaik **mee** (subject) **oo** (object) fo'n*
> *villey-figgagh*
> Because I said to thee that **I** (subject) saw **thee** (object) under the
> fig tree   [John i.50]

3.2   Possessive pronouns/particles

3.2.1   Ownership or possession

*my**	my	*nyn*	our
*dty**	your (fam. sing)	*nyn*	your
*e***	his	*nyn*	their
e	her		

* before vowels, *my* and *dty* may be abbreviated to *m'*, *dt'*
** *e* masculine singular 'his' causes lenition in the word that follows it:

> *e ven*   his wife

3.2.2   Possessive pronouns/particles used with state verbs such as
'stand', 'sit, 'lie'

*Ta mee **my hassoo***	I am standing
*Er y voayl ta mee **my lhie***	On the place whereon I lie
	[*Padjer Colum Killey*, traditional]

> *as honnick ee Yeesey **ny hassoo**, as cha row fys eck dy nee Yeesey v'ayn*
> she saw Jesus standing, and knew not that it was Jesus
>   [John xx.14] (*ayn*, see 4.1.2; *ny hassoo*, see 11.2)

3.2.3   Possessive pronouns/particles used with nouns to describe a
semi-permanent state or quality

> *dty yoarree, as **dty** wagaantagh vees oo er yn ooir*
> a fugitive and a vagabond shalt thou be in the earth
>   [Genesis iv.12]

Note: **Possession** is frequently expressed by the definite article (*y, yn,*
ny) + noun + the appropriate personal form of the preposition
ec, 'at':

y cass aym	my foot (literally: 'the foot at me')
*Ta'n bluckan **ec** Gerrard nish*	Gerrard has the ball now

Ownership is expressed with *lesh*, 'with' (see 4.1.11):

> *Ta'n lioar echey nish, agh cha nel ee lesh-hene*
> He has the book now, but he does not own it

Note: The ambiguous plural *nyn*, which can mean 'our', 'your' or 'their', may be clarified when necessary by the addition of the pronominal forms of the preposition *ec* (see 4.1.4)

nyn dhie oc	their house
nyn dhie eu	your house

Later speakers often use *yn thie oc.*

'mine, yours, ours, theirs' is expressed with a pronoun-preposition (*ec, da, lesh*):

Singular

first person	*S'lhiams yn thie shoh*	This house is mine
second person	*S'lhiats y thie shoh*	This house is thine/yours
	Ny ta lhiams, s'lhiats eh	What's mine is thine
third person (m)	*Ta'n thie shoh lesh/*	
	S'lesh yn thie shoh	This house is his
third person (f)	*yn fer ecksh*	her husband
	carrey jeeish	a friend of hers

Plural

first person	*S'lhiens eh!*	It's ours!
	carrey dooin	a friend of ours
	yn mac shen ain	that son of ours
	thie ain	a house of ours
second person	*T'eh lhieuish!*	It's yours!
third person	*Ta shen lhieusyn!*	That's theirs!
	Yn mac shen oc	That son of theirs
	S'lhieu yn thie shoh	That house is theirs

3.3   Alternative construction when the object of a sentence is a pronoun

a) When the object of the sentence is a pronoun (in sentences such as *t'eh fakin mee*, he sees me), and the Manx auxiliary verb is *ve*, 'be', especially in written language, there is the alternative construction

Singular		Plural	
T'eh dy my akin	He sees me	*T'eh dyn vakin* he sees us/you/them	
T'eh dy dty akin	He sees you		
*T'eh dy akin**	He sees him, it		

*T'eh **dy** fakin**   He sees her, it
*T'ad dy **my** choyrt*   They send me
*T'ad er **dty** choyrt*   They have sent you
*T'ad er **my** choyrt*   They have sent me
*V'ad er **dty** choyrt*   They had sent you ('thee', singular)

b) The possessives cause changes to the initial sound of the verbnoun
Lenition occurs in the verbnoun after *my, dty, dy* (masculine) (see 1.1)

> *V'ad er **my** (or m') **akin** (fakin)*   They had seen **me**
> *T'eh er **dty** chlashtyn (clashtyn)*   He has heard **you**

c) Nasalisation (see 1.6) occurs in the verbnoun after *dyn*

> *T'eh **dyn** vaagail (shin)* (= *t'eh faagail shin*)   He is leaving us

* Note: The only way of telling whether the meaning is 'they see **him**'
or 'they see **her**' is that the verbnoun lenites after *dy* when the person
referred to is masculine.

Exception: When the auxiliary verb used is *jannoo, dy* is omitted.

> *Ren shin fakin eh, ren shin eh y akin*   we saw him

3.4   Emphatic forms

3.4.1   Reinforced forms

a) Personal pronouns may be stressed by using the following
reinforced forms (see also 14.4)

	Singular	Plural
first person	*mish*	*shinyn*
second person	*uss*	*shiuish*
third person (m)	*eshyn*	*adsyn*
third person (f)	*ish*	

b) The emphatic pronoun may be used for contrast
I myself do this, while he, on the other hand, does that:

> *Ta **mish** bashtey lesh ushtey; agh ta fer shassoo nyn mast'eu, nagh vel
> enney eu er*
> I baptize with water; but one is standing among you whom you
> do not recognise   [John i.26]

c) The emphatic pronoun may be added to the imperative

> *Dooyrt e voir rish y vooinjer, Jean-jee* **shiuish** *cre-erbee jir eh riu*
> His mother said unto the servants, Whatsoever he says unto you,
> do it   [John ii.5] (*jir*, future of *gra*, see 9.6.7)

d) The emphatic pronoun may be attached to a pronoun which
introduces a relative clause
Because in Manx, unlike English, relative pronouns such as 'whom' are
not required, the emphatic pronoun identifies and stresses just who is
referred to in the relative clause. In the example below, the relative
clause is: 'of whom Moses in the law, and the prophets, wrote':

> *Ta shin er gheddyn* **eshyn**, *jeh ren Moses ayns y leigh, as ny*
> *phadeyryn scrieu, Yeesey dy Nazareth, macYoseph*
> We have found him, of whom Moses in the law, and the
> prophets, wrote, Jesus of Nazareth, the son of Joseph   [John i.45]

In the next example two relative clauses, 'that have done good' and 'that
have done evil', are linked with the emphatic pronoun '*adsyn*':

> *As hig ad magh:* **adsyn** *t'er n'yannoo dy mie, gys irree-seose-reesht y*
> *vea; as* **adsyn** *t'er n'yannoo dy olk, gys irree-seose-reesht y*
> *choayl-anmey*
> And shall come forth; **they** that have done good, unto the resur-
> rection of life; and **they** that have done evil, unto the resurrection
> of damnation   [John v.29][2]

d) The English relative 'that which' corresponds to the Manx *ny* in
cases where there is no noun to attach the relative clause to. This
tends to happen after '*ooilley*' and prepositions like '*jeh*' in the second
example as well

> *Tar-jee as hee shiu dooinney t'er n'insh dou ooilley* **ny** *ren mee rieau*
> Come and you will see a man who has told me all that I ever
> did   [John iv.29]

> *Ta shin loayrt shen ta fys ain er, as gymmyrkey feanish* **jeh ny** *ta shin*
> *er vakin*
> We speak that which we know, and bear witness of **that which**
> we have seen   [John iii.11]

---

[2] 'The pronoun to which a relative clause is attached, is necessarily somewhat stressed
and is therefore likely to occur in the emphatic form.' [R. L. Thomson, *Lessoonyn Sodjey*]

3.4.2   *-hene* and *-pene*

The emphatic *-hene* added to a noun or pronoun, and *-pene* added to a pronoun-preposition (typically, the first person singular) ending in *-m* (see 4, pronoun-prepositions), means 'self' in both reflexive and emphatic constructions:

mee-hene	myself
aym-pene	at myself
orrym-pene	on myself
jeem-pene	of myself
oo-hene	yourself (sg) thyself, etc.
shoh yn dooinney hene	this is the man himself

son 'naght myr ta ec yn Ayr bioys ayn **hene**
for as the Father hath life in Himself   [John v.26]

Cha voddym jeem **pene** *nhee erbee y yannoo*
I can of mine own self do nothing   [John v.30]

As shee Yee orrym **pene**   And the peace of God upon myself
[*Padjer Colum Killey*, traditional]

The following example contains two emphatics, *mish* and *ee hene*:

Chammah's my chree boght brisht as **mish** *as ee* **hene**?
As well as my poor, broken heart, and me, and her very self?
[R. C. Carswell, 'Ushag y Tappee', *Shelg yn Drane* 1994]

The emphatic intent of the second example above is revealed by the author's own English translation, with 'very.' He uses *hene* for 'very' in other cases, such as:

Ayns treisht
Dy assaghey my annym's hene.

In the hope
To feed my very soul.
[R. C. Carswell, 'Duillagyn ny Fouyir', *Shelg yn Drane* 1994]

But *ee-hene* could just mean 'herself'. *Hene* also forms the reflexive pronouns in Manx, as 'self' does in English:

Cha hreisht Yeesey eh-hene orroo
Jesus did not trust himself to them   [John ii.24]

Lhiggey jee hene
Injillaghey reesht
Letting herself
Descend again
[R. C. Carswell, 'Ushag y Tappee', *Shelg yn Drane* 1994]

3.4.3   The word *hene* added to a noun preceded by a possessive
The word *hene* added to a noun which is preceded by a possessive has
the meaning 'own':

> *Haink eh gys e vooinjer **hene***   He came to his own people
> [John i.11]

Note: -*hene* may only follow the unemphatic form of the pronoun. So
    mee-hene is possible, but not *mish hene

3.5   Indefinite pronouns

a) The Manx equivalents for English indefinite pronouns (and also
adverbs, see 6.15) ending in -ever (whoever, whatever) or preceded by
'any-' (anybody, anything, etc.) are usually formed by adding *erbee*,
sometimes hyphenated and sometimes not

> *quoi erbee*   whoever
> *cre erbee*   whatever
> *cre-erbee jir eh*   whatever he says   [John ii.5]
>
> *n'egooish cha row nhee erbee jeant*
> without him nothing (= not anything) was made   [John i.3]

b) The Manx equivalents for English indefinite pronouns (and also
adverbs) beginning with 'some-' (someone, somebody, something,
somewhere, etc.) are formed with *ennagh*

> *peiagh ennagh*   someone, somebody
> *red ennagh, nhee ennagh*   something

3.6   Interrogative pronouns

> *Quoi?*   Who? Whom?
> *Cre? C'red?*   What?
> *C'red ta shen?*   What's that?
> *Quoi s'lesh?*   Whose?
> *Quoi s'lesh ny guoiee shoh?*   Whose are these geese?
>   [Ned Maddrell (1877–1974)]

4 Prepositions
Roie-ocklyn

4.1 Pronoun-prepositions

Pronoun-prepositions formed from a fusion of preposition and personal pronoun are a main feature of the Celtic languages. Pronoun-prepositions contribute to many idiomatic expressions in Manx:

> *lesh* with-it, with-him

> *S'mie **lhiam** ushtey, s'mie **lhiam** soo*
> I like water, I like juice
> (literally: 'is good with me water, is good with me juice)

> *Ta'n gheay sheidey raad saillee*
> The wind bloweth where she listeth[3]   [John iii.8]
> (literally: 'where she wishes')

When the preposition is governed by a noun rather than a pronoun, the 'default' or unmarked form (the masculine singular) is used:

> *ersooyl **lesh** y gheay*   away (= gone) with the wind
> ***harrish** yn awin*   over the river
> *mie **rish** e gharran*   good to his pony

4.1.1 *Ass* (out of)

Ass is set out in greater detail so as to show how the two different elements fuse to form the compound. The other pronoun prepositions are more simply set out, just as they appear in written Manx. Masculine and feminine forms are identical in the plural.

Singular		Plural	
ass + *mee* → first person *assym*		*ass* + *shin* → first person *assdooin*	
ass + *oo/ou* → second person *assyd*		*ass* + *shiu* → second person *assdiu*	

---

[3] Note: In this example, the copula *-ail*, desire, wish, which is not found separately, and the personal form of *lesh* (*lhee*) combine into a single unit (see 9.7.8)

Singular	Plural
third person (m) *ass*	*ass* + *ad* → third person *assdoo, assdaue*
third person (f) *ass* + *ee* → *assjee*	

Cre ass t'ou?	Where are you from?
feed meeiley ass shoh	20 miles from here
giu ass cappan	drinking from a cup

Note: Emphatic third person singular masculine *ass-syn*
When *ass* refers to motion from place, in constructions such as 'gone away from X', *ass* is often preceded by *magh*, 'out of', 'forth':

magh ass y vagher	out of the field

Honnick mee ooyl appee
As soo oor çheet magh ass
I saw a ripe apple
And fresh juice coming out of it
   [R. C. Carswell, 'Honnick mee ooyl appee', *Shelg yn Drane* 1994]

As cre haink magh
Ass y thalloo shen agh çhibber dy ushtey oor
And what came out
Of that ground but a well of fresh water
   [Same source, 'Kione Vaghal']

4.1.2   *Ayns* (in)

	Singular	Plural
first person	*aynym*	*ayn, ayndooin*
second person	*aynyd*	*ayndiu*
third person (m)	*ayn*	*ayndoo, ayndaue*
third person (f)	*aynjee*	

Note: Uses of *ayn*:

a) *ayn* is used to express the notion 'there exists', 'there is present', (rather like French 'il y a', German 'es gibt')

Vel arran ayn?	Is there any bread?
Cha nel eeym ayn	There's no butter
roish my row seihll ayn	before there was a world
	[John xvii.5]

b) *ayn* is used for 'there'

> *V'eh ginsh dou dy row eh ayn*
> He was telling me that he was there
>
> [Harry Boyde (c. 1870–1953)]

c) *ayn* is used with the copula (*she, nee*) to express 'that it was X who was there'

> *As honnick ee Yeesey ny hassoo, as cha row fys eck dy nee Yeesey v'ayn*
> And she saw Jesus standing, and knew not that it was Jesus
>
> [John xx.14]

> *Heill ish dy nee yn gareyder v'ayn*
> Supposing him to be the gardener   [John xx.15]

> *She eh-hene t'ayn!*   It's himself!
>
> [Nigel Kneale: 'Curphey's Follower', tr. Brian Stowell, Duillagyn 1, November 2005]

d) *ayn* can combine with *shoh*, this; *shen*, that; *shid*, yon, to form adverbs

> *aynshoh, ayns shoh* here; *aynshen, ayns shen* there;
> *aynshid, ayns shid* yonder

> *Va gobbraghey aynshen dooinney enmyssit Carey*
> There was a man called Carey working there
>
> [Ned Maddrell (1877–1974)]

4.1.3   *Da* (to, for)

	Singular	Plural
first person	*dou*	*dooin*
second person	*dhyt*	*diu*
third person (m)	*da*	*daue*
third person (f)	*jee*	

> *Cur **dooin** eh*   Give it to us
> *Hug mee **da** eh*   I gave it (to) him
> *Hug mee **jee** eh*   I gave it (to) her

Da sometimes corresponds to English 'for':

> *Va mee gobbraghey **da** Mnr Kelly*
> I was working for Mr Kelly

Note: The emphatic form of the first person singular is *dooys*:

> *agh lhig dooys loayrt jeh'n inneen gring*
> but let me speak of the fair maid   [Manx Traditionary Ballad 32]

4.1.4   *Ec* (at)

	Singular	Plural
first person	*aym*	*ain*
second person	*ayd*	*eu*
third person (m)	*echey*	*oc*
third person (f)	*eck*	

Note: The emphatic form of the third person singular feminine is *ecksh*.

Ec is a very important pronoun-preposition in Manx because Manx has no verb the equivalent of 'to have'. Ownership and possession are expressed in a different way in Manx:

a) Possession is often expressed with a form of *ec*

> *Ta thie aym*   I have a house;
> *Vel thie ayd?*   Have you a house?

(see 4.4.3)

b) Sometimes Manx also uses the appropriate form of *ec* in place of a possessive pronoun

> *Cha vel my hraa's foast er jeet; agh ta'n traa* **euish** *dy kinjagh jesh diu*
> My time is not yet come; but your time is always ready
>
> [John vii.6]

Note: *Eu* here takes the emphatic ending *-ish* to indicate contrast between my time/your time.

c) Many idiomatic expressions in Manx are formed with *ec*
To thank someone:

> *Gura mie ayd! Gura mie eu!* (literally: May it be well with you!)

(To) know (a fact) = *fys ec* + *er* (about/of) (literally: 'there is knowledge at me about/of):

> *Ta fys* **aym** *er shen*   I know (about) that
> *Cha row fys* **eck**   She did not know
> *Vel fys* **ayd** *er yn ennym (er)/echey* ?   Do you know his name?

To know (a person) = *enney*, enn (+ *er*)+ *ec* (see 11.7.3):

Ta enney **aym** *er*	I know him
Nagh vel enney ayd **urree?**	Don't you know her?
Nagh vel enney **eu** *er?*	Do you not recognise (know) him?
as cha row enney **aym** *er*	and I did not recognise (know) him
	[John i.31]

d) Partitive use

yn jees oc	the two of them

4.1.5 *Er* (on)

	Singular	Plural
first person	*orrym*	*orrin*
second person	*ort*	*erriu*
third person (m)	*er*	*orroo*
third person (f)	*urree*	

Er is used in many common phrases:
To ask or state names:

*Cre'n ennym t'***ort?***   What is your name?
(literally: What the name is on you?)

Ta'n ennym **orrym** *Thom*   My name is Tom
(literally: the name on me is Tom.)

cur shilley **er**, to visit:

Ren y saggyrt çheet dy chur shilley **urree**
The parson came to visit her

This could also be expressed with *lesh*: *ren y saggyrt çheet dy chur shilley lhee*

cur er, to don, put on:

Cur **ort** *dt'edd*   Put on your hat
(literally: 'put upon you your hat')

Geearree/shir/shirrey + er = to ask, request (something) of someone:

Shir yn argid **er** *y charrey ayd*   Ask your friend for the money
Shir **urree** *çheet mayrt*   Ask her to come with you

smooinaghtyn er = to think of:

Ta mee smooinaghtyn **er**   I am thinking of it

cooinaghtyn er = to remember:

> *Ta cooinaghtyn mie aym **urree***   I remember her well

Ve feme (echey) er = to need, have need of:

> *Nagh row feme echey er unnane erbee*
> And needed not anyone   [John ii.25]

Note: *'enney + ec + er'* means 'to know':

> *Cre'n enney t'ayd orrym's?*
> What is the acquaintance that thou hast with me?   [John i.48]

To express emotions:

> *T'a corree orrym*   I am angry
>
> *C'red ta jannoo ort?*   What's the matter
> (literally: What is doing on you?)

4.1.6   *Fo* (under, beneath)

	Singular	Plural
first person	*foym*, beneath me, etc.	*foin*
second person	*foyd*	*feue*
third person (m)	*fo*	*foue*
third person (f)	*foee*	

> *fo ushtey*   under water
> *fo-raad*   underway

Note: In certain set phrases, *fo* causes lenition in the noun which follows
   it:

> *fo ghlass*   under lock and key (*glass* lock)
> *fo halloo*   underground (*thalloo* ground)
> *fo lieau*   under a mountain (*slieau* mountain)

Ta foym can mean 'to intend, undertake':

> *Er-y-fa dy vel mee er loayrt eh, ta **foym** dy bee eh jeant, as cha jean-ym*
> *arrys y ghoaill, chamoo nee'm shen y chaghlaa*
> Because I have spoken it, I have purposed it, and will not repent,
> neither will I turn back from it   [Jeremiah iv.28]

4.1.7   *Gollrish* (like)

The double 'l' is often written, but is not pronounced, so that '*gollrish*', for example, sounds like '*gorrish*'.

	Singular	Plural
first person	*gollrym*	*gollrin*
second person	*gollryt*	*gollriu*
third person (m)	*gollrish*	*gollroo*
third person (f)	*gollree*	

> *V'eh taaley ass e veeal* **gollrish** *ushtey*
> It (Manx) flowed from his mouth like water   [WC]

> *goll-ry-cheilley*   like one another, alike

> *Vel eh jooigh* **gollrhyt**'s?   Is he keen like you?
>   [Ned Maddrell (1877–1974)]

> *Va ny eayin gee yn conney noa* **gollrish** *shugyr*
> The lambs were eating the new gorse like sugar
>   [Thomas Christian (1851–1930)]

> *Tra v'eh ny wooinney aeg v'eh* **gollrish** *sleih aeg elley*
> When he was a young man he was like other young people
>   [Thomas Christian (1851–1930)]

> *Ren mee baghey red* **gollrish** *shey bleeaney ayns Skyll Andreays*
> I lived something like six years in Kirk Andreas
>   [John Kneen, 'The Gaaue' (c.1852–1958)]

4.1.8   *Gys* (literary), *dys* (popular), *hug* (to)

	Singular	Plural
first person	*hym*	*hooin**
second person	*hood*	*hiu*
third person (m)	*huggey, hug*	*huc*
third person (f)	*huic*(k) (emphatic *huicksh*)	

> *Hie mee* **hug** (*dys*) *yn talhear**   I went to the tailor
> *Ren eh goll* **hug** (*dys*) *yn traie**   He went to the shore
> *Ta'n muc cur lesh yn argid* **hym**   The pig brings the money in to me
>   [John Tom Kaighin (1862–1954)]

> *Quoi yn schoill ta shiu goll* **hug/huggey**? (normally **huic**)
> Which school do you go to?   [same source]

> *agh cha jed oo harrish* **huggey**
> but thou shalt not go over thither   [Deuteronomy xxxiv.4]

Vel oo son goll **gys** *shen reesht?*
Art thou intending to go thither again?   [John xi.8]

Note: *Gys, dys* are always used with place names: these examples * are
unusual too: *dys/gys* would be expected.

goll **dys** *Doolish*   going to Douglas
(*dy Ghoolish*, commonly found, is not strictly correct)

* *hooin* (to us), especially in the expression '*hooin roin*' is often used to
mean 'let's go!' instead of the more logical but less Manx '*lhig dooin
goll*', let us go
Note: The new preposition *hug* was created on the basis of *huggey*.

4.1.9   *Harrish* (over, across, over and above, past)

	Singular	Plural
first person	*harrym*	*harrin*
second person	*harryd*	*harriu*
third person (m)	*harrish*	*harroo, harrystoo*
third person (f)	*harree*	

My ta fir-ynsee elley er ghoaill y phooar shoh harriu?
If other teachers are partakers of this power over you?
                                   [Corinthians I ix.12]

There are several idiomatic expressions with *harrish*:

Harrym!	Pass!
Lheim eh harrish yn awin	He leapt across the river;
harrish as tarrish	over and over
harrish ny sleityn	batty
harrish as erskyn shen	over and above that
harrish boayrd	overboard
*harrish ny *hAlpyn*	trans-Alpine
harrish yn cadjinys	exceptionally

* *h-* is not often written, but usually pronounced (see 1.8).

4.1.10   *Jeh* (of)

	Singular	Plural
first person	*jeem*	*jin*
second person	*jeed*	*jiu*
third person (m)	*jeh*	*jeu*
third person (f)	*j'ee**	

* The apostrophe distinguishes written forms of *j'ee, j'eeish,* from *jee, jeeish,* from *da,* to (4.1.3).

*quoi **jeu**?*   which of them?

*My vees shiuish myr ta shinyn, dy bee dy chooilley mac dooinney **jiu** ny yiarey chymmylt*
If ye will be as we be, that every male of you be circumcised
[Genesis xxxiv.15]

4.1.11   *Lesh* (with)

	Singular	Plural
first person	*lhiam*	*lhien*
second person	*lhiat*	*lhiu, lhieu*
third person (m)	*lesh*	*lhieu*
third person (f)	*lhee*	

ersooyl lesh y gheay   gone with the wind
dellal lesh Nerin   trading with Ireland

lesh is used in several common phrases (see 3.2.3 and 4.4)
In idiomatic expressions it may be used with persons:

Ersooyl lhiat!   Away with you!   [WC]

Also see 4.4.2 and 4.4.3.

4.1.12   *Marish* ((in company) with somebody)

	Singular	Plural
first person	*marym*	*marin*
second person	*mayrt*	*mêriu*
third person (m)	*mârish*	*maroo*
third person (f)	*maree*	

*Shir urree çheet **mayrt***   Ask her to come with you
*Ta mee gobbraghey **marish***   I work with him
*Foast tammylt beg ta mish **mêriu***
A little while yet I am with you   [John vii.33]

Note: Sometimes all these forms except *mayrt* are written with a circumflex on the 'a': *mârym,* etc.

4.1.13   *Mysh* (about (concerning))

Sometimes *mysh* is reinforced by *mygeayrt*, around*, usually when referring to place:

	Singular	Plural
first person	*moom*	*mooin*
second person	*mood*	*miu*
third person (m)	*mysh*	*moo, mymboo*
third person (f)	*mooee*	

> She **mooee**(ish) v'ad loayrt
> It was about her that they were speaking

> Ta mish er chlashtyn **mysh** shen   I have heard about that
> Ren mee clashtyn mygeayrt-y-**mysh**   I heard about him

Mysh may be encountered in other equivalents of English 'about':

a) *mysh* = about (approximately)

> T'eh **mysh** kiare er y chlag   It is about four o'clock

b) *mysh* = about to, on the point of

> Va shin **mysh** goll   We were about to go

> Ta mee mysh giu my haie dy yough
> I am about to drink my fill of ale

* *mygeayrt* is more correctly used with the meaning 'around', *mychione* for 'concerning'.

> Veagh yn Cholloo **mysh** shoh   The Calf would be about here
> mygeayrt-y-**moom**   round about me
> mygeayrt-y-**mood**   round about you, etc.

> Va my noidyn ooilley mygeayrt-y-**moom**
> My enemies were all about me

> Rio as geay mygeayrt y **moo**   Frost and wind surrounding them
> [R. C. Carswell, 'Ta mee buinn Blaaghyn Braew',
> *Shelg yn Drane* 1994]

> jeeaghyn mysh, mygeayrt-y-mysh to look after, take care of
> T'eh jeeaghyn mysh hene   He looks after himself

> Va'n ven echey jeeaghyn mygeayrt-y-**mysh**
> His wife was looking after him

4.1.14 *Rish* has a number of different meanings, depending on the
context

	Singular	Plural
first person	*rhym*	*rooin*
second person	*rhyt*	*riu*
third person (m)	*rish*	*roo*
third person (f)	*r'ee**	

to (listening to, etc.)	*clashtyn rish kiaull* listen to music
by (in place names, etc.)	*rish cassey yn phost* by return of post

at, towards   *Ta'n oaie echey rish y cheayn*
It faces towards the sea   [Fargher 1979: 790]

for (a time)	*rish tammylt*	for a while, for some time past
with	*loayrt rish*	speak with
along	*rish y traie*	along shore
with, against	*caggey rish*	fighting with/against

*Ta mee loayrt **r'ee***   I am speaking to her
*mie **rish** e gharran*   good to his pony
*Cha nel mee ayns graih **r'ee***   I am not in love with her

*Cha row ad (ayns) coardail **rooinyn***
They did not agree with us

*V'ad caggey rish y cheilley **rish** hoght bleeaney*
They were fighting (against/with) each other for eight years

*Er-y-fa dy dooyrt mee **rhyt**, dy vaik mee oo fo'n villey figgagh*
because I said to thee that I saw thee under the fig tree
[John i.50]

*Dyll eh magh as cheau eh yn edd echey **r'ee***
He shouted and flung his hat at it (*thunnag* (f) duck)
[Nigel Kneale, 'Curphey's Follower', tr. Brian Stowell,
Duillagyn 1, November 2005]

* The apostrophe in *r'ee* distinguishes the written form from *ree*, king
Note: The original form of *rish* was *ry*, which is still found in some
adverbial compounds:

ry-foddey dy hraa   for a long time (see 6.14.1, n.)

4.1.15   *Roish* (before)

	Singular	Plural
first person	*roym*	*roin*
second person	*royd*	*reue, rhymbiu**
third person (m)	*roish*	*roue, rhymboo**
third person (f)	*roee, rhymbee**	

> *roish* yn aile   before (= in front of) the fire
> yn vlein *roish* shen   the year before (= previous year)
> *roish* my vow my lhiannoo baase before my child dies   [John iv.49]
> *roish* my deie Philip ort   before Philip called thee
>   [John i.48]

> *Immee royd!*   Get lost!
>   [Joseph Woodworth (1854–1931)]

* These forms appear frequently in the idiom *hie eh roish*, he went on his way;

> *hie ad rhymboo*, they went on their way, departed, etc.

> *Hooin roin!*   Let's go! (see 4.1.8)
> *Fow royd!*   Go on!
> *Tar royd as hee oo*   Come on and thou shalt see
>   [John i.46]

> *Hie ee rhymbee*   She went off/went on her way
>   [John iv.28]

4.1.16   *Shaghey* (past), which is really an adverb, is sometimes fused with the personal pronouns

	Singular	Plural
first person	*shaghym*	*shaghin*
second person	*shaghyd*	*shaghiu*
third person (m)	*shaghey*	*shaghoo*
third person (f)	*shaghee*	

> *Ta mee goll shaghee gagh laa*   I pass her (go past her) every day
>   [Thomson and Pilgrim: Outline of Manx Language
>   and Literature: YNC: 8]

> *Lhig da'n cappan shoh goll shagh-ym*   Let this cup pass from me
>   [Matthew xxvi.39]

Note: Cregeen (1984 repr.: 171) suggests that *shaghey* is here fused with the pronoun-preposition *ec*.

4.1.17 *Veih, voish* (from)

	Singular	Plural
first person	*voym*	*voin*
second person	*voyd*	*veue*
third person (m)	*voish, veih*	*voue*
third person (f)	*voee*	

> *Gow **voee** eh!*   Take it from her!
> *Chionnee mee **voyd** eh,*   I bought it from you
> *Faag-jee **veue** ee,*   Leave her alone   [John xii.7]
> (literally: leave her from you)

4.2   Emphatics
The emphatic forms of the pronoun-prepositions occasionally add the following suffixes:

	Singular	Plural
first person	-s	-yn
second person	-s	-ish
third person (m)	-syn	
third person (f)	-ish	-syn

This system produces, for instance, the following emphatic forms for *ec*: *ayms, ayds, echeysyn, ecksyn, ainyn, euish, adsyn.*

Note: Where the masculine singular simple ends in *-sh*, the suffix *-syn* is usually simplified to *-yn*, *liorishyn* (rather than *liorishsyn*, *liorish-syn*).

4.3   Phrasal prepositions
Phrasal prepositions are made up of several elements, one of which is usually a preposition* and one of which is often a possessive particle like '*my*', '*dty*'.
* although not always

Manx phrasal prepositions are formed in one of two ways:

4.3.1   Preposition + definite article/possessive particle
Most common of this type are the 'fixed' prepositional phrases:

Erskyn (above):

	Singular	
first person	*er-my-skyn*	above me
second person	*er-dty-skyn*	above you
third person	*er-e-skyn*	above him/her

All Plurals   *er-nyn-skyn*   above us/you/them

mychione (concerning, about):

Singular

first person	*my-my-chione*	about me
second person	*my-dty-chione*	about you
third person (m)	*my-e-chione*	about him
third person (f)	*my-e-kione*	about her

All Plurals   *my-nyn-gione*   about us/you/them

son (for the sake of):

Singular

first person	*er-my-hon*	for my sake
second person	*er-dty-hon*	for your sake
third person (m)	*er-e-hon*	for his sake
third person (f)	*er-e-son* (frequently *son eck*) for her sake

Note: *son aym* etc. are equally frequent in late Manx.

All Plurals *er-nyn-son* (frequently *son ain, son eu, son oc*), for our/your/
    their sake

> *Ta mee guee ort* **er nyn son**   I pray for them   [John xvii.9]

> *Chamoo ta shiu goaill eu hene kys dy vel eh ymmyrçhagh* **er nyn son ain**
> Nor consider that it is expedient for us   [John xi.50]

> *Kionneeym's ny lioaryn shid* **er-dty-hons***
> I'll buy those books for you   [JC] (see 14)

*   Hyphenation is variable: *er my hon*, etc.

4.3.2   Possessive particle + preposition
Mutation occurs where necessary:
The preposition *cour, gour*, has a number of meanings depending on the
context: these include: towards, by, along, for the purpose of, provided
for, according to, in the direction of:

Singular

first person	*my chour*	for me
second person	*dty chour*	for you
third person (m)	*ny chour*	for him
third person (f)	*ny cour*	for her

All Plurals: *nyn gour*   for us/you/them

cour y raad	along the road
cour yn aile	by the fire
cour yn imbagh	according to the season
cour-y-laa	daily, day by day
cour-y-traa	as the time comes
V'eh roie **cour** *y dorrys*	He was running for the door

cour y ghoaill eh with a view to seizing him [John xi.57]

Cour *laa my oanluckey t'ee er reayll shoh*
Against the day of my burying hath she kept this   [John xii.7]

Kionnee ny vees mayd feme **cour** *y feailley*
Buy what we shall need for the festival   [John xiii.29]

Hie ad **gour** *nyn drommey, as huitt ad gys y thalloo*
They went backward, and fell to the ground   [John xviii.6]

Fegooish (without):

Singular

first person	*m'egooish*	without me
second person	*dty'egooish*	without you
third person (m)	*n'egooish*	without him
third person (f)	*ny fegooish*	without her

All Plurals: *nyn vegooish* without us/you/them

n'egooish cha row nhee without him nothing
erbee jeant va er ny yannoo was made that was made [John i.3]

A modern alternative is to use the appropriate form of *ec* (at):
fegooish aym, without me, *fegooish eck*, without her, etc. This happens with most other compound prepositions too, for example *erskyn aym* above me, *mychione aym*, about me, etc.
This has the advantage of removing the ambiguity in the plural, where *nyn* corresponds to first, second and third person.

Note: The simple preposition *gyn* (without), has no personal forms:

   gyn caarjyn   without friends

gyn may also be used to negate the main verb where there is no *nagh*:

   dy vod dooinney gee jeh   that a man may eat thereof
   as **gyn** *baase y gheddyn*   and not die   [John vi.50]

Fud (among, amid, throughout): *nyn vud/nyn vud ain, eu, oc*:

   ny gobbagyn raipey ny vud ny lhieenteenyn
   the dogfish tearing amongst/amidst the nets

fud ny hoie		all (through the) night
fud-y-cheilley		confusedly

Lurg (after, following):

Singular

first person	*my lurg*	after me
second person	*dty lurg*	after you
third person	*ny lurg*	after him/her

All Plurals:	*nyn lurg*	after us/you/them

Note: 'After' may also be expressed by *yei* with a possessive particle:

my yei, dty yei, ny yei (m) *ny jei* (f), *nyn yei* (pl)

ny yei y cheilley, jei y cheilley, lurg y cheilley = one after the other

ny yei *shen*	after that
V'eh roie **my yei**	He was running after me
	[Thomas Christian (1851–1930)]

Mastey (among): *Mastey* is usually only found in the plural. It is abbreviated to *mast'* before a vowel:

first person	*ny mast'ain*
second person	*ny mast'eu*
third person	*ny mast'oc*

as ren eh baghey nyn **mast'ain**   and he lived among us [John i.14]

ta fer shassoo nyn **mast'eu**
one standing amongst you   [John i. 26]

As blaa ny **mast'oc,** *blaa er-lheh*
And a flower amongst them, a special flower
                    [R. C. Carswell, 'Ta mee Buinn Blaaghyn Braew',
                                                   Shelg yn Drane 1994]

Mastey may occur in the singular with collective nouns:

Bee ny moddee ny **mast'ayd,** *ashoon aym*
The dogs will be amongst thee, my nation
                                                  [Fargher 1979: 27 cit.]

Va lane argane **mastey** *yn pobble*
There was much argument among the people

                                                           [John vii.12]

It may also occur with uncountable nouns such as 'bread', 'beer':

> *Va'n thunnag puhttey lurg ny grineyn* **mastey'n** *lhune slishit*
> The duck was nuzzling after the grain among the slopped beer
> [Nigel Kneale: 'Curphey's Follower', tr. Brian Stowell,
> *Duillagyn* 1, November 2005]

Note: Cregeen (repr. 1984: 123) notes the use of *mast'* in the singular,
        mast'echey, mast'eck.

Noi (against):

	Singular	Plural
first person	*m'oi, noi aym*	*nyn oi, noi ain*
second person	*dt'oi, noi ayd*	*nyn oi, noi eu*
third person (m)	*n'oi, e oi*	*nyn oi, noi oc*
third person (f)	*ny hoi, e hoi*	

noi-*ry-hoi*   against one another;
shass **noi**'*n voalley*   stand against the wall

Cha vel ad gra veg **n'oi**   They say nothing against him
                                        [John vii. 26]

ta (fer) ayn ta plaiynt **nyn'oi eu** there is one that accuseth you
                                        [John v.45]

Note: the ambiguous *nyn* here has an added *eu* for clarification.

Trooid (through):

	Singular	
first person	*my hrooid*	through me
second person	*dty hrooid*	through you
third person (m)	*ny hrooid*	through him
third person (f)	*ny trooid*	through her
All Plurals:	*nyn drooid*	through us/you/them

trooid *dorrys*   through a door
gynsagh **trooid** *Gaelg*   teaching through Manx

Note: *eddyr* (between), is followed by a simple or emphatic personal
        pronoun:

eddyr *mish as eshyn*   between me and him

Other phrasal prepositions include:

beealloo	in front of
çheu my veealloo, er-my-veealloo,	in front of me,
çheu dty veealloo, er-dty-veealloo	in front of you, etc.
beeal, mouth (see 2.4.4)	

neealloo (towards):

> *T'ad getlagh magh myr urley **neealloo** yn aer*
> They fly away as an eagle towards heaven   [Proverbs xxiii.5]

> *cooyl, cooylloo*, behind (*my chooyl, er-my-chooylloo*, etc.)

In modern Manx, these phrases are often replaced by a construction using *ec*:

> *noi oc*   against them

'Towards' can also be expressed with *cour* + possessive particle (see 4.3.2).

4.4   'Fixed' prepositional phrases with *lesh*

4.4.1   *lesh* agrees with the subject
The form of the pronoun-preposition *lesh* agrees with the subject in fixed prepositional phrases such as:

er + *lesh* =   I think, it seems to me:

Er-lhiam *dy vel*	I think so
*Cre er-**lhiat**?*	What do you think?

cooinee- + *lesh*, remember:

*Cha gooin **lesh***	He does not remember
*S'cooin **lhiam***	I remember
*Nagh by chooinee **lhiu**?*	Did they not remember?

Cooney + *lesh*, help:

*Cooin **lhiam**!*	Help me!
*Cha jean shen cooney **lhiat***	That will not help you
*Cooin **lhiat**!*	Help yourself!

Verb (copula or *ve*) + *treih*, sorry + *lesh*, be sorry:

*S'treih **lhiam***	I am sorry
*Cha dreih **lhiam***	I am not sorry
*By hreih **lhiam***	I was sorry

Closing formula for letters:

Lhiat's	Yours (to one person, informal)
Lhiuish, lhieuish	(to more than one person, or formal)

cur + lesh = bring:

*Cur **lhiat** arran hym*	Bring me bread
*Verym **lhiam** y lioar mairagh*	I'll bring the book tomorrow
*Hug mee **lhiam** eh*	I brought it
*t'ou cur **lhiat***	you are bringing
*cha derragh shiu **lhiu***	you would not bring
*v'ad er chur **lhieu***	they had brought

4.4.2   *lesh* with copula expressing 'liking'
The English 'like', 'prefer' (= like more), may be expressed with the copula (see 9.7) + *taittin* (delight, satisfaction) *mie* (*good*), or *mooar*, big, + the appropriate form of *lesh*:

*S'mie **lhiam** eh*	I like him
*Share **lhiam** yn fer elley*	I prefer the other one
	[Thomas Christian (1851–1930)]

(literally: 'is better with me the other one')

*By vie **lhiat** cosney £2,500?*   Would you like to win £2,500?

*My s'mie **lhiat** screeu bardaght ayns Gaelg oddagh oo!*
You could, if you like to write poems in Manx!
[Paul Rogers, *Dhooraght* 36, December 2004]

*S'mie **lhiam** ... nagh row mee ayns shen*
I am glad that I was not there   [John xi.15]

*Er-y-fa ... nagh mooar **lesh** son ny kirree*
Because ... he does not care about the sheep   [John x.13]

*s'taittin **lhiam***	I delight in, I am pleased
*S'taittin **lhiam** fakin oo*	I am delighted to see you
	[Fargher 1979: 225]

*By vie **lhiat** cappan dy hey?*	Would you like a cup of tea?
*Share **lhiam** feeyn na lhune*	I prefer wine to ale

(literally: 'is better with me wine')

*Bare **lhiam** feeyn*
I preferred/used to/would prefer wine

*Cha nhare **lhiam** feeyn*	I do not prefer wine

Note: Use of *lesh* signifies the individual's emotions, whereas *da* is less
personal:

Share **lhiam** *eh*	I prefer it
Share **dou** *eh*	It is better for me
S'cummey **lhiam** *eh*	I do not mind
S'cummey **dou**	It is no business of mine

4.4.3 *lesh* expressing ownership
Ownership is expressed with *lesh*, as distinct from possession, which is
expressed with *ec* (see 4.1.4):

Ta'n lioar **lhiam**	I own the book
*Quoi s'***lesh** *yn thie?*	Who owns the house?

Cha vel my ynsagh **lhiam** *pene, agh* **leshyn** *t'er my choyrt*
My teaching belongs not to me but to him who sent me

[John vii.16]

nagh vel ny kirree **lesh** *hene*
to whom the sheep do not belong   [John x.12]

5 The article
Art

The definite article has three forms *yn, ny* and *nyn*:

> *yn* is the normal singular form
>
> *ny* is the plural and the form used for the feminine genitive singular (f gen sg)
>
> *nyn* is an archaic form sometimes found in place names

Manx has no indefinite article:

dooinney	man, a man
ben	woman, a woman, wife, a wife

5.1 The singular definite article *yn* applies to both masculine and feminine, nominative and accusative (acc) cases and to the masculine genitive singular (m gen sg)

yn ushtey (m)	the water
yn ushag happagh (f)	the lark
*sollan **y cheayn***	the salt of the sea (m gen sg)
*shelg **yn drean***	hunt the wren (m acc sg)

5.1.1 The *n* of the article may be dropped

a) between consonants in mid-sentence

> *Vel y noo ny lhie 'syn ooir shoh?* Is the saint lying in this soil?
> > [R. C. Carswell, 'Kione Vaghal', *Shelg yn Drane* 1994]

b) initially when the following word starts with a consonant

y dooinney	the man
y dorraghys	the darkness

5.1.2   The *y* of the article may be dropped following an unstressed word

a) after a particle or preposition

da'n dooinney	to the man
veih'n dooinney	from the man
fo'n ghrian	under the sun

b) after a word ending in a vowel, '*h*', or '*y*'

Balley 'n Ard Ainle	Archangel
brishey'n laa	daybreak

c) after *ta* and *va*, the independent present and past forms of *ve*, to be

Va'n dooinney roie cour y dorrys
The man was running towards the door

Ta'n doodee feer ghroamagh   The girl is very dejected

5.2   The genitive case of the definite article, feminine singular, is *ny*

broogh ny hawin   the bank of the river

The genitive of the definite article, feminine, is generally used only when the noun has a distinct genitive form:

kione ny bleeaney (*blein*)	end of the year
eaghtyr ny hooirey (*ooir*)	the earth's surface
but *bing* y *çheshaght* (*sheshaght*)	the committee of the society

5.3   The plural definite article for both genders is normally *ny*

ny stubbinyn	the Manx cats
ny quallianyn	the pups
ny meeghyn	the months

In a number of set phrases and place names the archaic form of the genitive plural *nyn* is used. In nouns, nasalisation is still sometimes found after this genitive plural form in old placenames:

Bwoaillee nyn **Giark**   Hens' fold

5.4   Mutation after the article
The initial sound of a word may change after the article (see 1.1):

5.4.1   Most feminine nouns in the nominative, vocative and accusative mutate after the article

*Honnick mee yn **ven** (ben)*   I saw the woman

*cummal ghaa ny three dy firkinyn y **pheesh** (peesh)*
containing two or three firkins apiece   [John ii.6] (see 8.3.3)

5.4.2   Feminine nouns beginning with dentals *t-, d-, çh-, j-* do not mutate

*Honnick mee yn **doodee***   I saw the girl

*Va'n **thunnag** puhttey lurg ny grineyn*
The duck was nuzzling after the grain
            [Nigel Kneale, 'Curphey's Follower', tr. Brian Stowell,
                        Duillaghyn 1, November 2005]

5.4.3   Masculine nouns in the vocative or genitive singular mutate after the article

*laa yn **chaggey** (caggey)*   the day of the battle

*V'eh raad y **vaaish** (baaish)*
He was on the way of death   [John iv 47]

5.4.4   Singular nouns of either gender may mutate after preposition + article

*er y **cheayn** (keayn* m)   on the sea
*harrish y **vooir** (mooir* f)   over the sea

5.5   Uses of the article

5.5.1   before some abstract nouns

y vea   life
y baase   death
yn irriney   truth, the truth
y dooinney   (hu)mankind

5.5.2   in questions, placed between the interrogative and the noun

Cre'n ennym t'ort?   What is your name?
(literally: what the name is on you?)

Quoi'n cabbyl ren oo reih?   Which horse did you choose?
(literally: who the horse did you choose?)

5.5.3   before a noun followed by the demonstratives *shoh, shen* and
shid

y ven shoh	this woman
yn dooinney shoh	this man
ny paitçhyn shen	those children
yn dooinney mooar shen	that big man
yn dooinney beg shid	yonder little man;

Exception: proper   nouns   do   not   require   the   article   with
demonstratives:

Yeesey shoh   this Jesus

5.5.4   before established compound nouns

y dooinney-poosee	the bridegroom
ny fir-reill	the rulers
yn çheshaght-chaggee	the army

5.5.5   sometimes after *lheid* (such) and *veg* (in the sense of 'any')

lheid ny deiney	such men
veg yn argid	any money

son lheid y graih shen hug Jee da'n theihll
for such love did God give to the world   [John iii.16]

Kys ta lheid yn ynsagh ec y dooinney shoh?
How has this man such learning?   [John vii.15]

*lheid y *cabbyl*   such a horse

* In older usage, *cabbyl* would be lenited, because *lheid* is in reality a
noun (meaning 'the like'; '*as y lheid*' means 'and the like', 'et
cetera')

5.6   The article used to express 'of' or possession

5.6.1   'of' expressed with the article + personal pronoun-preposition
ec instead of a possessive pronoun (3.2.3, 4.1.4)

my hie/y thie aym	my house
e braar /y braar eck	her brother
e vac shinney /yn mac shinney echey	his eldest son

This construction is especially useful in clarifying the ambiguous plural form *nyn*, our/your/their:

y thie ain	our house
yn obbyr eu	your (pl or formal) work
Ta shoh yn argid oc(syn)	this is their money

5.6.2   'of' expressed with a nominative noun + article + nominative or genitive noun

Bayr ny Hayrey	The road of the Ayres
Va ennym y voidyn Moirrey	the virgin's name was Mary
	[Luke i.27]
thie yn vainshtyr-sc(h)oill	the schoolmaster's house
reayrt ny marrey	view of the sea

Note: Few nouns still have separate genitives. There is also uncertainty surrounding gender (see 2).

5.6.3   'of' in compound nouns
In compound nouns made up of two nouns, the article or possessive is used only with the second noun:

cass y stoyl	the leg of the chair (chair-leg)
mwannal my laue	my wrist
(literally: the neck of my hand)	
thie my huyrey	my sister's house
ben y dooinney	the man's wife
ushtey yn çhibber	well water

5.6.4   The article used instead of a possessive
The article may be used instead of a possessive with:

a) persons, usually relatives

yn jishig	the (my) father

b) parts of the body

y cass aym	my foot

c) clothing

Ta fys ec dagh ghooinney c'raad ta'n vraag gortagh eh
Every man knows where the (his) shoe hurts him

5.7   The article with collective nouns

Collective nouns take a singular article but a plural adjective:

yn sleih	the people
yn ollagh	the cattle
yn vooinjer veggey	the little folk

Hooar eh ayns y çhiamble feallagh va creck dew ... as y vooinjer va caghlaa argid

He found in the temple people who were selling oxen ... and he found the people who were changing money   [John ii.14]

cur coonlagh dys yn ollagh   giving straw to the cattle

[Tommy Leece (1859–1956)]

6 Adjectives and adverbs
Marenmyn as rovreearyn

6.1 The formation of adjectives

Adjectives may be formed from nouns by adding suffixes such as *-agh*, *-oil*:

meanagh	average, central	(*mean*	centre, average)
fuilltagh	gory, bloody, confounded	(*fuill*	blood) [WC]
scanshoil	important	(*scansh*	importance)
çhiarnoil	lordly	(*çhiarn*	lord)

A few adjectives are formed from nouns using the suffixes *-ar*, *-ey*, *-yr*:

aigh	luck	*aighar*	lucky
leagh	price, value	*leaghar*	valuable
lhieen	number	*lhieenar*	numerous
airh	gold	*airhey*	golden
dooinney	man	*deiney*	human
grayn	horror	*graney*	ugly, horrible
bio	live, living	*bioyr*	lively, brisk
loo	activity	*looyr*	active, nimble

6.1.1 The form of Manx adjectives

Manx adjectives are usually identical in form in both singular and plural:

dooinney mie a good man   *deiney mie* good men

Manx adjectives may change their initial sound according to whether the noun they accompany is feminine or masculine gender (see 2), or (sometimes) plural:

ben vooar   a big woman *dooinney mooar*   a big man
deiney mooarey big men

6.1.2   Adjectives with a separate plural
In Classical Manx, when they follow the noun, in attributive function, a few monosyllabic adjectives ending in a consonant form a plural by adding *-ey*:

aeg, aegey	young	*ard, ardey*	high
beg, beggey	little	*boght, boghtey*	poor
bwoyagh/bwaagh, bwaaghey	pretty	*ching, chingey*	sick
glass, glassey	green, grey, pale	*jiarg, jiargey*	red
mooar, mooarey	big	*bane, baney*	white
mynn, mynney	fine, small	*roauyr, roauyrey*	fat
trome, tromey	heavy		

6.1.3   Adjectives with collective nouns
Collective nouns (2.3) take a singular article but a plural adjective. This adjective is lenited (see 1.1) where possible:

sleih aegey	young people, the young
mooinjer veggey	little people

Tra va ny skibbyltee boghtey cheet, v'ad beaghey ayns ny thieyn mooarey
When the visitors (the poor nimble folk) came, they stayed in the big houses   [WC]

6.1.4   Adjectives with duals
Following duals (see 8.3), the adjective is plural, even though the noun itself remains singular in Manx:

*daa eeast veggey   two small fishes   [John vi.9]

* (R. L. Thomson notes (*Lessoonyn Sodjey*, 79) that in this last example the plural adjective is normal, but the lenition ($b \rightarrow v$) is rare. Lenition, see 1.1)

6.1.5   Adjectives with a feminine noun
   Adjectives following a feminine noun often lenite (see 1.1.):

ben vooar   a big woman   *oie vie*   good night

6.2   Predicative adjectives
Predicative adjectives are invariable in form:

cha nel shin aeg agh yn un keayrt   we are only young once
(*aeg* (young) when used attributively, forms the plural *aegey*, see 6.1.2)

Predicative adjectives, which follow the noun, can complement the subject or the object.

6.2.1 Subject complement

Ta'n ghrian gial jiu	The sun is bright today
Ta'n thie mooar feayr	The big house is cold
Va mee fliugh	I was wet [WC]

6.2.2 Object complement

Ta shin fakin shin hene aeg foast We see ourselves young still

Predicative adjectives follow the noun in both Manx and English in cases such as the equative comparison, where one thing is equated with another:

T'eh cho shenn as ny sleityn He's as old as the hills

Where English would have: 'Leslie was funny, modest, kindly', Manx puts the verb first: **Va** *Leslie aitt, imlee, caarjoil*

6.3 Changing the meaning of an adjective through prefixes

6.3.1 Prefixes meaning the contrary
Chief among these 'contrary' prefixes in Manx are:

aa-	*aaghowin*	shallow	(*dowin*	deep)
am-	*amloayrtagh*	mute, dumb	(*loayrtagh*	articulate)
an-	*anleighalagh*	illegal	(*leighalagh*	legal)
do-	*do-chorree*	imperturbable	(*corree*	angry)
mee-	*mee-chadjin*	uncommon	(*cadjin*	common)
neu-	*neuagglagh*	fearless	(*agglagh*	fearful)

6.3.2 Other prefixes change the meaning or make it more specific

lieh (half):

lieh-wuigh	yellowish	(*buigh*	yellow)
lieh-yerrinagh	penultimate, semi-final	(*jerrinagh*	last)
lieh-foshlit	ajar	(*foshlit*	open/opened)

myn- (diminutive, little):

mynchooishag	petty, meticulous, pernickety	(*mynchooish*	trifling matter)
mynvrisht	shattered	(*brishey*	break)
mynyiarrit	shredded	(*giarrey*	cut)

so- (-able, -ible):

so-chlashtyn	audible	(*clashtyn*	hear)
so-lhottey	vulnerable	(*lhottey*	injure)
so-vrishey	fragile, breakable	(*brishey*	break)

yl- (multi-, poly-):

yl-çheeragh	cosmopolitan	(*çheeragh*	indigenous)
yl-ghaait	colourful, multi-coloured	(*daah*	colour)
yl-phoosee	polygamous	(*poosey*	marry)

ym- (around, peri-, circum-):

ym-lioarlagh	voluminous	(*lioar*	book)
ym-schleoil	versatile (of mind)	(*schleoil*	talented, skilful)
ym-scruit	circumscribed	(*screeu*	write)

yn- (-able):

yn-ee	edible, fit to eat	(*ee*	eat)
yn-arganey	debatable	(*arganey*	argue)
yn-troo	enviable	(*trooaghey*	grudge, envy)

Prefixes often trigger lenition in Manx (see 1.1).

6.4   The verbal or participial adjective

The verbal adjective is a past participle used adjectivally, that is, used as an adjective to describe or 'qualify' a noun. In Manx the past particple is formed from a verb and usually ends in *-it*, or sometimes *-t* (see 9):

caillt, caillit (*coayl*) lost	*Pargys **caillit*** Paradise lost
*ben **reilt***	nun (literally: 'a ruled woman')
*ooh **vroieit***	boiled egg
*thalloo **traauit***	ploughed land

An earlier participial form ending in *-jey* survives in a few fixed phrases:

*cooid **chailjey***	lost property
*skeddan **sailjey***	salt(ed) herring (*sailjey* salted)

6.4.1   Uses of the participial adjective

attributive use:

*Honnick mee yn dorrys **jeight***	I saw the closed door
*T'eh ny loayreyder **cliaghtit***	He is an experienced speaker

Nagh vel dagh ooilley red eck – my clane theihll: Chammah's my chree boght **brisht** *as mish as ee hene?*
Does she not have everything – my whole world: As well as my poor broken heart, and me, and her very self?
    [R. C. Carswell, 'Ushag y Tappee', *Shelg yn Drane* 1994]

predicative use, with *ta, va,* to indicate a state which is the result of an action:

ta'n dorrys **jeight**	the door is closed
ta'n chree aym **brisht**	my heart is broken

Ta mee **cliagh**tit *rish nish*
I am accustomed to it now (*cliaghtey* accustomed)

V'eh **currit** *da'n jough*   He was addicted to drink

6.5   Nominalised adjectives

Some adjectives, including all those ending in *-agh* denoting living beings, can be used as nouns in both the singular and plural:

S'booiagh **yn voght** *er yn veggan*
How contented is the poor man with little

[Manx proverb]

When Manx adjectives are used as nouns in this way they form noun-type plurals:

marroo	a dead person	*ny merriu*	the dead
baccagh	a lame person	*ny baccee*	the lame
asslayntagh	a sick person	*ny asslayntee*	the sick
ny doail (doal)	the blind	*ny boghtyn (boght)*	the poor

6.6   Mutation after adjectives

6.6.1   Preceding adjectives and possessive adjectives trigger mutation
Those few Manx adjectives which (exceptionally) precede the noun, and also the possessive adjectives such as *my, dty,* usually cause lenition in the following noun (see 1.1):

drogh (bad):

drogh hraghtalagh	smuggler	(*traghtalagh*, trader)
drogh chaaynt	bad or strong language	(*caaynt*, spoken language, talk)
drogh 'uill	bad blood	(*fuill*, blood)

Drogh always needs a noun with it; it cannot be used independently or predicatively, to say 'he is bad', 'that's too bad', etc.

shenn (old):
Shenn also precedes the noun, causing it to lenite, except for dentals:

my henn charrey	my old friend	(*carrey* friend)
shenn chumraag	old comrade	(*cumraag* comrade)
shenn chretoor	old crock (of a person)	(*cretoor* creature)

ard (high, chief, main):
Ard usually precedes a noun or another adjective only in hyphenated compounds. Lenition then occurs in the second half of the compound:

yn Ard-Vaylee	the High Bailiff	(*Baylee*)
ard-varriaghtagh	triumphal	(*barriaght* victory)
ard-charrey	patron	(*carrey* friend)
ard-chiaull	classical music	(*kiaull* music)
ard-wannalagh	high-faluting	(*mwannal* neck)

But when there is no hyphen, and the meaning of *ard* is 'high', *ard* follows the noun in the usual way:

cronk ard	high hill
ynnydyn ardey	high places
mwannal ard	high neck

reih (choice):
Reih is listed by some authorities as an adjective when it functions adjectivally and precedes a noun to form compounds such as *reih-feeyney* (vintage), *reih-ghuilley* (blue-eyed boy, favourite). However, *reih* is more common as a noun or verb, although Fargher (1979: 152) suggests *yn reih red dy yannoo* as 'the choice thing to do'.

6.6.2   Possessive adjectives
They usually cause mutation (see 1.1):

my	my (lenition)
dty	your (singular informal) (lenition)
e	his (lenition)
e	her (no mutation)
nyn	our, your (plural or singular formal), their (nasalisation)

My and *dty* may appear as *m'* and *dt'* before vowels.
Often, possessives are replaced by *y* with a noun and the appropriate form of *ec*:

y chass aym	my foot

This strategy usefully clarifies the ambiguous situation in the plural, where the single form *nyn* corresponds to our/your/their.

6.7   Adverbs

6.7.1   Forming adverbs in Manx

Most Manx adverbs which are derived from adjectives are formed by simply placing the particle *dy* before the adjective. The adjective does not mutate:

mie	good	*dy mie*	well
gennal	cheerful	*dy gennal*	cheerfully

*shegin dou jus jeeaghyn **dy dowin** er y chooish shoh*
I ought to look into this matter thoroughly   [JC]

Although the adverbial particle *dy* does not in principle cause lenition, in practice, an extra *h-* is pronounced (and occasionally written) before initial vowels:

dy holk	badly	(*olk* bad)
dy hamlagh	ironically	(*amlagh* ironic)
dy helgysagh	spitefully	(*elgysagh* spiteful)
dy himneagh	anxiously	(*imneagh* anxious)

and, by analogy:

dy çhennoil	vehemently	(*çhennoil* vehement)
ta jannoo dy holk	that doeth evilly	[John iii.20]

6.7.2   Position of adverbs

In Manx, most adverbs follow the word they intensify:

*mie **dy liooar***	good enough
*çhing **agglagh***	terribly sick
*graney **atçhimagh***	horribly ugly

*V'ad feayr **agglagh**, nagh row*
They were awfully cold, weren't they?   [JC]

*Va'n cretoor graney **agglagh***   The creature was amazingly ugly
[Nigel Kneale: 'Curphey's Follower', tr. Brian Stowell,
Duillagyn 1, November 2005]

A few adverbs precede the word they qualify: *braew* (fine, wonderfully), *bunnys* (almost), *feer* (very), *(s)lane* (quite), *ro* (too):

*T'eh **braew** çheh aynshoh*   It's very warm here
[John Tom Kaighin (1862–1954)]

*Va shin goll sheese er y traie **bunnys rooisht***
We used to go down to the beach almost naked   [WC]

*Ta shen skeeal **feer vie**!*	That's a very good story!	[LQ]
*T'ou **slane keoie**!*	You're completely mad!	[WC]
*V'ee **ro vie** da*	She was too good for him	
	[Mrs Emily Lowey (1867–1947)]	

Position of adverbs in the sentence:
Adverbs derived from adjectives are placed either:

a) within the verbal phrase

*Ta mee **dy kinjagh** faagail y moddey ec y thie*
I always leave the dog at home

b) at the end of the clause

*Ren eh eh **dy tappee***   He did it quickly
(with the more Gaelic variant *ren eh dy tappee eh*)

c) in a relative clause
an adverb in the comparative or superlative takes the form of an adjective
in the comparative or superlative and follows the noun or pronoun it
relates to (the antecedent):

Y	charvaant	**smoo**	ta	cur geill	da	goan	e	vainshter
The	servant	most	is	attending	to	words	his	master

the servant who pays most attention to his master's words

yn	fer	**share**	ren	eh
the	man	best	did	it

the man who did it better/best

6.7.3   Omission of the adverbial particle *dy* in the following cases

a) when the adjective is in the comparative/superlative form only the
predicative *ny* is used

*Dreggyr eh **ny s'gennal** na roie*
He replied more cheerfully than before

*Haink mee **ny sodjey** na Juan noght*
I came further than John tonight

*Bee Juan dy valley **ny s'leaie** na mish*
John will be home sooner than myself

b) with certain adverbs, such as

çhelleeragh	immediately
*Freggyr **çhelleeragh**, my sailliu*	please answer immediately

doaltattym	suddenly
foast	still, yet, however, nevertheless
eisht, nish	now
reesht	again
arragh	ever again
sodjey	further
wass	on this side, below
hoal	over, beyond
noon as noal	to and fro
ny jean peccah **arragh**	sin no more = never again
abbyr shen **reesht**	say that again = repeat
vel eh **foast** *bio?*	is he still alive?
kinjagh	constantly (Biblical Manx)

6.7.4   Permanently lenited adverbs
Some adverbs begin with a permanently lenited consonant:

hoshiaght   first(ly), from *toshiaght*, beginning
Hooar eshyn **hoshiaght** *e vraar hene, Simon*
He first found his brother, Simon   [John i.42]

hannah   already (*c-* permanently lenited to *h-*)
T'eh **hannah** *jeant aym*
I've already done it.   [Joseph Woodworth (1854–1931)]

6.8   Adverbs of direction
Manx has six main adverbs of direction:

heese	*heose*
neese	*neose*
sheese	*seose*

6.8.1   *h-*: at rest
Those beginning with *h-* have the meaning stationary, at rest.
Heese, down (there), and *heose*, up (there), are used after *ve*, to be, and after prepositions without motion:

Ta dooinney **heese** *y traid*	There is a man down the road
heese *er y cheer*	down in the country
veih neese dy seose	from bottom to top
	(English: from top to bottom)

6.8.2   *n-*: towards
Those beginning with *n-* have the meaning 'towards the speaker':

neese	up towards the speaker from below
neose	towards the speaker from above

Tar neese!   Come up!
Tar neose!   Come down!

*V'ad çheet **neose** jeh'n clieau*
They were coming down from the mountain

*Honnick mee yn Spyrryd çheet **neose** veih Niau*
I saw the spirit coming down from heaven   [John i.32]

6.8.3   *s-*: away from

Those beginning with *s-* have the meaning 'away from the speaker':

sheese	down
seose	up

*Soie **sheese**!*	Sit down!
*Ta mee goll **sheese** y traid*	I am going down the road
*Huitt eh **sheese***	He fell down
*Irree **seose**!*	Get up!

*Lhie mee **sheese**, as dirree mee **seose***	
I lay down and I got up	
*Ceau eh **seose** 'syn aer!*	Throw it up in the air!
*Lheim eh **seose***	He jumped up

*V'eh shooyl neese as **sheese***
He was walking up and down (a hill; if the meaning is 'walking
up and down on the flat', pacing the floor, etc., usually Manx
has *huggey as veih*, 'back and forth', 'to and fro' or *noon as noal*)

Note: The English 'he's up', meaning 'he's out of bed', is translated by
the idiom *t'eh ry-chosh, er e chosh* ('on foot').

6.8.4   Compass points

The original naming of the points of the compass took place with the
speaker facing east: hence, the root *-ar* means 'front', the root *-eear* means
'back':

eastwards, to the east	*shiar, my-hiar*
from the east	*niar*
westwards, to the west	*sheear, my-heear*
from the west	*neear*
northwards, to the north	*twoaie, my-hwoaie*
from the north	*veih'n twoaie*
southwards, to the south	*jiass, my-yiass*
from the south	*veih'n jiass*

N *twoaie*
↑
↓
S *jiass*

← *sheear*   W
→ *neear*

E   → *shiar*
← *niar*

6.8.5   Other adverbs of direction

At rest	Motion away from speaker	Motion towards speaker	Prepositional use
wass here, this side	*noon, harrish* from this side to the other side	*noal, harrish* over to this side, over to the other side	*çheu-wass-jeh* this side of
hoal the far side, other side of			*çheu-hoal-jeh* the far/other side of
mooie outside	*magh* out	*magh* out	*çheumooie jeh* outside of
sthie inside	*stiagh* in	*stiagh* in	*çheusthie jeh* inside of

6.9   Adverbial clauses

An adverbial clause is a group of words clustered around a verb giving information about such things as time, place and manner:

a) When: he visits every Friday evening (*fastyr Jeheiney*)

b) Where: they sit in the garden (*ayns y gharey*)

c) How: he speaks in a low voice (*ayns coraa dowin*)

6.9.1   Adverbial clauses of time may be introduced by *tra* (when), *neayr's* (since), *derrey, gys* (until)

All of the above are used with either the relative or the independent form of the verb:

Tra *va mish jeeaghyn er-ash*   When I looked back   [LQ]
Tra *va mee aeg*   When I was young

Tra *hug ny Hewnyn saggyrtyn veih Jerusalem*
When the Jews sent priests from Jerusalem   [John i.19]

C'red t'ou er ve jannoo **neayr**'*s ren mee fakin oo?*
What have you been doing since I saw you?

[Ned Maddrell (1877–1974)]

neayr'*s y traa shoh nurree*   since this time last year

[Joseph Woodworth (1854–1931)]

Manx future or future relative is often, logically enough, used for events that have not yet taken place, in cases where English uses the present tense, see 9.

Fuirree **derrey** *higym*   Wait until I (shall) come

derrey *vees oo erreish yn farling sodjey magh y eeck*
until you (will) have paid the last farthing   [Fargher 1979: 829]

Adverbial clauses of time may also be introduced by *roish my*, before, usually with a dependent verb, but sometimes with relative verb through confusion with *my*, if (see 4.1.15)

roish my *deie Philip ort*   before Philip called you [John i.48]
roish my *vow my lhiannoo baase*
before my child (will) die(s)   [John iv.49]

Vow is the future dependent of *geddyn*. Here again Manx uses the future tense for events that have not yet occurred, where English has the present.

Note: Originally, *roish my*, 'before', was simply '*my*' followed by a dependent verb, whereas *my*, 'if', was followed by a relative verb. But this distinction could not always be made clearly and led to confusion, so *roish* was added to distinguish *my*, 'before', and in late Manx was often used without *my*.

6.9.2   Adverbial clauses of place are introduced by *raad* (where) used with a relative or an independent verb

ayns Bethabara … **raad** *va Ean bashtey*
in Bethabara, where John was baptizing   [John i.28]

6.9.3   Adverbial clauses of cause are introduced by *er-y-fa dy/nagh* (because) and *er yn oyr dy/nagh* (because). The dependent form of the verb is used

Hie eh dy valley, **er-yn-oyr** *dy row eh ching*
He went home because he was ill

Some people prefer the hyphens, others omit them. Hyphens are unstable in both Manx and English and their use changes over time and with different language habits and fashions.

6.9.4   Adverbial clauses of purpose and result may be introduced by
dy/nagh (so that ... not) and *er-aggle* (in case, lest), *dy/nagh* (for
fear that/lest)

er aggle *ny haggle*   to be on the safe side
er-aggle *dy jig red smessey ort*   lest a worse thing happen to you
                                                                            [John v.14]

Note: *Son* is sometimes used to reinforce *dy/nagh* of purpose:

Hug eh yn soilshey sterrym dou **son dy gholl** *thie*
He gave me the storm lantern (for) to go home (= so that I might
get home)

son nagh jig *brah er ny obbraghyn echey*
so that judgment may not come on his works

Hooar eh yn cappan **son dy** *chur da fys*
Cre'n aght ta niau bannaghey giastyllys

He received the cup, in order to teach him
How heaven blesses charity
                                                                            [Thomas Parnell, The Hermit 258–9]

6.9.5   Adverbial clauses of 'concession' may be introduced in Manx
by *ga, ga dy/nagh* (negative) (although) but see 7.2.7, *ga*
(Some speakers now use the dependent form of the verb after *ga: ga dy
vel ad, ga dy beagh*. Others still use the independent form: *ga t'ad, ga
veagh*)

Ga dy vel *mee shooyl ayns coan scadoo yn vaaish*
Though I walk through the valley of the shadow of death
                                                                            [Psalm 23 v.4]

Less usually, adverbial clauses of concession may be introduced by *er
be dy*, were it not that, had it not been that:

er-be dy *row yn Çhiarn hene er nyn lieh*
were it not that the Lord himself was on our side [Psalm 124 v.1]

(*er-be*, see 7.3)

6.9.6   Adverbial clauses of condition may be introduced by

a) *my* (if) with the independent form of the verb if the condition is
fulfillable

my *t'eh clashtyn shoh*   if he is hearing this
my *ta fys ayd*   if you know (and perhaps you do)

> *my t'ou jannoo ny reddyn shoh*   if you are doing these things
> [John vii.4]

More rarely this is used with past:

> *my v'eh ayns shoh,*   if (as you say), he really was here

b) For future or hypothetical present, the relative form of the verb is used

> *my ee-ys dooinney erbee jeh'n arran shoh*
> if any man [shall] eat of this bread   [John vi.51]
>
> *my vees eh goll, hem marish*
> if he goes (literally: 'will go'), I'll go with him

c) Hypothetical conditions less likely of fulfilment take the conditional tense of the verb

> *my chredjagh oo*   if you were to believe   [John xi.40]
> *my ghoghe dooinney erbee rish*   if any man were to admit
> [John ix.22]

In these examples, exceptionally, *dy* is replaced by *my* + conditional verb, to avoid ambiguity.

d) *mannagh* (if not, unless) is used with the dependent form of the verb

> *mannagh vel shen firrinagh*   if that isn't true, unless that's true

or with conditional in unreal conditions:

> *Mannagh beign er ve ayns shen, cha beign er chredjal eh*
> if I hadn't been there I shouldn't have believed it

e) *dy* (if) is used with conditional only and expresses unreal conditions

> *dy beagh eh ayns shoh*   if he were here (but he isn't)
> *dy beagh eh er ve ayns shoh*   if he had been there (but he wasn't)
>
> *Dy beagh shiu nyn gloan da Abraham, yinnagh shiu obbraghyn Abraham,*
> If you were the children of Abraham, you would do the works of Abraham   [John viii.39]

f) *myr dy/nagh* (as if, as if not) is used with the conditional tense functioning as a subjunctive

> *myr dy beagh eh*   as if it were   [John vii.10]
>
> *myr nagh beagh eh dy nyn glashtyn*
> as if he did not hear them   [John viii.6]

6.9.7   Adverbial clauses of comparison are introduced by *myr* (as) used with relative or independent form of verb

> *myr share as dod eh*   as best he could
>   [Fargher 1979: 43]

6.10   Preceding adverbs: mutation
Adverbs which precede the adjective or adverb they intensify or otherwise modify, cause lenition, changing the first sound of the following word:

> *braew*, extremely (literally: 'fine')
>   *braew vie*   very good, well (*mie*, good)
>
> *feer*, very   *feer vie*   very good
> *lane*, quite   *lane vie*   quite good
> *ro*, too   *ro vooar*   too large
>
> *mie*, good, well
>   *mie chiune*   well calm (*kiune*, calm) (compare
>   English 'nice and calm')

Note: words beginning with *s-, sh-, d-, t-, j-, çh-* do not change after *feer* and *lane*.

6.11   Intensifiers without *dy*
Adverbs which follow the adjective or adverb they intensify drop the adverbial particle *dy*:

> *Va mee çhing agglagh*   I was terribly ill
> *V'eh taggloo ard agglagh*   He was speaking awfully loudly
> *V'eh olk agglagh!*   It was terribly bad!   [LQ]

6.12   Prominence
In some constructions the present affirmative of the copula *she*, abbreviated to *'s*, precedes the adjective:

> *S'mooar va nyn moggey**   (how) great was their joy
> *S'mie shen!*   That's good!
> *S'quaagh shen!*   That's strange!

* Earlier Manx has: *by vooar nyn moggey*.

6.13   *er-çhee, er çhee, mysh* (about) can be followed by the verbnoun and then give the meaning 'about to' 'on the point of' doing something

*Va shin **er çhee** goll*	We were about to go
*Va shin **mysh** goll*	We were about to go

*Ta'n lioar **er çhee** goll er screeu*
The book is about to be written

*Cha nel mee **er-çhee** geddyn baase!*
I'm not about to die

6.14   Adverbs with *ry-*

6.14.1   *ry-hoi* or *ry-oi*, (reserved) for, can also be used to mean 'about to'
Ry-hoi is made up from the older form of the preposition *rish + oaie*, 'in the face of', with a prefixed *h-* to the vowel. It now means 'about to' or 'for the purpose of':

*shey siyn cloaie **ry-hoi** ushtey*   six stone vessels for water

[John ii.6]

***ry-hoi** y vrah eh*   about to betray him   [John xiii.11]

*va **ry-hoi** çheet gys y theill*
who was about to come into the world   [John xi.27]

Note: the same original form of *rish* is found in the expression *ry foddey dy hraa*, 'for a long period of time'

6.14.2   *ry-lhiattee* (aside)

*Bee oo abyl dy chur y blein shoh **ry-lhiattee***
You'll be able to put that year aside

[Thomas Christian (1851–1930)]

6.14.3   *ry-cheilley* (together)

*Lhig dooin goll **ry cheilley***   let's go together

[Thomas Christian (1851–1930)]

*gys unnaneys **ry-cheilley***
to unity with one another, together,   [John xi.52]

6.15   Indefinite adverbs
erbee, ennagh (any, ever) are often used to form indefinite adverbs

6.15.1 *erbee* (any-, -ever)

traa **erbee**	whenever, anytime at all
raad/boayl **erbee**	anywhere, wherever
ansherbee	anyhow
er chor **erbee**	for whatever reason

6.15.2 *ennagh* (some-)

traa **ennagh**	sometime
er aght **ennagh**	some way, somehow or other
raad/boayl **ennagh**	somewhere

6.15.3 *erbee* (no-) uses a negated verb

Cha jagh *mee boayl* **erbee**
I went nowhere (= I didn't go anywhere)

Cha nel *mee er aght* **erbee** *scoorit*
I am in no way drunk

6.15.4 *rieau, dy bragh, çhioee* (ever, never)
When referring to the past *rieau* is used:

Naik oo **rieau** *ee?*	Did you ever see her?
Cha dooyrt mee **rieau** *eh*	I never said it
Cho dowin as v'ad **rieau**	As deep as ever they were
	[*Kirree fo 'niaghtey*, Traditional Ballad]

When referring to the future *dy bragh* or *çhioee* is used:

Cha bee'm **dy bragh** *heose ayns shoh*
I'll never be up here again

son **dy bragh** *as dy bragh*	for ever and ever[4]

Bee'n fockleyr shoh aarlee **çhioee**?
Will this dictionary ever be ready?   [Fargher 1979: 287]

Cha jigym **çhioee**	I shall never come
	[Fargher 1979: 519]

---

[4] R. L. Thomson says of '*dy bragh*': 'the etymologically absurd but very long established *dy bragh*.' (The Manx Traditionary Ballad: *Etudes celtiques* X, p. 73) Etymologically absurd or not, the phrase is included in many prayers as the equivalent of the English 'for ever and ever', so there would not appear to be any need to feel embarrassed about using it.

6.15.5   *sheer* (ever/never) as an intensifier

Originally an adjective meaning 'long', *sheer* can be prefixed to other words to give the sense of duration, as in English 'never-ending', 'everlasting', etc.

sheer-accanyn	never-ceasing complaints
sheer-geearree	importuning
sheer-rio	permafrost

tra v'ad sheer fênaght jeh
when they were continually enquiring of him [1763], as they
pressed him for an answer   [John viii.7]

adsyn va sheer geiyrt er
those who were continually following him, meaning Jesus'
disciples   [R. L. Thomson, *Lessoonyn Sodjey* 98]

Note: *dy bragh farraghtyn*, 'continuing for ever', is used in religious
contexts in imitation of the English expressions 'everlasting', 'for
ever and ever'.

6.16   Interrogative adverbs

Questions like 'where?' 'when?' are introduced by interrogative adverbs:

c'raad?	where?
cre'n traa, cuin?	when, what time?
cre'n fa, cre'n oyr?	why?
kanys, kys?	how?
cre'n aght?	how, in what way?
quoid? c'woad?	how much?
cre whilleen, c'woad?	how many?
cre wheesh?	how big?
cammah?	why? for what reason?
kevys (= cre/cre'n fys) da?	how does he know?
kevys dou?	how do I know?
cre choud?	how far? how long?
cre'n lheead?	how wide?

6.17   Comparison of adjectives and adverbs

Manx comparatives and superlatives are formed using the copula *she*, abbreviated to *'s* (see 9.7). Most adjectives do not change their form between the comparative and superlative, but there are exceptions (see 6.19):

yn dooinney mooar	the big man
yn dooinney smoo	the bigger man, the biggest man

6.17.1   -*y* with attenuated vowel
Many adjectives add -*ey* in the comparative and superlative, and the vowel is attenuated, that is, it becomes slender:

> *Share as fer* **s'gilley** *jeh mooinjey y vadran* (*gial*)
> Brightest and best of the sons of the morning
> > [Hymn 75, Epiphany]

6.17.2   *smoo, sloo*
The alternative periphrastic construction with *smoo* (greater, more) and *sloo* (less, least) may always be used, especially with longer adjectives, and those beginning with *s-*, except with irregulars:

> *yn dooinney* **smoo scanshoil**   the most important man

> *yn red* **smoo agglagh** *va rieau jeant ayns Doolish*
> the most dreadful thing that ever was done in Douglas   [BC]

> *Va ny Hewnyn wheesh shen* **smoo shleeit** *er cur baase da*
> The Jews sought the more to kill him
> (literally: 'were all the keener on putting him to death')
> > [John v.18]

> *yn dooinney* **smoo ynsit**   the most learned man
> *yn dooinney* **sloo ynsit**   the least learned man

The periphrastic construction with *ny sloo … na* is the only means of expressing 'less than':

> *Tra va mee* **ny sloo na** *daa vlein d'eash*
> When I was less than two years old   [LQ]

> *Son v'eh feer veshtal; shen-y-fa cha dinsh ee veg da,* **ny sloo ny ny smoo**, *derrey'n voghrey*
> For he was very drunk; wherefore she told him nothing, neither less nor more, until the morning light   [I Samuel xxv.36]

> *Ta mee jerkal nagh bee ee* **ny sloo ymmydoil na** *ny shenn Lessoonyn*
> I hope it will not be less useful than the old Lessons
> [R. L. Thomson, First Lessons in Manx, third, revised edition, 1965]

6.17.3   Attributive comparison
The comparative/superlative is in reality a relative clause introduced by the present tense of the copula, *s'* (see 9.7.2), or occasionally the past copula *by*:

> *V'ee yn inneen* **s'bwaaee** *'sy theihll*
> She was the prettiest girl in the world
> (= she was the girl who was prettiest)

*Vel shen y thie **syrjey**?*   Is that the highest house?
(= is that the house which is highest?)

*Ta Glion Sulby y fer **s'bwaaee** er yn Ellan*
Sulby Glen is the most beautiful in the Island

*Ta shoh yn lioar **s'çhee** ayns my hie*
This is the thickest book in my house

*Daag mee yn thie lhionney **s'girroo** 'sy Jiass*
I left the roughest pub in the South

***S'troshey** yn theay na'n çhiarn*
The people are stronger than the lord

*yn vooinjer **b'ardey** as **by niartal***
the highest and strongest people   [Psalm 78 52]

Note: This last form is rare, and is found in Classical Manx only.

6.17.4 Predicative adjectival comparative/superlatives
Predicative comparatives and superlatives are preceded in Manx by *ny*
+ copula *s'* and occasionally *by**. After a comparison, *na* = than:

*Ta'n dooinney shoh **ny share na** eh shen*
This man is better than that one

*Ta'n Thames **ny shlea na**'n Awin Sulby*
The Thames is wider than Sulby River

*Ta'n dorrys shoh **ny shinney na**'n dorrys shen*
This door is older than that door

* The form with '*by*' is found only in older Manx:

By hroshey *eshyn*   He was the strongest
Yn *dooinney* **by hroshey**   The man who was strongest

6.17.5 Adverbial comparative/superlatives
The comparative and superlative forms of adverbs are formed along the
same lines and are also preceded by *ny* + copula *s'*, occasionally *by*:

*Roie yn moddey **ny s'bieau na** eshyn*
The dog ran faster than he did

6.18   Changes may occur in adjectives and adverbs in the comparative/superlative

6.18.1 Monosyllabic adjectives (and some others)
Changes of form between the positive or ordinary form of the adjective or adverb and the comparative/superlative occur chiefly in monosyllabic adjectives and adverbs. Technically, these changes involve:

a) the raising of the stem vowel + palatalization of the following consonant: the effects of this are shown by the examples below

b) and/or addition of the suffix -*ey*

> *Share as fer **s'gilley** jeh mooinjey y vadran (gial)*
> Brightest and best of the sons of the morning
> [Hymn 75, Epiphany]

Note: *share* is the irregular comparative/superlative of *mie* (good), see
6.19.

Positive		Comparative/superlative
aalin	fair, beautiful,	*aaley*
annoon	weak	*annooiney*
anvennick	infrequent	*anvenkey*
bog	soft	*buiggey*
çhionn	tight	*çhenney*
deyr	precious	*deyrey*
dowin	deep	*diuney*
eddrym	light (weight)	*edrymmey*
gial	white, bright	*gilley*
giare	short	*girrey*
glen	clean	*glenney*
injil	low	*inshley*
jeean	vehement	*jeeaney*
liauyr	long	*lhiurey*
meen	fine	*meeney*
millish	sweet	*miljey*
moal	slow	*melley*
ooasle	noble	*ooashley*
roauyr	fat	*riurey*
thanney	thin	*theinney*

*Ta Mannin **ny s'aaley** na Lerphoyll*
Mann is prettier than Liverpool

*yn ven **s'aaley***   the most beautiful woman

Note: *S'jerree* (last) has the form of a comparative/superlative although there is no corresponding positive form in either Manx or English:

*Ec toshiaght yn chaggee **s'jerree***
At the start of the last World War   [JC]

6.18.2   Stem changes
Some adjectives change the stem without apparent addition:

çheh	hot	*çhoe*	hotter
çhiu	thick	*çhee*	thicker
garroo	rough	*girroo*	rougher
broghe	dirty	*broiee*	dirtier
bwaagh	pretty	*bwaaee*	prettier

*Ta fuill **ny s'çhee** na ushtey*   blood is thicker than water

6.18.3   *-agh* → *-ee*
Final *-agh* becomes *-ee* in Classical Manx, but not usually in Modern Manx:

arryssagh	repentant	*arryssee*	more repentant
berçhagh	rich	*berçhee*	richer
booiagh	pleased	*booie*	more pleased

6.19   Irregular comparative/superlative
Some common adjectives have irregular comparative/superlative forms to which the copula *s* is prefixed without the apostrophe:

aashagh	easy	*sassey*	easier
lhean	broad	*shlea*	broader
aeg	young	*saa*	younger
mie	good	*share*	better
ard	high	*syrjey*	higher
olk	bad	*smessey*	worse
beg	small	*sloo*	smaller
shenn	old	*shinney*	older
faggys	near	*sniessey*	nearer
trome	heavy	*strimmey*	heavier
foddey	far	*sodjey*	further
leah	sooner	*sleaie*	sooner
lajer	strong	*stroshey*	stronger
ymmodee	many	*shlee*	more (in number)
mooar	big	*smoo*	more (in quantity)

Ta airh **ny s'trimmey na** *argid*   Gold is heavier than silver

Myr **sniessey** *da'n oie,* **shlee** *mitchoor*
The nearer the night, the more rogues

Tra **s'reaie** *yn chloie,* **share** *faagail jeh*
When the play is merriest, it is best to leave

Myr **smoo** *yn çheshaght,* **s'reaie** *yn chloie*
The more the merrier,
(literally: 'the larger the company, the merrier the play')

6.20   Equative comparatives
The comparison is expressed with *cha* or *cho*, the latter often written in this way to distinguish it from *cha* meaning 'not':

Ta mee **cha mie** *as eshyn*   I am as good as he is
(*cha mie* often becomes *chammah*)

Roie yn guilley **cho bieau** *as y moddey*
The boy ran as quickly as the dog

V'eh **cho roauyr** *as muck*   He was as fat as a pig

Shen yn oyr ta'n Ghailck aym's **cho moal**, *cha nel mee son giu!*
That's why my Manx is so poor as it is, I'm not for drinking!
                                                                [LQ]

V'eh **cho çhing**, *dooyrt eh*   He was so very sick, he said [WC]

Cha row mee rieau fakin dooinney **cho jiarg** *as va Alec!*
I never saw a man as red as Alec!   [JC]

6.21   Comparative constructions

6.21.1 *chammah* etc.
Comparative constructions may feature the following elements:

a) *chammah* (as good, as well), derived from *cha mie*

Ta ushag ayns laue **chammah** *as jees 'sy thammag*
A bird in the hand is as good as two in the bush

Ta **chammah** *enney eu orrym's, as ta fys eu cre-voish ta mee*
Ye both know me, and ye know whence I am   [John vii.28]

As va **chammah** *Yeesey cuirt, as e ynseydee, gys y vannish*
And both Jesus was called, and his disciples, to the marriage
                                                        [John ii.2]

b) *foddey* (much, far)

    foddey smessey   much worse; *foddey share*   far better

Note: also *dy mooar*:

*Er-lhiam dy bee fer ny ghaa ayn chreidys dy vel ee **ny smessey dy mooar***
I think there will be one or two people who will think it is far worse

[R. L. Thomson, Gys y Lhaider, First Lessons in Manx,
third, revised edition, 1965]

c) *lane* (full, quite, much more)

*Ta mee **lane** saa na Juan*   I am much younger than John
*(V'ad) **lane arryltagh***   they were quite willing   [JC]

*Ta'n lessoon shoh **lane sassey** na'n lessoon y çhiaghtin shoh chaie*
This lesson is much easier than the lesson last week

*Honnick mee dy row eh **lane trimshagh***
I saw he was very sad   [JC]

d) *monney* (much, more), used especially in negatives

***Cha** row mee **monney smessey na** my charrey*
I was not much worse than my friend

***Cha** nel eh **monney shinney na** shen*
He is not much older than that

e) *myr* (or); – 'the' in 'the … the' constructions

    myr s'leaie share   the sooner the better

***Myr sloo** yn çheshaght, **smoo** yn ayrn*
The smaller the company, the bigger the share

***Myr sniessey** da'n oie, **shlee** mitçhoor*
The nearer the night the more rogues

f) *ro, roud, rou(y)r* (too much)

    *V'ee **ro vie** da*   She was too good for him
[Mrs Emily Lowey (1867–1947)]

*Va **rou(y)r** sleih ayn*   There were too many people there

Rouyr *moddee as beggan craueyn*
Too many dogs and few bones

g) *whilleen* (as many)

*agh **whilleen** as ren soiaghey jeh*
but as many as esteemed him   [John i.12]

h) *wheesh* (as much, as many, that much = all the more)

*Tamain freayll **wheesh** kirree as v'ad freilt son veg*
We keep as many sheep as could be kept for nothing
                              [John Tom Kaighin (1862–1954)]

*bunnys jeih bleeaney, **cho wheesh** as shen*
almost 10 years, as long as that   [JC]

*Va ny Hewnyn **wheesh** shen **smoo shleeit** er cur baase eh*
The Jews were that much more keen on putting him to death
                              [John v.18]

Whilleen and *wheesh* are permanently lenited 'equatives' which compare
equal qualities, degrees, quantities, etc.
Note: Before a pronoun, *as* may be replaced by *rish*:

*Cha row clagh ayns Mannin chammah **rish***
There wasn't a bell in Man as good as it

6.21.2 Concessive comparison
The ordinary Manx comparative/superlative, using the copula *she*,
abbreviated to *'s*, expresses the concessive comparison:

Myr s'doo *yn feeagh yiow eh sheshey*
(As) black as the raven is, he'll find a mate

6.21.3 Inversion
The compared adverb in the relative clause (introduced in English by
'who') is attached to the antecedent as an adjective.
Some examples from *Pargys Caillit*:

*Quoi **s'creeoil** yinnagh booise*
Who would give thanks most heartily   [*Pargys Caillit* 248]

*Tra **smoo** veagh magher çheh*
When most a (battle) field would be hot
(= when the battle would be hottest)   [*Pargys Caillit* 532]

Aile, jaagh as feiyr v'ayn myr streeu quoi oc **smoo** *yinnagh misreill as coayl da'n çheshaght noa*
Fire, smoke and noise there were, as contesting who should wreak most havoc on the new company   [*Pargys Caillit* 827]

She'n soilshey **smoo** *ta freayll as veih meehreishteil*
The sun, first and foremost, keeps away despair
                                                [*Pargys Caillit* 1120]

7   Conjunctions
Co-whingyssyn

Manx employs both co-ordinating and subordinating conjunctions.

7.1   Co-ordinating conjunctions
The principal co-ordinating conjunctions in Manx are *as* (and), *agh* (but),
ny (or):

7.1.1   *as* (and)

> *V'eh jeant feayr ec aer yn oie **as** ghow eh toshiaght dy chur reddyn my
> ner*
> He was chilled by the night air and beginning to notice things
> > [Nigel Kneale, 'Curphey's Follower', tr. Brian Stowell,
> > *Duillagyn* 1, November 2005]

> *Jeh reiltys niau lhig toiggal cooie ve ayd*
> ***As** da dooyteilys ny cur arragh raad*

> Then know the truth of government divine
> And let these scruples be no longer thine
> > [Thomas Parnell, The Hermit 194–195]

7.1.2   *agh* (but)

> *Va graih aym urree – cha row niart aym er –*
> *Agh ish gyn graih, nagh ren goaill tastey jeem.*

> I loved her – I couldn't help myself –
> But she was without love for me.
> > [R. C. Carswell, 'Ushag y tappee', *Shelg yn Drane* 1994]

7.1.3   *ny* (or)

> *Cha s' aym's vel mee er jannoo mie **ny** dyn*
> I don't know whether I've done well or not
> > [Ned Maddrell (1877–1974)]

In the last example, in both Manx and English, only one single word follows the conjunction, so it doesn't look much like a real clause. But both Manx '*ny dyn*' and English 'or not' in this context correspond to a full clause, meaning 'or whether I have not done well,' so *ny* counts as a co-ordinating conjunction.

7.1.4   The modern use of co-ordinating conjunctions
There is a tendency for Manx speakers and writers, certainly since the middle of the twentieth century, to use many more main clauses linked by *as* (and), or *agh* (but), where earlier usage might prefer subordinate clauses. This means that the co-ordinating conjunctions in modern Manx enjoy a disproportionate degree of exposure.

7.2   Subordinating conjunctions
Some of the 'subordinating conjunctions' most commonly encountered in Manx are the following:

7.2.1   *chamoo* (neither = and not)

> ... *gys e raad ta mee er chummal, as cha vel mee er hreigeil eh.*
> **Chamoo** *ta mee er hyndaa veih slattys e veillyn.*
> ... his way have I kept, and not declined. Neither have I gone back from the commandment of his lips
>
> > [Job xxiii:11–12]

7.2.2   *choud, choud's (choud as)* (while, whilst)

> *Jean traagh* **choud** *as ta'n ghrian soilshean*
> Make hay while the sun shines
> > [Proverb, A. Cregeen: repr. 1984 cit.]

> ... *eayin veggey geamagh magh ec dagh gass birragh,* **Choud***'s t'ad shirrey bayr dy hooyl gyn gortey*
> Little lambs calling out at each sharp stalk, whilst they seek a way to walk without wound
> > [R. C. Carswell, 'Er y Çheer 'sy Çheeiragh', *Shelg yn Drane* 1994]

7.2.3   *derrey* (until)

> ... *cha jig Crestee Raueagh erbee dy lhie* **derrey** *nee eh fakin yn ghrian girree moghrey Laa yn Ollick*
> ... no Roman Catholic could go to bed until he saw the sun rise on Christmas Day
> > [Clague, Manx Reminiscences 1911: 38–39]

7.2.4   *Dy*, like *my*, *ny*, has many different meanings and functions in Manx. When *dy* is used as a conjunction, these are some of its chief uses

a) *dy* (that)

> *Ayns Ceredigion, ta 51.8% gra **dy** vel Bretnish oc*
> In Ceredigion, 51.8% say that they speak Welsh
> > [Brian Stowell, *'Bretnish: Neose Seose'*,
> > *Dhooraght* 29, April 2003]

> *Dooyrt eh **dy** jinnagh shin goll dys Purt le Moirrey*
> He said that we'd be going to Port St Mary
> > [Ned Maddrell (1877–1974)]

b) *dy* (so that)

> ***Dy** vod mayd ansoor y choyrt dauesyn […] t'er choyrt shin*
> So that we may give an answer to them that sent us
> > [John i.22]

Note: The second 'that' in the English phrase, represented by […] in the Manx, is a relative pronoun (corresponding to 'who' or 'which'). This, like other relative pronouns, does not appear in the Manx:

> *… ayns ny troaryn […]*
> *Ta mee gee, as ayns yn ushtey […] ta iuit aym*

> in the crops
> that I eat, and in the water that is drunk by me
> > [R. C. Carswell, 'Kione Vaghal', *Shelg yn Drane* 1994]

> *Ayr ain t'ayns niau*   Our Father, who art in heaven

c) *dy, nagh* (so that, not)

> *… dubbey **dy** ushtey moanagh, cho aaghowin **dy** goan choodee eh ny stroanyn echey*
> … a puddle of brown mountain water, so shallow that it barely covered his nostrils
> > [Nigel Kneale, 'Curphey's Follower', tr. Adrian Pilgrim 2006]

> *Ta ny bodjallyn chiu dy choodaghey eh, **nagh** vel eh fakin*
> Thick clouds are a covering to him, that he seeth not
> > [Job xxii:14]

d) (*son*) *dy* (that, in order that, to, in order to)

> *Hooar eh yn cappan **son dy** chur da fys*
> *Cre'n aght ta niau bannaghey giastyllys*

> He received the cup, in order to teach him
> How heaven blesses charity
> > [Thomas Parnell, The Hermit 258–9]

> *V'eh laccal yn dooinney … **son dy** gheddyn yn gunn as goll son dy*
> *varroo eh*
> He wanted the man … to get the gun and to go and kill him
> > [Ned Maddrell (1877–1974)]

> ***Dy** voddagh cooish chassid y ve oc n'oi*
> So that they might have a subject of accusation against him
> > [John viii.6]

7.2.5 *fakin dy/nagh* (seeing (that), seeing (that … not))

> ***Fakin nagh** vel ny traaghyn keillit veih'n Ooilley-niartal, cre'n fa*
> *nagh vel adsyn oc ta enney er cur geill da e laghyn?*
> Why, seeing times are not hidden from the Almighty, do they
> that know him not see his days?
> > [Job xxiv:1]

> *Agh **fakin** dy row yn stoo heose clouit 'sy vlein 1873 …*
> But seeing that the above excerpt was printed in the year 1873 …
> > [R. C. Carswell, 'Padjer Colum Killey',
> > *Dhooraght* 16, December 1999]

7.2.6 *ny-yei* (yet, nevertheless)
This is sometimes seen written *ny-yeih*, and is always spelled this way
in the Manx Bible:

> ***Ny-yeih** lhieen eh nyn dhieyn lesh nheeghyn mie*
> Yet he filled their houses with good things   [Job xxii:18]

> *… va foddeeaght orrym dy gheddyn obbyr 'syn Ellan, ny-yeih, cha*
> *jinnin cur seose m'obbyr myr fer-ynsee keirdee.* (sic)
> … I longed to get work in the Island, yet I would not give up
> my job as a craft teacher.
> > [Juan y Geill, *Cooinaghtyn Elley* 1977: 25]

7.2.7 *ga* (though)

a) In earlier Manx, and in modern Manx if *ga* is not followed by *dy* or
nagh, the independent form of the verb occurs

*Ga feer ard hoshiaght corree'n Bwaagaght **va***
Though loud at first the Pilgrim's passion grew
[Thomas Parnell, The Hermit 220]

*'s **ga** t'eh gyn oie foast* and though yet without eve (it is)
[*Pargys Caillit* 166]

b) *ga dy* (although) plus dependent verb

*'Agh **ga dy vel** myn-chengaghyn goll sheese dy mooar ayns gagh ayrn jeh'n teihll, t'eh cur taitnys feer vooar dooin dy vel Bretnish goll seose.'*
'But although minority languages are declining rapidly all over the world, we are delighted that Welsh is increasing.'
[Brian Stowell, 'Bretnish: Neose Seose',
Dhooraght 29, April 2003]

*... **ga dy vel** mee shooyl ayns coan scadoo yn vaaish, cha goym aggle roish olk erbee*
... though I walk through the valley of the shadow of death, I will fear no evil

[Psalm xxiii]

c) *ga nagh* (although ... not) plus dependent verb

*... **ga nagh row** 'n hermit loayrt...* although the hermit did not speak
[Thomas Parnell, The Hermit 155]

*"**Ga nagh** jig y stubbin dy ve ny heelrey feer ennoil, s'cosoylagh, t'eh er chummal ynnyd feer rea ayns seihll ny taishbynyssyn."*
"Although the Manx cat will *not* come to be a very popular breed, it has probably kept a clear place in the show world."
[Animal Pictorial, quoted by Mona Douglas, This is Ellan Vannin, tr. Brian Stowell, 'Vel stubbinyn Manninagh dy firrinagh?', *Dhooraght* 37, March 2000]

7.2.8   *er-y-fa, er yn oyr* (because)
Both these expressions appear written with and without hyphens:

*Neayr's shen, ghow Robert Thomson ny focklyn 'anaase' ('interest') as 'anaasagh' ('interesting') voish Gaelg Albinagh **er y fa** dy row eh boirit dy row 'sym' ayns Gaelg çheet er 'sum' ayns Baarle.*
Since then, Robert Thomson took the words *anaase* ('interest') and *anaasagh* ('interesting') from Scots Gaelic, because he was worried by the relationship between *sym* and the English 'sum'.
[Brian Stowell, 'Cooish veih'n Eddyr Voggyl',
Dhooraght 28, December 2002]

er-y-fa *nagh row agh beggan jeh ny sampleyryn va prentit 'sy vlein*
1947 foast er-mayrn
because only a few of the copies printed in the year 1947 remain
[R. L. Thomson, *Gys y Lhaihder*, First Lessons in Manx,
third revised edition, 1965]

S'cosoylagh dy vel y red jerrinagh firrinagh, **er yn oyr** *s'cosoylee dy*
row whilleen jeu ayn ...
It is probable that the latter is true, because it is more probable
that there were so many of them ...
[Mona Douglas, This is Ellan Vannin, tr. Brian Stowell,
'Vel stubbinyn Manninagh dy firrinagh?',
Dhooraght 37, March 2005]

7.2.9   *dyn, gyn* (not to)

Dooyrt eh rhym **dyn** *jannoo eh*   He told me not to do it
[Ned Maddrell (1877–1974)]

As guee ad er **gyn** *eh dy oardaghey daue goll sheese gys y diunid*
And they besought him that he would not command them to go
out into the deep   [Luke viii.31]

7.2.10   *myr* (while, as)
When 'as' means 'while', as in 'as I was going to the fair':

Myr *v'ad goll er*   While hence they walk
[Thomas Parnell, The Hermit 155]

Myr *lhie ad er son ansoor*
As they pressed him for an answer   [John viii.7]

Harragh sleih gys dorrysyn ny cottyn **myr** *hie ad shaghey.*
People would come to cottage doors as they passed.
[Nigel Kneale, 'Curphey's Follower', tr. Brian Stowell,
Duillagyn 1, November 2005]

7.2.11   *son* (for)
When 'for' means 'because', as in 'she did not speak to him, for he was
not at home', etc.:

Son *va mee accryssagh, as hug shiu beaghey dou*
For I was an hungered, and ye gave me meat

[Matthew xxv:35]

V'ad toiggal feer vie yn laa dy gholl, **son** *v'ad geddyn skeddan dy liooar.*
They knew very well which day to go, for they would get plenty
of herring.   [John Kneen, 'The Gaaue' (1852–1958)]

7.2.12 *tra* (when)

> *Ta cooinaghtyn aym* **tra** *va mee abyl loayrt y Ghaelg cha mie as y Vaarle*
> I remember when I was able to speak Manx as well as English
> [Ned Maddrell (1877–1974)]

> *Va Daniel shey bleeaney d'eash* **tra** *ren eh yn obbyr shoh*
> Daniel was aged six when he produced this piece of work
> [*Dhooraght* 36, December 2004]

7.3 Conditions

Conditional clauses are introduced by *dy* (if), *my* (if), *er-be* (if ... not), *mannagh* (unless, if ... not) and *myr* (as if, as though):

7.3.1 *dy* (if)

Dy is used to introduce conditional clauses where fulfillment is unlikely, uncertain or impossible:

> **Dy beagh** *fys ayd's er gioot Yee*
> If thou knewest the gift of God – (subtext: but you don't know)
> [John iv.10]

> **Dy beagh** *shiu er chredjal ... veagh shiu er chredjal*
> If you had believed ... you would have believed – (subtext: but you didn't, and it's too late now)
> [John v.46]

Note: The verbs following *dy* in these two examples are in the dependent form of the conditional tense, which is acting like a subjunctive here. The English equivalent would be 'if you were to believe'.

7.3.2 *my* (if)

My is used with open, fulfillable conditions:

> **My ee-ys** *dooinney erbee jeh'n arran shoh*
> If any man [shall] eat of this bread (subtext: and it is to be hoped that some will)
> [John vi. 51]

> *Mârym's* **my** *vees my Yee*
> If my God is with me (subtext: as I hope He will be)
> [Mrs Sage Kinvig (1870–1962), quoting from
> *Lioar dy Hymnyn as Arraneyn Spyrrydoil* 27, 1830]

Note: The verbs in these two examples (*ee-ys* and *vees*) are in the future relative (see 9) because the reference is to some indeterminate time in the future – and there may also be a shadow of doubt.

Cha beem*'s ayns aggle geddyn baase*
I shall not fear to die
> [*Lioar dy Hymnyn as Arraneyn Spyrrydoil*, Hymn 27, 1830]

My *t'ou jannoo ny reddyn shoh* If you are doing these things
(subtext: you may well be doing them; I wouldn't put it past
you: a distinct possibility)
> [John vii.4]

Kionnee eh **my ta** *fort ayd*   Buy it if you can afford it
(subtext: maybe you can, maybe not; I don't know the state of
your finances but this looks like a good buy to me)
> [Brian Stowell, *Dhooraght* 36, December 2004]

Cur fys dou my sailt **my ta** *anaase ayd*
Please let me know if you are interested
(in fact, this would make more sense the other way round in
English: 'interested parties please get in touch. If you aren't
interested, don't bother!')
> [Philip Gawne, '*Mooinjer Veggey*',
> *Dhooraght* 16, December 1999]

Note: *My sailt* means 'please'. The English 'politeness' expression
'please' was originally 'if you please': in Manx the equivalent
phrase retains the 'if' in the form of *my*:

my sailt	if you please (one person, familiar)
my sailliu	if you please (plural or formal)

7.3.3 *My* can be used instead of *dy* in cases where ambiguity might
otherwise arise

Nagh dooyrt mee rhyt, my chredjagh oo, **dy** *vaikagh oo gloyr Yee?*
Said I not unto thee, that, if thou wouldst believe, thou shouldst
see the glory of God?   [John xi.40]

If *dy gredjagh* were used here in the Manx translation instead of
my chredjagh, in the same way as *dy* was used in the examples
listed above, under *dy*, (if), then the Manx version of John xi.40
could equally well translate: 'Did I not say to you that you
would believe if you were to see the glory of God?' The use of
my removes any ambiguity.
> [R. L. Thomson, *Lessoonyn Sodjey* 1981: 118]

7.3.4   *erbe, er-be*

The fixed expression *'erbe, er-be'* means 'if it were not for the fact that',
'were it not that'.

This is, technically, a fossilized clause containing the conditional of the
copula plus the third person singular masculine of the pronoun *er*. It is
followed by the dependent form of the verb. It is included here because it
functions like a conjunction in such examples as:

> **Er-be** *dy vel y dooinney shoh veih Jee, cha voddagh eh nhee erbee y*
> *yannoo*
> If this man were not of God, he could do nothing
>
> > [John ix.33]

> **er-be** *dy nee drogh-yantagh eh*
> were it not that he is an evil-doer
>
> > [John xviii. 30]

> *'be hug eh mian da ooilley*
> were it not that he lusted for all
>
> > [*Pargys Caillit* 279 (*''be'* for *'er-be'*)]

> *V'eh kiart gollrish ben* **erbe** *dy row cooat er.*
> He was just like a woman were it not that he had a coat on.
>
> > [Brian Stowell, *Dhooraght* 36, December 2004]

7.3.5   *mannagh* (unless, if … not)

> **Mannagh** *bee oo coyrt laa jeh cha jean oo geddyn stiagh*
> If you don't give us a day off you won't get in
>
> > [John Kneen, 'The Gaaue' (1852–1958)]

> **Mannagh** *row uss er goaill eh*   If you had not taken it
>
> > [Harry Kelly (1853–1935)]

> **Mannagh** *noddagh eh jannoo baghey er y Colloo cha noddagh eh*
> *jannoo eh ayns Balley Yelse*
> If he could not make a living on the Calf he wouldn't be able to
> make one in Ballayelse
>
> > [Ned Maddrell (1877–1974)]

7.3.6   *myr* (as if, as though)

> *Va'n thie cho fast as fea* **myr** *v'eh fo halloo*
> The house was as quiet and still as though it was underground
>
> > [R. C. Carswell, 'Gyn Ansoor', *Shelg yn Drane* 1994]

> **Myr** *nagh beagh eh dy nyn glashtyn*
> As if he did not hear them
>
> > [John viii.6]

*Hie eshyn myrgeddin seose ... cha nee dy foshlit, agh **myr** dy beagh eh dy follit*
He went ... not openly, but as it were in secret   [John viii.10]

Myr *veagh saveenagh kiune*   As if it were a peaceful slumber
                                                                  [*Pargys Caillit* 269]

*Ny ainleyn, **myr** dy beagh ad booiagh lesh,*
Chroym sheese nyn gione ...

The angels, as if therewith content,
Bowed their heads ...

                                                                  [*Pargys Caillit* 217–18]

*V'ad **myr** dy beagh ad streeu quoi smoo*
Yinnagh lhieu cooney gys y randivoo

As if they strove who most should help them
With the rendez-vous

                                                                  [*Pargys Caillit* 1266–7]

Note: *myr dy beagh* is the usual construction, as in the last 2 examples, but the author of *Pargys Caillit* generally preferred the shorter form *myr veagh*.

7.3.7   *ny slooid* (unless)

*Ta keeayll ommidjys **ny slooid** ny t'ee ec dooinney creeney dy reayll*
Wit is foolishness unless a wise man has it to keep
                                                                  [Cregeen, repr. 1984: 180]

*Ny poose eirey-inneen **ny slooid** ny ta'n ayr eck er ny ve croghit*
Don't marry an heiress unless her father has been hanged
                                                                  [Kneen, *Idiomyn as Raaghyn* 75]

7.4   Conjunctions used with *dy* or *nagh*
Where a conjunction is used with *dy* or *nagh*, the following verb is in the dependent form in Manx. *Dy* and *nagh* themselves, unaccompanied by other conjunctions, are also followed by the dependent form:

Dy *vod mayd ansoor y choyrt dauesyn t'er choyrt shin*
So that we may give an answer to them that sent us   [John i.22]

Dooyrt ee **nagh re agh Sostnee ad*
She said [that] they were only Englishmen
                                                                  [Ned Maddrell (1877–1974)]

* The alternative dependent form of the copula, *re*, is only found after *dy* and *nagh* (see 9.7)

8   Numerals
Earrooyn

Manx cardinal and ordinal numerals can occur with or without a noun.

8.1   Cardinal numbers

8.1.1   Cardinal numbers without a noun from 0 to 20

0	*neunhee, veg*		
1	*unnane, 'nane*	11	*nane-jeig*
2	*jees*	12	*ghaa-yeig*
3	***t(h)ree troo(a)r*	13	*t(h)ree-jeig*
4	*kiare*	14	*kiare-jeig*
5	*queig*	15	*queig-jeig*
6	*shey*	16	*shey-jeig*
7	*shiaght*	17	*shiaght-jeig*
8	*hoght*	18	*hoght-jeig*
9	*nuy*	19	*nuy-jeig*
10	*jeih*	20	*feed*

un and *daa* are used before nouns: *un laa* (one day)
* *'nane, unnane* are interchangeable and are used in counting: *'nane, daa, tree …*
** *tree* is sometimes written with an 'h': *three*
  trooar is found as an alternative to *troor* in some dictionaries.
Note: *jees* and *troo(a)r* may be used on their own to mean two persons, three persons.

    Ny neesht is used for 'the two', 'both'

    *ren shin **ny neesht** gra*   the two of us said

    *Va **troor** dy vraaryn ayn*   There were three brothers   [LQ]

    *T'ad shen nyn **droor** ayns Keeill Marooney*
    The three of them are in Marown Church

                                       [Traditional Ballad 20]

Note: When pronouncing the cardinal numbers between 11 and 19, the
stress falls on the first element of the number.

8.1.2   Cardinal numbers without a noun from 21 to 30
The single units precede *as feed* (and twenty). Thus *nane as feed* means
'one and twenty', and so on:

21 *'nane as feed*	22 *daa as feed*	23 *t(h)ree as feed*
24 *kiare as feed*	25 *queig as feed*	26 *shey as feed*
27 *shiaght as feed*	28 *hoght as feed*	29 *nuy as feed*
30 *jeih as feed*		

Note: When pronouncing numerals from 21 onwards, the stress falls on
the final element *'feed'*.

8.1.3   Cardinal numbers without a noun from 31 to 39
The single units precede *jeih as feed* (ten and twenty). Thus, thirty-one
is *'nane jeig as feed* (eleven and twenty) and so on:

31 *'nane jeig as feed*	32 *daa yeig as feed*	33 *t(h)ree jeig as feed*
34 *kiare jeig as feed*	35 *queig jeig as feed*	36 *shey jeig as feed*
37 *shiaght as feed*	38 *hoght as feed*	39 *nuy jeig as feed*

8.1.4   Cardinal numbers without a noun from 40 to 59

Forty is *daeed* (two twenties).

[*Daeed* is *daa 'eed* with the *'f'* of *feed* lenited after *daa*. Expect to find
lenition after *'daa'* in compounds like *'daa yeig'* (twelve) (see 8.2.1)]
To obtain the numbers from 41 to 59, the numbers from one to nineteen
are placed in front of *daeed*.

41 *'nane as daeed*	51 *'nane jeig as daeed*
42 *daa as daeed*	52 *daa yeig as daeed*
43 *t(h)ree as daeed*	53 *t(h)ree jeig as daeed*
44 *kiare as daeed*	54 *kiare jeig as daeed*
45 *queig as daeed*	55 *queig jeig as daeed*
46 *shey as daeed*	56 *shey jeig as daeed*
47 *shiaght as daeed*	57 *shiaght jeig as daeed*
48 *hoght as daeed*	58 *hoght jeig as daeed*
49 *nuy jeig as daeed*	59 *nuy jeig as daeed*

8.1.5   Cardinal numbers from 60 to 100

The Manx system continues to count in twenties but the tens and twenties (ie 60, 70, 80 and 90) are usually placed before the units:

60 *t(h)ree feed*	61 *t(h)ree feed as 'nane*
62 *t(h)ree feed as jees*	67 *t(h)ree feed as shiaght*
70 *t(h)ree feed as jeih*	71 *t(h)ree feed as 'nane jeig*
72 *t(h)ree feed as daa yeig*	77 *t(h)ree feed as shiaght jeig*
80 *kiare feed*	81 *kiare feed as 'nane*
82 *kiare feed as jees*	87 *kiare feed as shiaght*
90 *kiare feed as jeih*	94 *kiare feed as kiare jeig*
96 *kiare feed as shey jeig*	99 *kiare feed as nuy jeig*
100 *keead*	

Note: The expression *lieh-cheead* (half a hundred) may be used for 50.

8.1.6   Cardinal numbers greater than 100

After 100 the larger numbers still go first, so the hundreds precede

101 *keead as nane*	110 *keead as jeih*
120 *keead as feed*	229 *daa cheead nuy as feed*

8.1.7   Counting in scores

Counting in scores like this may continue right up to 200

120 *shey feed*	140 *shiaght feed*	180 *nuy feed*
200 *daa cheead*	500 *queig cheead*	

Note: *keead* is lenited, changing the initial 'k' to 'ch', pronounced like 'ch' in Scots 'loch', after *daa*, *t(h)ree*, etc.

8.1.8   A modern counting system

An alternative system of counting is now in use by some modern speakers, in line with Scottish and Irish, and to simplify the teaching of mathematics through Manx:

30	*treead*
40	*kiarad*
50	*queigad*
60	*sheyad*
70	*shiaghtad*
80	*hoghtad*
90	*nuyad*
21 men	*feed-'nane deiney*
35 degrees	*treead-queig keimyn*
122 women	*keead as feed-jees mraane*

8.2   Cardinal numbers with a noun

8.2.1   Lenition after *un, daa*, etc.
Lenition occurs in nouns and adjectives following the cardinal numbers
un, daa, either alone or as part of a larger number (see 1.1):

daa hie vooarey	two big houses	(*thie, mooarey*)
daa ghooinney	two men	(*dooinney*)
daa ghooinney yeig	twelve men	

8.2.2   Singular noun after numerals
The noun remains singular after *un, daa, feed, daeed,* and all multiples of
feed, keead and *thousane*:

un laue	one hand
daa laue	two hands
t(h)ree laueyn	three hands
un laue jeig	eleven hands
un dooinney as feed	twenty-one men
keead blein	one hundred years

8.3   Duals 'two of something'

8.3.1   Singular article
The article remains singular before *daa*

as cheayll yn daa ynseydagh eh loayrt
and the two disciples heard him speaking   [John i.37]

8.3.2   Plural adjectives
Following duals, although the noun and article remain singular, any
accompanying adjective has to be plural

daa eeast veggey[5]   two small fishes   [John vi.9]

8.3.3   '*ghaa*' when no noun directly follows
'*ghaa*', the lenited form of *daa*, is used when the noun does not directly
follow the numeral:

ghaa ny three dy firkinyn y pheesh
two or three firkins apiece   [John ii.6]

ghaa ny three   two or three
                                        [John Tom Kaighin (1862–1954)]

---

[5] R. L. Thomson notes that the plural adjective in this example is regular but the lenition
rare (*Lessoonyn Sodjey* 79)

8.3.4 *'jees'* used instead of *daa*
'jees' is used instead of *daa* when the numeral is used as a noun in the
sense of 'the two of us' (8.1.1), followed by *jeh*, of:

jees **jeh** e ynseydee	two of his disciples	[John i.35]
fer **jeh**'n jees	one of the two	[John i.40]

ren jees jin goll as giarrey eh sheese	
two of us went and cut it down	[Ned Maddrell (1877–1974)]

8.4 Nouns of measure after numerals
Nouns of measure usually remain singular after any numeral:

t(h)ree **punt**	three pounds
t(h)ree **laa**	three days
hoght **punt** jeig	eighteen pounds

8.5 Numerals preceding nouns
One-word numerals or inseparable numerals such as *t(h)ree feed* (sixty),
kiare feed (eighty) precede the noun:

T'eh **feed** blein dy eash	He is twenty years old
T'eh **t(h)ree feed** blein dy eash	He is sixty years old

8.6 Nouns embedded in compounds
From 11 to 59, the noun follows the first element of the compound
number:

daa **vaatey** yeig	twelve boats
un **dooinney** as feed	twenty-one men
jeih **bleeaney** as daeed	fifty years
t(h)ree **baatyn** jeig as daeed	fifty-three boats

8.7 Numerals with *dy*

8.7.1 *feed* (twenty) and *keead* (hundred) may occur in the plural to
mean 'scores' and 'hundreds', with the preposition *dy*

feedyn dy 'leih aegey,	scores of young people
keeadyn dy vagheryn,	hundreds of fields

8.7.2 Plural nouns preceded by *dy*
Sometimes a plural noun preceded by *dy* stands apart from the
compound number:

jeih as feed **dy laadyn**	thirty loads

*ghaa ny three **dy firkinyn** y pheesh*
two or three firkins apiece [John ii.6]

8.8 Numerals used as nouns
When numerals are used as nouns, the article is singular:

yn *nuy* the nine [Luke xvii.17]

yn *Chiare-as-Feed* the 24
(the 24 members of the House of Keys)

fer * *jeh'n jees* one of the two [John i.40]
(for *jees*, see 8.1.1)

V'eh ny s'onnoroil na'n jees
He was more honourable than the two

[I Chronicles xi.21]

* *fer*, man, is used as a pronoun ('one')

8.9 Ordinal numbers
The ordinal numbers precede the noun.

8.9.1 The first three ordinal numbers are *yn chied* (first), *yn nah* (second) and *yn trass* (third)

*Ec **y chied** cheayrt va mee goaill booise dy row eh foast bio, as ec **yn** nah cheayrt va mee goaill booise dy row eh foast bio reeshtagh!*
The first time I was giving thanks that he was still alive, and the second time I was again giving thanks that he was still alive!

[JC]

Note: *yn nah laa*, the second day, can also mean 'the next day':

Yn nah laa *honnick Ean Yeesey çheet ny-whail*
The next day John saw Jesus coming towards him [John i.29]

8.9.2 The remaining ordinal numbers are formed by adding the suffix '-oo' to the cardinal numbers

4th	*yn chiarroo*	5th	*yn whieggoo*
6th	*yn çheyoo*	7th	*yn çhiaghtoo*
8th	*yn hoghtoo*	9th	*yn nuyoo*
10th	*yn jeihoo*	20th	*yn 'eedoo*

*Nish haink **y chied** lot magh er Jehoiarib, **yn nah** lot er Jedaiah*
Yn trass *er Harim*, **yn chiarroo** *er Seorim*
Yn whieggoo *er Malchijah*, **yn çheyoo** *er Mijamin ...*
Yn nuyoo yeig *er Pethahiah*, **yn eedoo** *da Jehezekel*
Yn trass *lot **as feed** er Delaiah.*

Now the first lot came forth to Jehoiarib, the second to Jedaiah,
The third to Harim, the fourth to Seorim
The fifth to Malchijah, the sixth to Mijamin ...
The nineteenth to Pethahiah, the twentieth to Jehezekel
The three and twentieth to Delaiah   [I Chronicles xxiv.7–18]

8.9.3   Lenition after ordinals
Nouns are lenited after all the ordinal numbers, except where the initial sound is one of the dentals *t-*, *d-*, *çh-*, *j-*, which do not change after *chied*

yn chied vaatey	the first boat
(but *yn chied dooinney*)	
yn hoghtoo vaatey	the eighth boat

8.9.4   Compound ordinal numbers with a noun
In compound numbers with a noun, the noun follows immediately after the first element of the numeral:

*yn chied **vaatey** jeig*   the eleventh boat
(literally: the first boat ten)

*yn trass **vaatey** jeig*   the thirteenth boat
(literally: the third boat ten)

*yn jeihoo **vaatey** as feed*   the thirtieth boat
(literally: the tenth boat and twenty)

8.10   Fractions   *corrillaghyn*

slane earroo	whole number
ayrn (pl *ayrnyn*)	part
lieh (f) (pl *liehghyn*)	half
treen (m) (pl *treenyn*)	third
kerroo (m) (pl *kerrooyn*)	quarter
queigoo	fifth
tree dy leih	three and a half
kiare queigoo	four fifths

8.10.1   *lieh* (half) causes lenition

lieh-ghooint	half-closed (*dooney*)
lieh-varroo	half-dead (*marroo*)
lieh-hyndaa	half turn (*çhyndaa*)
lieh-hraa	half time (*traa*)
dy lieh	'and a half'

oor dy lieh	an hour and a half
nuy punt dy lieh	nine and a half pounds

8.10.2 *kerroo* (quarter)

kerroo s'jerree ny heayst	the last quarter of the moon
kerroo yn thunnag	a quarter of the duck

Sometimes *kerroo* is used with *dy*:

kerroo dy guiy	a quarter goose

8.11 Telling the time

8.11.1 Whole hours
Whole hours are expressed by the number followed by *er y chlag* (o'clock):

hoght er y chlag	eight o'clock
'nane jeig er y chlag	eleven o'clock

8.11.2 Half-hour and quarter past the hour are usually expressed with *lieh* (half) *oor* (hour) and *kerroo* (quarter) + *lurg* (after)

lieh oor lurg kiare	half-past four
kerroo lurg hoght	quarter past eight

8.11.3 Minutes past the hour are also expressed with *lurg* (after)

shiaght minnid jeig lurg hoght	seventeen minutes past eight

8.11.4 Minutes and quarter to the hour are expressed with *dys, gys*

feed minnidyn dys shey	twenty to six
kerroo dys t(h)ree	quarter to three

8.11.5 Seconds
grig, m, and *tullagh*, f, both mean 'second' when telling the time

*Kiare minnidyn as shiaght **tulleeyn** lurg jees*
Four minutes and seven seconds past two

Grig is also used in expressions where it corresponds to 'moment':

*Cha bee eh agh **grig** ny jees*
He/it will only be a second/moment or two

8.11.6 Days
Laa (day) is singular after all numerals up to about ten:

kiare laa	four days	[John xi.17]
shey laa	six days	[John xii.1]

8.12   Mathematical terms

maddaght	mathematics	*earrooaght*	arithmetic

2 + 2 = 4	*jees as jees/jees plus jees, shen kiare*
6 − 5 = 1	*shey minus queig/shey loojey queig, shen 'nane*
3 x 8 = 24	*tree bishit liorish hoght, shen kiare as feed*
20 ÷ 2 = 10	*feed rheynnit liorish jees, shen jeih*
6 > 5	*ta shey ny smoo na/ na shlee na queig*
5 < 6	*ta queig ny sloo na shey*
$8^2 = 64$	*ta hoght kernit tree feed as kiare*
x3	*x gys y trass phooar*
x = 2.35	*ta x corrym rish jees point tree queig*
v =	*fraue cherrinagh*
$2^3 = 8$	*jees kioobit, shen hoght*
35°	*queig keimyn jeig as feed*

8.12.1 Geometrical figures

troorane (pl *trooraneyn*)	triangle
kioob (pl *kioobyn*)	cube
kiare-chuilleig (f) (pl *kiare-chuilleigyn*)	rectangle
kerrin (m) (pl *kerrinyn*)	square
queig-lhiatteeane	pentagon
shey-lhiatteeane	hexagon
shiaght-lhiatteeane	septagon
hoght-lhiatteeane	octagon

8.12.2 Decimals

jeihoil	decimal
point (m) (pl *pointyn*)	point
ynnyd jeihoil	decimal place
nuy point kiare	9.4 (nine point four)

8.12.3 Other mathematical expressions

ard-sym	total
bishaghey	multiplication
bun-earroo (m) (pl *bun-earrooyn*)	digit
corrym rish	equals (=)

ta x corrym rish jees point tree queig	x = 2.35
cur gys	add (verb)
goaill veih	subtract
minus/loojey	minus
neunhee/veg	zero, nil
plus/moojey	plus
rheynn	divide (verb)
rheynn (f)	division
sym (m) (pl *symaghyn*)	sum
symey (m) (pl *symaghyn*)	addition
unnid	unit

9 Verbs
Breearyn

Affirmative sentences use the independent form of the verb. Negative and interrogative sentences, and constructions with *dy*, *nagh*, use the dependent form.

9.1 The inflected tenses and the imperative of regular verbs
The future, conditional and simple past or 'preterite' may be formed by inflection. In addition, the verb-noun is formed by inflection of the imperative (see below).

9.1.1 The future tense
The regular inflected future tense is formed by adding suffixes to the verb stem:
The future independent fuses the first person pronoun, both singular and plural, with the verb, to give the ending *-ym* in the singular and *-mayd* in the plural.
Often, all the other future independent forms of the verb (second and third person, both singular and plural) add *-ee*:
The future dependent is usually preceded by the negative *cha*: this causes nasalisation of an initial unvoiced consonant. For example:

coayl (lose):

	Independent		Dependent
caillym	I shall lose	*cha gaillym*	I shall not lose
caillee oo	you will lose	*cha gaill oo*	you will not lose
caillee eh	he will lose	*cha gaill eh*	he will not lose
caillee ee	she will lose	*cha gaill ee*	she will not lose
*caillmayd**	we shall lose	*cha *gaillmayd*	we shall not lose
caillee shiu	you (pl) will lose	*cha gaill shiu*	you (pl) will not lose
caillee ad	they will lose	*cha gaill ad*	they will not lose

* sometimes written in two words in Classical Manx: *caill mayd, cha gaill mayd*

tilgey (throw):

	Independent		Dependent
tilgym	I shall/will throw	*cha dilgym*	I shall/will not throw
tilgee oo	you will throw	*cha dilg oo*	you will not throw
tilgee ee	he will throw	*cha dilg eh*	he will not throw
tilgee ee	she will throw	*cha dilg ee*	she will not throw
tilgmayd	we shall/will throw	*cha dilgmayd*	we shall/will not throw
tilgee shiu	you will throw	*cha dilg shiu*	you will not throw
tilgee ad	they will throw	*cha dilg ad*	they will not throw

Regular verbs beginning with a vowel or with *f-* prefix *n'* in the future dependent:

ee (eat):

> *T'ee credjal dy n'eeym*   She believes that I shall eat
> *T'eh credjal dy n'ee oo*   He believes that you will eat, etc.

faagail (leave):

> *T'ee credjal dy n'aagym*   She believes that I shall leave
> *T'eh credjal dy naag oo*   He believes that you will leave, etc.

Sometimes there is instead nasalisation of the *f-* to *v-*: *vaagym, vaag oo*, etc.

Exception: The future dependent does not always add *-ee*. Even where it does, this ending may disappear after negatives (*cha, mannagh*), unless the verbnoun contains *-aghey*:

> *Mannagh **leigh** shiu veih nyn greeaghyn*
> if ye from your hearts forgive not
> (= unless you from your hearts (will) forgive)   [Matthew xviii.35]

[This example also sometimes appears as: *mannagh leihee shiu veih nyn greeaghyn*, with the ending *-ee* retained.]

Cha nynsee oo (*ynsaghey*, teach or learn), you will not teach (or learn) retains the *-ee* ending because the verbnoun *ynsaghey* contains the element *-aghey*

Verbs in *-agh*, with initial vowel or *f-*: *ooashlaghey* (worship), *follaghey* (hide):

	Independent		Dependent
ooashlee eh	he will worship	*cha n'ooashlee eh*	he will not worship
follee eh	he will hide	*cha vollee eh*	he will not hide

9.1.2   The conditional tense

The conditional tense is formed by adding the fused pronoun ending -*in* to the stem to form the first person singular. All other forms except the first person add -*agh* to the verb stem, and are then followed by the appropriate pronoun.

Conditional dependents which begin with an unvoiced consonant have nasalisation after *dy*:

coayl (lose):

Independent		Dependent	
chaillin	I should lose	*dy gaillin*	that I should lose
chaillagh oo	you would lose	*dy gaillagh oo*	that you would lose
chaillagh eh	he would lose	*dy gaillagh eh*	that he would lose
chaillagh ee	she would lose	*dy gaillagh ee*	that she would lose
chaillagh shin	we should lose	*dy gaillagh shin*	that we should lose
chaillagh shiu	you (pl) would lose	*dy gaillagh shiu*	that you (pl) would lose
chaillagh ad	they would lose	*dy gaillagh ad*	that they would lose

tilgey (throw):

Independent		Dependent	
hilgin	I should throw	*dy dilgin*	that I should throw
hilgagh oo	you would throw	*dy dilgagh oo*	that you would throw
hilgagh eh	he would throw	*dy dilgagh eh*	that he would throw
hilgagh ee	she would throw	*dy dilgagh ee*	that she would throw
hilgagh shin	we would throw	*dy dilgagh shin*	that we should throw
hilgagh shiu	you would throw	*dy dilgagh shiu*	that you would throw
hilgagh ad	they would throw	*dy dilgagh ad*	that they would throw

Regular verbs beginning with a vowel prefix *n*, in the conditional dependent. Those beginning with *f* either lenite this and prefix *n* or nasalise *f* to *v*:

ee (eat), *faagail* (leave):

dy n'eein	that I should eat	*dy n'eeagh oo*	that you would eat, etc.

> *dy n'aagin* that I should leave *dy naagagh oo* that you would leave, etc.
>
> or: *dy vaagin* or *dy vaagagh oo*

eaishtagh[ey] (listen):

> **Dy neaishtagh** *shiu agh rish my Skeayll*
> If you would only listen to my tale
>
> [Manx Traditional Ballad 1]

Verbs in -*agh*, with initial vowel or *f*-:
ooashlaghey (worship), *follaghey* (hide):

Independent

ooashleeagh eh	he would worship
olleeagh eh	he would hide

Dependent

T'eh credjal dy nooashleeagh eh   He believes that he would worship

There was a tendency in Late Manx for the first person singular of the conditional to assimilate to the pattern and adopt the -*agh* ending too, but often speakers corrected themselves and reverted to the traditional -*in* ending.

9.1.3   Past tenses: the preterite

Manx inflected verbs have one simple past tense, the preterite, with independent and dependent forms.

The regular preterite is usually formed by stem with lenition:
coayl (lose):

chaill mee	I lost	*chaill shin*	we lost
chaill oo	you (sg) lost	*chaill shiu*	you (pl) lost
chaill eh	he lost	*chaill ad*	they lost
chaill ee	she lost		

tilgey (throw):

hilg mee	I threw	*hilg shin*	we threw
hilg oo	you threw	*hilg shiu*	you threw
hilg eh	he threw	*hilg ad*	they threw
hilg ee	she threw		

This tense corresponds to English simple past:

Vrish *eh yn uinnag*	He broke the window
Ghreim *eh yn oikan faase*	He seized the feeble infant

Chass *eh e chione*   He twisted his head
                                    [Thomas Parnell, The Hermit, 189–190]

Lesh padjer **hug** *ad jerrey er y laa*   They ended the day with prayer
                                                        [ibid 182]

Verbs with an initial vowel or *f* add *d-*, or sometimes *j-* (before *-ee* or *-i*), to form the Preterite:

aase	grow	*daase*	grew
irree	rise	*dirree, jirree*	rose
ee	eat	*d'ee, jee*	ate
faagail	wait	*daag*	waited

The independent and dependent preterite of verbs in *-agh*, with initial vowel or *f-*: *ooashlaghey* (worshipped), *follaghey* (hide)
For example:

    dooashlee mee   I worshipped   *dollee mee*   I hid

9.1.4   Future relative
Regular verbs, and also *ve* (be), *clashtyn* (hear), *foddym* (be able) and *goaill* (take), have a distinct future relative form. All other irregular verbs lack a relative form. The relative and simple forms of the verb are identical in all tenses except in the future of regular verbs.

The future relative is formed by leniting the initial consonant of the stem and then adding the endings: *-ym* in the first person singular, *-ysmayd* in the first person plural and *-ys* for all other persons.
coayl (lose):

chaillym	I shall lose	*chaillysmayd*	we shall lose
chaillys oo	you shall lose	*chaillys shiu*	you shall lose
chaillys eh	he shall lose	*chaillys ad*	they shall lose
chaillys ee	she shall lose		

Similarly,

tilgey (throw):	*hilgym, hilgysmayd, hilgys*
troggal (lift, build):	*hroggym, hroggysmayd, hroggys*
cooinaghtyn (remember):	*chooineeym, chooineeysmayd,*
	chooineeys (the verb stem is *cooinee*)
foddym (can, am able):	**oddym, oddysmayd, oddys*

*   Although lenition usually removes the initial *f-*, in other cases it may be retained:

    Freillym   I shall keep (*freill*), perhaps to
avoid confusion with *reill*, rule or govern

Eeys, the relative of the verb *ee* (eat), is often used for the future independent to avoid *ee ee*.

9.1.5 Subjunctive

The subjunctive sense in all inflected verbs is expressed by means of the future dependent or future perfect, stating a general or hypothetical case, or by the conditional:

> *Ny jean peccah arragh, er-aggle dy jig red smessey ort*
> Sin no more, lest a worse thing come upon thee   [John v.14]
> (*jig* = future dependent of *çheet*, come)

> *Son nagh jig brah er ny obbraghyn echey*
> So that judgment may not come on his works   [John iii.20]

> *Mannagh bee dooinney er ny ruggey reesht*
> Unless a man be born again   [John iii.3]
> (*bee* = future dependent of *ve*)

> *Myr dy beagh eh*
> As if it were, as it were (conditional)   [John vii.10]

> *Er-lhieu hene dy beagh ayn keead*
> So you would think there were a hundred
> [Manx Traditional Ballad 5]

9.1.6 The past subjunctive is expressed by the conditional

> *Nagh jinnagh quoi-erbee credjagh aynsyn cherraghtyn*
> So that whoever might believe in him might not perish
> [John iii.16]

> *Er-aggle dy voghe e ghaltyn oghsan*
> For fear that (lest) his actions should find reproof
> [John iii.20 tr. Ph.]

> (*voghe* = conditional dependent of *geddyn*, get, find)

> *Dy beagh shiu er chredjal ... veagh shiu er chredjal*
> If you had believed ... you would have believed   [John v.46]
> (unfulfilled condition in the past, using past conditional in both clauses, the first functioning as pluperfect subjunctive)

> *Saillym dy beagh yn geurey hannah harrish*
> I wish the winter were already over

9.1.7 Imperative

The imperative is only found in the second person of the present tense. It is formed with the stem of the verb to address one person informally, and with the stem of the verb with -*shiu*, or, in older Manx, -*jee*, to address more than one person, or one person more formally. Some verbs add -*ee* to the stem.

> *coayl* (lose):   *caill!* lose!   *caill-shiu!* lose!   (older: *caill-jee!*)
> *tilgey* (throw):   *tilg!* throw!   *tilg-shiu!* throw!   (older: *tilg-jee*)

> **Clasht**, *o inneen, as* **smooinee** *ort,* **croym** *dty cleaysh;* **jarrood**
> *myrgeddin dty phobble hene*
> Hear, O daughter, and remember and incline thine ear; forget
> also thine own people   [Psalm 45.11]

> **Shooill-jee** *mysh Sion, as* **immee-jee** *mygeayrt-y-moee, as* **gow-jee**
> **coontey** *ny tooryn eck*
> Walk ye about Zion and go ye about her, and count her towers
>   [Psalm 48.11]

A periphrastic imperative may be formed using the imperative of *jannoo*, *jean/jean-shiu*
For the special imperative forms of irregular verbs see the individual paradigms (see 9.6).

9.1.8   Optative and jussive
Optative and jussive are expressed by the future dependent, usually after the conjunction *dy*, or with the dependent preterite form *row*, from *ve*. Also occasionally with *dy bee*.

Optative:

> *shee* **dy row** *marin*   peace be with us

> *shee* **dy row** *shiu* (Ph. *shee* **dy row** *erriu*)
> peace be with you   [John xx.19]

> **dy jig** *dty reeriaght*   thy kingdom come

Note: *gura mie ayd* (thank you: literally 'may good be upon you') is a unique fixed optative phrase. '*Gura*' is part of the copula

Jussive:

> **kiangl e mayd** *eh*   let us bind him

Optatives and jussives may also be formed with the subjunctive.
Imperatives and first and third person optative may now be formed in Manx as in English, with *lhig*, the singular imperative of *lhiggey*, let + the appropriate form of the preposition *da*, to:

> *lhig da coayl*   let him lose
> *lhig dooin coayl*   let us lose

agh lhig dooys loayrt jeh'n inneen gring
but let me speak of the fair maid   [Manx Traditional Ballad 32]

Lhig da'n cronk Sion goaill boggey, as inneen Yudah ve gennal
Let the hill of Zion rejoice, and the daughter of Judah be glad
[Psalm 48.10]

Lhig dooin brishey ny kianglaghyn oc
O lhig da ny arraneyn eu ve jehsyn!
Let us break their bonds
O let your songs be of him!   [Psalm 105.2]

In this construction the *lhig* remains singular and does not add -*shiu*, -*jee* to form a plural imperative like other Manx verbs, in contrast to the fixed expression:

lhig-jee'n raad daue   let them go, allow them to depart

9.1.9   Negative imperative and optative are formed with *ny* (*nagh* before vowels)

O ny treig mee!   Oh do not forsake me!

Ny lhig da jymmoose ve ny mast'eu
Let not anger be among you   [John i:43]

O ny lhig da my chree ve er ny lhoobey gys drogh obbyr erbee!
O let not my heart be inclined to any evil work!

The first person plural of the preposition *gys, hooin*, is used as a sort of first person plural imperative of *goll*. Thus, instead of *lhig dooin goll, hooin* or *hooin roin*, are used for 'let us go': (*goll* (go) + *roish* (before = go away, depart).

9.2   Past tenses: perfect, pluperfect, future perfect and past conditional

The perfect and the pluperfect, together with the future perfect and the past conditional, are periphrastic or compound tenses and are formed with the auxiliary *ve* + *er* + verbnoun (+ mutation):

Perfect
   ta mee er dilgey (*tilgey*)   I have thrown

Pluperfect
   va mee er dilgey   I had thrown

Future perfect
   tra veesmayd er dilgey   when we (shall) have thrown

Past conditional
> *veign er dilgey*   I would have thrown

9.3   The verbnoun
The verbnoun is formed on the basis of the verbal stem, which is usually exactly the same as the imperative singular.

Most verbnouns are formed by adding a suffix to the verbal stem. The commonest suffixes are the following:

-ey	*bwoaill* → *bwoalley*	strike
	dooin → *dooney*	shut*
	follee → *follaghey*	hide **
-agh	*etl* → *etlagh*	fly **
-tyn	*benn* → *bentyn*	touch
-al	*cred* → *credjal*	believe
-t	*freggyr* → *freggyrt*	answer
-dyn	*giall* → *gialdyn*	promise
-yn	*jeeagh* → *jeeaghyn*	look
-eil	*leeid* → *leeideil*	lead
-ys	*togher* → *togherys*	wind
-oo	*shass* → *shassoo*	stand
-iu	*toill* → *toilliu*	deserve
-lym	*çhaggil* → *çhaglym*	meet, gather
-çhyn	*toill* → *toillçhin*	deserve

* The final consonant of the stem may be depalatalised.
Depalatalisation of one consonant may bring about vowel changes:

> *dooin, dooney* (shut)   *caill, coayl* (lose)

** The *-agh-* verbs, (verbs ending in *-aghey, -aghyn, -aght, -aghtyn*) form the stem by changing *-agh* to *-ee*. This *-ee* remains throughout the tenses. It absorbs the *-ee* of the future independent, avoiding forms such as **cooineeeeym*:

cooinaghtyn (to remember):

Future: Independent: *cooineeym*   Dependent: *gooineeym*

Relative: *chooineeys*

Preterite: *chooinee mee*

Conditional: Independent: *chooineein*   Dependent: *gooineein*

Imperative: *cooinee* (sg); *cooinee-shiu, cooinee-jee* (pl)

Past Participle: *cooinit*

Sometimes the verbnoun itself is identical with the stem:

creck (sell); *insh* (tell); *lhie* (lie down); *lhaih* (read); *soie* (sit)

Auxiliary verbs

The main auxiliary verbs used in Manx are *ve* (be), *jannoo* (make or do) and the modals. Tenses which must be formed with auxiliaries are: the present, the imperfect, the perfect, the future perfect and the pluperfect, and also the rare continuous future.

All other tenses – the conditional, the future, and the simple past tenses, and also the imperative mood, may also be formed by means of auxiliaries as an alternative option to inflected tenses.

The verbnoun does not change its form (apart from mutations, see 1) in constructions formed with auxiliaries.

The various options for forming the passive involve auxiliaries (see 9.11).

Ve and *jannoo* function as full lexical verbs as well as auxiliaries. This means that they can form a sentence without a verbnoun as well as with one:

Te	It is
Ta mee braew	I am well
Ta mee goll dy valley	I am going home
Ren mee jannoo brock jeh	I made a mess of it
Ren mee goll dy valley	I went home
Cha jeanym eh	I shall not do it

9.4   *ve* (to be): simple and habitual present
The present tense of all verbs, both simple and habitual, is formed with the present tense of *ve* + noun, or the present tense of *ve* + pronoun + verbnoun.

No present tense can be made without the auxiliary *ve*:

9.4.1   Present
In the present, *ve* has three forms: *ta* (independent) and *vel*, *nel* (dependent). These are the same for all persons:
The independent form is used in affirmative statements:

ta mee goll	I go, I am going
ta shin goll	we go, we are going
t'ou goll	you (sg) go, you are going
ta shiu goll	you (pl) go, you are going

t'eh goll	he goes, he going
t'ad goll	they go, they are going
ta'n inneen goll	the girl goes, she is going

The dependent forms are used in relatives, interrogatives and negatives, and after *dy* and *nagh*, in both the present and the past:

Vel shiu goll?	Are you going?
Vel ee goll?	Is she going?
Cha nel mee goll	I am not going

Cha can take both *nel* and *vel*; *nagh* and *dy* (and interrogatives) only take *vel*:

Nagh vel shiu fakin yn brattagh?	Don't you see the flag?
Nagh vel oo goll?	Aren't you going?
Vel shiu clashtyn mee?	Do you hear me?

In all tenses formed with auxiliary *ve*, *g-* is added to the initial vowels of verbnouns:

ta mee gaase (*aase* grow)	I am growing

The first person plural form *-mayd* has the emphatic form *-main*, which is also used in 'Late Manx' in the present tense of *ve*:

tamain cur ad dys yn clieau	we put them to the mountain [John Tom Kaighin (1862–1954)]

9.4.2 Simple past (preterite)

Independent: *va*	Dependent: *row*
Va mee ayns shoh I was there	*Row ad ec y thie?* Were they at home?
V'ad ayns shoh They were there	*Cha row ad ec y thie* They were not at home
	Ta mee gra dy row mee ec y thie I am saying I was at home

The imperfect (habitual past) tense of other verbs is formed using the preterite of *ve* (*va/row*) + verbnoun:

V'ee creck eeym	She was selling butter/she used to sell butter
Cha row ad jannoo eh	They weren't doing it
V'ad niee	They were washing/they used to wash
myr v'eh shooyl	as he was walking [John i.36]

Row shiu rieau goll er y 'Quaaltagh?'
Did you ever use to go as the 'quaaltagh?

Va, dy jarroo!	I did, indeed!	[John Gell 1977]

V'eh sheidey creoi fud ny-hoie
It was blowing hard all night long   [same source]

9.4.3   Future
In the future tense, the independent and dependent forms of *ve* are identical:

bee'm	I shall be	*beemayd*	we shall be
bee oo	you (sg) will	*bee ad*	you (pl) will be
bee shiu	he will be	*bee ad*	they will be
bee ee	she/it will be		

The continuous future is formed with the future tense of *ve* + verbnoun:

bee ad fuirraghtyn   they'll be waiting

Alternatively, Manx uses the future relative of *ve* after an interrogative + verbnoun:

*Cuin **vees** shiu cur mynjeigyn gys Lerphoyll?*
When will you be sending parcels to Liverpool?

Compare this with the inflected future of *cur*:

*Nagh **der** oo veg mairagh?*	Won't you send [any] tomorrow?

The future relative of *ve*:

vee'm	I shall be
veesmayd	we shall be
vees	(you/he/she/they) will be

*Liorish shoh **vees** fys ec dy chooilley ghooinney*
By this every man will know   [John xiii.35]

9.4.4 Conditional[6]

Independent	Dependent
veign I should be	*(dy) beign* I shouldn't be
All others: *veagh oo, eh*, etc.	*(dy) beagh oo, eh*, etc.

> *Cha **beagh** farscaadagh oc* They wouldn't have an umbrella
>
> *Cha **beagh** eh jeant ayns y çheer shen*
> It wouldn't be made in that country [WC]
>
> *Saillym **dy beagh** yn Ollick hannah ayn*
> I wish it were already Christmas
>
> ***Dy beign** slane, **raghin** maroo* If I were well, I'd go with them

* (present conditional of *ve*, with *raghin*, present conditional of *goll*)
The past conditional of *ve*: present conditional + *er* + *ve*:

> *veign er ve* I sh/would have been,
> *veagh oo er ve* you (sg) would have been, etc.

The past conditional of other verbs is formed with the present conditional of *ve* + *er* + verbnoun:

> *veagh oo er jeet* you would have come
> *veagh shin er n'ghoaill* we would have taken
> *cha beagh shiu er n'gheddyn* you would not have got

> ***Dy beagh** eh er aght elley, **veign** er n'insh diu*
> If it were otherwise, I should have told you [John xiv.2]
> (present conditional followed by past conditional)

---

[6] Sometimes this is given as the imperfect: but Manx has a full array of past tenses without the need to use the conditional for repeated actions in the past. R. L. Thomson notes (*Lessoonyn Sodjey* 142) that in John xix.17 *gys ynnyd yiarragh ad ynnyd y vollag rish*, a place they called the place of the skull, 'the use of the conditional as an imperfect is quite exceptional'. This usage may have resulted from confusion about the meaning of English habitual 'would', or with older usage where there was an element of hypothesis and doubt about the events described: one example is verse 4 of the Manx Traditionary Ballad (ca. 1490–1530):
> *Cha nee lesh e Chliwe ren eh ee reayll*
> *Cha nee lesh e Hideyn, ny lesh e Vhow*
> *Agh tra aikagh eh Lhuingys troailt*
> *Oallagh eh mygyeayrt lesh Keaue*
'Not with his sword did he defend it, nor with his arrows nor his bow (shield?) but when he saw a fleet sailing he would hide it round with mist.' The *tra* in the third line is sometimes given as *nar*, which has a more hypothetical sense, or *my*, if: 'this is what he (Manannan) would do, if such an event should ever come to pass.'

veagh trimshey orrym **dy beagh** shiu er ve soit er
I should be sorry (simple conditional: literally 'sorrow would be upon me', hence third person singular of the conditional) if you had been attacked (past conditional)

veagh blass share er ve er ny plumbisyn shoh **dy beagh** ad er ve ny s'appee
those plums would have tasted better if they had been riper (past conditional: literally: 'there would have been a better taste on')

9.4.5 Perfect
The perfect is formed using the present tense of *ve + er*:

ta mee er ve	I have been	*ta shin er ve*	we have been,
t'ou er ve	you have been, etc.:		

Ta shiu er ve cooid veg ardvooaralagh
You have been rather presumptuous

Ta my vraar er ve yn cloieder share
My brother has been the best player

Ta mee er ve harrish yn ushtey I've been over the water
[Mrs Eleanor Karran (1870–1953)]

The perfect of other verbs is formed using the present tense of *ve + er, er n'*, or *er ny ve* + verbnoun:

Ta mee hannah er n'insh dhyt I've already told you

Vel peiagh erbee rieau er loayrt lesh ny smoo dy yesh-focklaght?
Has anyone ever spoken more eloquently?

Ta'n fer tootagh er duittym sheese The silly fellow has fallen down

Cha nel mee er chur jerrey er shennaghys
I have not finished the history

t'eh er n'aase	he has grown
ta mee er n'ghoaill arrane	I have sung
t'eh er gheddyn baase	he has died
t'eh er n'gholl	he has gone
vel ee er vakin?	has she seen?
cha nel shiu er ghraa	you have not said

Ta shin ooilley er gheddyn ayrn
We have all received a part   [John i.16]

Cha nel unnane er vakin Jee
No-one at all has seen God   [John i.18]

English uses the auxiliary 'have' to form the perfect tenses. Manx has no verb 'to have'.

9.4.6   Future perfect
The future perfect is formed with the future tense of *ve* + *er* + *ve* or verbnoun:

beeym er ve	I shall have been
bee oo er ve	you (sg) will have been
beemayd er niee	we shall have washed

*S'gerrid **vees** ooilley my vlaaghyn **ushtit** aym*
I shall soon have watered all my flowers

*S'gerrid **vees** ooilley nyn Vrangish **jarroodit** ain*
We shall soon have forgotten all our French

9.4.7   Pluperfect
The pluperfect is formed with the preterite of *ve* + *er* + (*ve* or verbnoun):

va mee er ve   I had been

Va mee er ve e ynseydagh rish foddey
I had been his pupil for a long time

Va'n cloie er ve liauyr   The performance had been long

Va shin er ve er nyn lhottey ayns y Chaggey Mooar
We had been wounded in the Great War

Va'n jaagh er ghooaghey yn farvoalley
The smoke had blackened the ceiling

Row eh er ve e noid?   Had he been his enemy?
Cha row!   He had not!

Va mainshter … er vlashtyn er yn ushtey
The master … had tasted the water   [John ii.9]

V'eh er ve ny lomarcan   He had been alone
Va shin er ve taggloo   We had been talking

liorish dy row ad er vakin ooilley ny ren eh ec Jerusalem
because they had seen all that he had done in Jerusalem
[John iv.45]

tra va shin er n'aase   when we had grown

un vaatey shen va ny ostyllyn er n'ghoaill
that one boat which the apostles had taken   [John vi.22]

In all the perfect tenses, the perfect particle *er* now causes lenition in most verbs. In the commonest verbs, and in older use, it causes nasalisation. *n-* is prefixed to an initial vowel:

veagh oo er **jeet**	you would have come	(*çheet*)
t'eh er **n'gholl**	he has gone	(*goll*)
v'ee er **chur**	she had given	(*cur*)
cha nel shiu er **ghra**	you have not said	(*gra*)
row ad er **ghra?**	had they said?	(*gra*)
cha beagh shiu er **n'gheddyn**	you wouldn't have got	(*geddyn*)

The perfect, pluperfect and future perfect tenses may be formed with the appropriate tense of auxiliary *ve* + *erreish* or *lurg* (after) + usually *y* + verbnoun:

Future perfect:

> *tra* **vees** *shiu* **erreish** *yn Mac dooinney* **y hroggal** *seose*
> when you shall have lifted up the Son of Man   [John viii.28]

Pluperfect:

> *tra v'eh erreish ny goan shoh y loayrt*
> he had spoken the words   [John xviii.22]

> *tra v'eh erreish shoh y loayrt*   when he had said this   [John ix.6]
> *tra v'ad erreish bee*   when they had eaten [John xxi.15]
> (elsewhere rendered as: *erreish daue v'er n'ee*)

After *erreish* the past tenses may be reinforced by preceding *v'er*; often the appropriate form of the preposition *da* is used:

> *erreish dhyt v'er loayrt*
> after you had spoken   [Exodus iv.10]

> *erreish da'n Chiarn v'er chur booise*
> after the Lord had given thanks   [John vi.23]

> *erreish daue v'er n'ee*   after they had eaten   [John vi.13]
> *erreish da v'er niee*   when he had washed
>   [John. xiii.12]

> *erreish da v'er n'irree veih ny merriu*
> after he had risen from the dead   [John xxi.14]

Exception: *Lurg* does not usually take a perfect construction: thus the following examples are really exceptions:

> *Lurg da ny cayrnyn goll er shellym*
> After the horns were (= had been) blown

Lurg da Nebuchadnezzar v'er chur ersooyl ayns cappeeys Jeconiah
After Nebuchadnezzar had sent Jeconiah into captivity
[Jeremiah xxvii.20]

9.4.8   Imperative

bee	be (sg)	*bee shiu, bee-jee*	be (pl):

Bee dty host!	Be quiet!
Bee shiu mie!	Be good!
Ny bee meeviallagh hym!	Do not disobey me!
Ny bee-shiu neuwooisal!	Don't be ungrateful!
Ny bee shiu myr shen!	Don't be like that!

9.5   *Jannoo*, like *ve*, functions as both verbnoun and auxiliary

A 'periphrastic construction' or 'complex verbal phrase' made up of auxiliary *jannoo* and a verbnoun is very commonly used and a convenient alternative to the inflected tenses of verbnouns:

9.5.1   The present tense of *jannoo*, like that of all other verbs in Manx, is formed with *ve*

ta mee jannoo	I do	*ta shin jannoo*	we do
t'ou jannoo	you (sg) do	*ta shiu jannoo*	you (pl) do
t'eh jannoo	he does	*t'ad jannoo*	they do
t'ee jannoo	she does		

9.5.2   Preterite

The preterite of *jannoo* can be used with a verbnoun instead of the inflected preterites of other verbs to form a complex verbal phrase in the past:

The independent and dependent form is *ren*:

ren ad gee	they ate
(verbnoun *ee*, adding *g-* to the initial vowel)	
ren ad clashtyn	they heard

9.5.3   Future

The future tense of other verbs can be formed with the future tense of *jannoo* + verbnoun:

Independent		Dependent
neeym, nee'm	I will do	*jeanym*
nee	you (sg) shall do	*jean*
nee	he, she, it will do	*jean*
neemayd	we will do	*jeanmayd*

	Independent		Dependent
	nee	you (pl) will do	*jean*
	nee	they will do	*jean*

*Cha **jean** ny fir-lhee dy-bragh **lheihys** eh*
The doctors will never cure him

*Nagh **jean** oo çheet?*   Will you not be coming?

9.5.4   Conditional
The conditional of *jannoo* can be used with a verbnoun instead of the inflected conditionals of other verbs to form a complex verbal phrase:

	Independent	Dependent
first person (sg)	*yinnin*	*jinnin*
All others:	*yinnagh*	*jinnagh*

yinnagh *eh chyndaa*   he would turn

yinnagh *oo **jannoo** mie dy liooar*
you would do well enough   [Ned Maddrell (1877–1974)]

9.5.5   Imperative
The imperative of *jannoo* is *jean, jean-shiu, jean-jee*. It may be used as an auxiliary with a verbnoun to form the compound imperative of other verbs:

Jean cummal *ayns y cheer*
Live in the country (Do live in the country!)

Jean-jee troggal!   Lift!

*O **jean** uss **farkiaght** er caa yn Çhiarn!*
O wait thou for the Lord's time!

In English, the imperative reinforced by 'do' is emphatic; in Manx this is not the case.

9.5.6   Past participle
The past participle of *jannoo* is *jeant*.

Jeant dy mie!   Well done!

9.5.7   Pluperfect

tra v'eh er n'yannoo kip dy choyrdyn keylley
when he had made a whip of thin cords   [John ii.15]

dooinney va er jannoo jerrey er hene
a man who had made an end of himself (= a suicide)
[Thomas Christian (1851–1930)]

9.6   The irregular verbs

Besides *jannoo* and *ve* there are seven irregular verbs in Manx. These are extremely common and also form a great number of phrasal verbs (see 10).

9.6.1   *çheet* (come)

Future independent		Future dependent
higym	I shall/will come	*jigym*
hig oo/eh/ ee	you (sg), he, she shall/ will come	*jig oo/eh/ee*
higmayd	we shall/will come	*jigmayd*
hig shiu/ad	you (pl)/they shall/will come	*jig shiu/ad*

Preterite independent: *haink mee*, etc. *Preterite* dependent: *daink*

Conditional independent:

harrin	I should come
harragh oo, etc.	you (sg) would come etc.

Conditional dependent:

darrin	I should not come
darragh oo, etc.	you (pl) would not come etc.

Imperative: *tar!*   come! (sg)   *tar-shiu, tar-jee*   come! (pl)

9.6.2   *clashtyn* (hear)

Future independent:

cluinnym	I shall/will hear
cluinnee oo/eh/ee	you (sg), he, she shall/will hear
cluinmayd	we shall/will hear
cluinnee shiu/ad	you (pl), they shall/will hear

Future dependent:

gluinnym	I shall/will not hear
gluin oo/eh/ee	you (sg), he, she shall/will not hear
gluinmayd	we shall/will not hear
gluin shiu/ad	you (pl), they shall/will not hear

Relative:

chlinnym	I shall hear

chlinnysmayd   we shall hear
chlinnys   you/he/she/they will hear

Preterite: Independent *cheayll mee*, etc.   Dependent *geayll*

	Conditional independent	Conditional dependent
first person (sg)	*chluinnin*	*gluinnym*
All others:	*chluinnagh oo*, etc.	*gluinnagh oo*, etc.

Imperative: (sg) *clasht*, (pl) *clasht-shiu, clasht-jee*

Perfect:

Ta mee er clashtyn jeh'n çhenn ven   I have heard of the old woman
                                        [Ned Maddrell (1877–1974)]

Cha nel mee rieau er n'akin eh, agh ta mee er clashtyn jeh
I've never seen him but I've heard of him   [ibid]

Past participle: *clui(n)nit*

9.6.3   *coyrt, cur* (put, give)

Future independent		Future dependent
verym	I shall give	*derym*
vermayd	we shall give	*dermayd*
ver oo, etc.	you (sg), etc. shall give	*der oo*, etc.

Preterite: Independent: *hug mee*, etc.   Dependent: *dug mee*, etc.

Conditional independent		Conditional dependent
verrin	I should give	*derrin*
verragh oo, etc.	you (sg), etc. would give	*derragh oo*, etc.

Imperative:

cur!   give! (sg)
cur-shiu, cur-jee!   give! (pl)

Past participle: *currit*

9.6.4   *fakin* (see)

Future independent		Future dependent
heeym, hee'm	I shall/will see	*vaikym*
heemayd	we shall/will see	*vaikmayd*
hee oo, etc.	you (sg), etc. shall/will see	*vaik oo*, etc.

Preterite independent   Preterite dependent

honnick mee, etc.   I saw   *vaik* mee*, etc.

Naik *shiu yn baatey çheet stiagh jiu?* **Honnick**
Did you see the boat come in today? I saw (= yes)

Conditional independent   Conditional dependent

heein   I should see   *vaikin**
heeagh oo, etc.   you (sg), etc. would see *vaikagh oo*, etc.

Imperative:

jeeagh, cur-my-ner!   see! (sg)
jeeagh-shiu, cur-shiu-my-ner, jeeagh-jee   see! (pl)

Past participle: *fakinit*

* Note that alternative dependent forms substitute *n-* for *v-*, especially
  after *cha*:

Cha naik mee eh   I did not see him/it

9.6.5   *geddyn, feddyn* (get, find)

Future independent   Future dependent

yioym   I shall get/find   *voym*
yiowmayd   we shall get/find   *vowmayd*
yiow oo, etc. you (sg), etc. shall/will get/find *vow oo*, etc.

Preterite: Independent: *hooar*   Dependent: *dooar*

Conditional independent   Conditional dependent

first person (sg)   *yioin*   *voin*
All others: *yioghe oo*, etc.   *voghe oo*, etc.

Imperative: (sg) *fow*, (pl) *fow-shiu, fow-jee*

Past participle: *geddynit, feddynit*

Note: Alternative dependent forms may substitute *n-* for *-v-*.
  After *dy* or *y* only *gheddyn* is found.

9.6.6   *goll*, go

Future independent   Future dependent

first person (sg)   *hem*   I shall go   *jem*
first person (pl)   *hemmayd*   *jemmayd*
All others: *hed oo*, etc.   *jed oo*, etc.

Preterite: Independent *hie*   Dependent *jagh*

Conditional: Independent and dependent, 1st sg. *raghin,*

All others *ragh oo,* etc.

Imperative: sg. *gow, immee* (pl) *immee-shiu, immee-jee, gow-shiu, gow-jee*

Past Participle: *ersooyl* (away) is used as the past participle of *goll*

> *T'ad ooilley ersooyl nish*   They're all gone now
> [John Kneen, 'The Gaaue' (c.1852–1958)]
>
> *ersooyl lesh y gheay*   gone with the wind

9.6.7   *gra* (say)

Future: Independent and dependent   Dependent only

first person (sg)	*jirym*	I shall say	*n'arrym, niarrym*
first person (pl)	*jirmayd*		*n'arrmayd, niarrmayd*
All others:	*jir oo,* etc.		*n'arr, niarr*

> Alternative independent future   Alternative dependent future
>
> *abbyrym,* etc.   *n'abbyrym,* etc.

Preterite: Independent and dependent: *dooyrt*

> Conditional independent   Conditional dependent

| first person (sg) | *yiarrin* | *niarrin* |
| All others: | *yiarragh oo,* etc. | *niarragh oo,* etc. |

Imperative: *abbyr, abbyr-shiu, abbyr-jee*

Past participle: *grait*

Note: In direct speech, when the exact words of the speaker are given, sometimes '*gra*' may be omitted, and '*as*' used instead:

> '*Er hen y thie,*' *as y dooinney*   'There is the house,' said the man
> '*Quoi oo hene?*' *as eshyn*   'Who are you?' said he.

Note: Here '*as*' does not mean 'and', but is related to the Irish verb '*arsa*', meaning 'said,' or the archaic 'quoth'.

9.6.8   *goaill* (take)
Goaill is used in many phrasal verbs. It is not a genuine irregular, despite its rather unusual appearance, but it is often included among irregulars:

Future independent and dependent

first person (sg) *goym*   I shall take
first person (pl) *gowmayd*
All others: *gowee oo*, etc.

Relative: *ghoym* or *ghowym*, I shall take; *ghoysmayd* or *ghowysmayd*; we shall take; *ghoys* or *ghowys*, you/he/she/they will take

Preterite: Independent and dependent: *ghow*

Conditional independent	Conditional dependent
first person (sg) *ghoin*	*goin*
All others: *ghoghe*	*goghe*

Imperative: (sg) *gow*, (pl) *gow-shiu, gow-jee*

Past participle: *goit*

9.7   The copula
The copula has but few forms and is only used in restricted circumstances.

Present independent: *she*

Present dependent: *nee*

after *dy*, *nagh* sometimes *re*

Sometimes it could be replaced by the symbol = without loss of meaning:

She *thie eh*	It's a house
Nee *uss yn fer lhee?*	Are you the doctor?
She	I am
She Tarzan mish	Me Tarzan
Nee uss Jinn?	You Jane?

9.7.1   Position of the copula
The copula is usually the first word in its sentence. It is used instead of *ve* (be) in certain specific cases, chiefly:
- the comparative and superlative of adjectives and adverbs (6), also used in exclamations (how great was my joy, etc.)
- for emphasis
- in statements equating one thing with another
- with certain verbs, or with certain predicates in place of a verb to form a compound which is used as a verb
- when adverb precedes verb (*dy* is omitted)

9.7.2   Tense of the copula

The copula generally occurs only in the present-future tense:

Independent: *she* (*s'* before an adjective or adverb)

Dependent: *nee* or, especially after *dy* and sometimes *nagh*, an alternative dependent form *re*.

'He is a big man' may be stated in three ways:

> With *ve* and *ny* expressing a state: *T'eh ny ghooinney mooar*

> With copula and inversion (the '*eh*' goes to the end): *She dooinney mooar eh*

> With the same word order as in English (except for the lack of indefinite article): *T'eh dooinney mooar*

In tenses other than the present, the verb *ve* must be used in this type of statement:

> *Shen va'n soilshey firrinagh*   That was the true light   [John i.9]

9.7.3   The copula is needed in comparisons and exclamations

> *y dooinney s'niartal*   the most powerful man

> *Ta'n dooinney shen ny s'niartal na mish*
> That man is more powerful than I

> *Roie y moddey ny s'bieau na eshyn*
> The dog ran faster than he (did)

s'mooar my haitnys	how pleased I am!
s'mooar va nyn moggey	(how) great was their joy!
ny s'melley na crammag	slower than a snail
myr s'creeney ad!	as wise as they are!
yn pibbyr s'çhoie	the hottest pepper
s'feayr va'n oie!	cold was the night!
s'atçhimagh vees yn laa shen!	how terrible will that day be!
er y laa s'jerree	on the last day [John vii.37]

9.7.4   The copula is used for emphasis in cases like the following

She eshyn ren eh	It is he that did it
She Manninagh mish	I am a Manxman
She Manninagh ta mish	It is a Manxman that I am
S'feer eh	It's true

> *She beishtag mish as cha nee dooinney*
> I am a worm and no man

Nee dooinney eh?	Is he a man?
She baagh cabbyl	The horse is an animal
S'doo geayl	Coal is black
Cha nee eshyn ren eh	It is not he that did it
Nee eshyn ren eh?	Is it he that did it?
She	Yes, it is

Dooyrt ad dy nee (or *re*) *eshyn ren eh*
They said that it was he that did it

Dooyrt ad nagh nee eshyn ren eh
They said that it was not he that did it

*Cha **nee** mish dooyrt shen*	It was not I that said it	
Jed oo?	Will you go?	
She mish hed!	That I will!	
She ooig v'ayn	It was a cave	[John xi.38]
Nee ass Galilee t'ou uss?	Is it from Galilee that thou art?	
		[John vii.52]

*Nagh **nee** shoh eh?*	Is not this he?	[John vii.25]
*Er-lhiam dy **re** shen eh!*	I think that's it	
		[Ned Maddrell (1877–1974)]

9.7.5 The copula in use

The copula is used in statements of this type:

*Heill mee dy **re** Manninagh oo*
I thought you were a Manxman

*Ta mee credjal dy **re** ayns y gharey hooar ad eh*
I think it was in the garden that they found it

9.7.6 Omission of the copula

The copula may be omitted in present tense constructions when one of the following elements is present:
a personal pronoun

Mish eh	I (am) he
Mish t'ayn	It is I
Eshyn yn ree	He is the king

Oo mac Yee, oo ree Israel
Thou (art) the son of God, thou (art) the King of Israel

[John i.49]

an interrogative

Quoi ad?	Who (are) they?
Quoi oo hene?	Who are you yourself? [John i.19]

a demonstrative

Shoh'n dooinney	This is the man
Shoh eh jeh ren mish loayrt	This is he of whom I spoke
	[John i.15]

9.7.7 The 'zero' copula

The 'zero' copula occurs where a copula might be expected but is 'understood', rather than overtly expressed. It was formerly more frequent in constructions where two nominal groups are equated, such as in situations where the copula could be expressed as = without loss of meaning, as in 'You Tarzan, me Jane':

Juan Mooar y fer share	Big John is the best man

Often *ve* is now used in this type of construction:

Ta Juan Mooar y fer share	Big John is the best man

The copula may only be omitted in present affirmative statements. In negatives or interrogative constructions, it must be expressed:

*Cha **nee** mish eh*	I am not he
***Nee** shoh'n lioar?*	Is this the book?

*Cha **nee** dy vel dooinney erbee er vakin yn Ayr*
There is no man who has seen the Father [John vi.46]

9.7.8 The copula with preposition: *saillym, baillym*

The copula combines with a predicate and the appropriate form of a preposition into a unit which can function as a verb. Thus, *s'* + *aill, ail,* ('desire', not found separately) + *lhiam, lhiat, lesh,* functions as a modal auxiliary meaning 'wish':

Present and future independent		Present and future dependent
saillym	I wish	*naillym*
saillt	you wish	*nailt*
saillish	he wishes	*naillish*
saillee	she wishes	*naillee*
saillin	we wish	*naillin*
sailliu	you wish	*nailliu*
sailloo	they wish	*nailloo*

Ta'n gheay sheidey raad **saillee** The wind blows where she wishes
[John iii.8]

Saillym *dy darragh oo*	I wish that you would come
Nailt *lhiat goll marin?*	Do you want to go with us?
Cha **naillish** *eh*	He does not wish it
My **saillt**, *my* **sailliu**	Please, if you please

Past and conditional, independent and dependent:

baillym	I would wish	*baillin*	we would wish
bailt	you would wish	*bailliu*	you would wish
baillish	he would wish	*bailloo*	they would wish
baillee	she would wish		

yn red **baillym** the thing that I would wish

'Wishes' may also be expressed with the copula + *mian* (wish, desire) + *lhiam, lhiat, lesh,* etc.:

s'mian lhiam gra or *saillym gra* I wish to say
ta shen kiart myr by vian lesh that's just as he would wish it

9.7.9 Necessity: copula + *egin* + *da*
'Must' can be expressed with the copula *s'* + *egin* (need, necessity, obligation) + *da*, etc.

Present and future independent Present and future dependent

shegin dou	I must, I have to	*negin dou* (or *nhegin*)
shegin dhyt	you (sg) must	*negin dhyt*
shegin da	he must	*negin da*
shegin jee	she must	*negin jee*
shegin dooin	we must	*negin dooin*
shegin diu	you must	*negin diu*
shegin daue	they must	*negin daue*
shegin dou goll	you must go	

Shegin dooin loayrt Gaelg, nagh nhegin dooin?
We must speak Manx, mustn't we?

Shegin diu v'er nyn ruggey reesht
You must be born again [John iii.7]

Cha negin daue ve cho sayntoilagh! They must not be so avaricious!

ad shen … shegin dou y chur lhiam
those … I must bring [John x.16]

Past and conditional, independent and dependent:

> *begin/beign dou,* I had to, etc.

> | *beign da goll* | he had to go | [John iv.4] |

> *as beign daue jannoo speinaghyn jeh fuygh*
> and they had to make spoons of wood [BC]

Necessity is often expressed with *t'eh orrym* (literally: 'it is upon me'):

> *Ve **er** dy uirraght daa oor*   He had to wait two hours

The English 'must' of supposition, as in 'That must have been a terrible sight!', 'You must be tired,' is best translated by 'doubtless' and a verb in the appropriate tense:

> **gyn ourys** *bee shiu skee*   no doubt you will be tired
> **gyn dooyt** *va shiu accryssagh*   you must have been hungry

9.7.10 *Shione, bione* (know)
Besides *enney, fys,* (4.1.4,) 'know' can be expressed with *shione* + *da*: (The origins of *shione, bione, nione* are uncertain).

Past and future independent	Dependent
Singular: *shione dou/dhyt/da/jee*	*nhione dou/dhyt/da/jee*
Plural: *dooin/diu/daue*	*dooin/diu/daue*

> *Shione dou eh*   I know him

> *Nagh nhione dhyt ee (nagh vel enney ayd urree?)*
> Don't you know her?

Past and conditional, independent and dependent: *bione dou/dhyt,* etc. (I knew):

> | *Shione dou yn boayl* | I know the place |
> | *Cha bione dou eh* | I did not know him |

> *Bione dou eh as mish my ghuilley*
> I knew him when I was a boy

> *Bione dou eh reesht*   I would know him again

> *yn ayr as y voir echey shione dooin*
> whose father and mother are known to us [John vi.42]

9.7.11 The copula with *lesh*: liking and preferring
The copula with the pronoun-preposition *lesh* forms expressions of liking, loving, preferring:

with *shynney* = 'love':

Present and future independent	Present and future dependent

Singular: *shynney lhiam/lhiat/lesh/lhee*   *nhynney lhiam/lhiat/lesh/lhee*
Plural: *shynney lhien/lhiu/lhieu*   *nhynney lhien/lhiu/lhieu*

Shynney lhiam eh	I love him/it
eshyn shynney lesh e ven	he who loves his wife
Cha nhynney lhiam ee	I don't love her

Past and conditional, both independent and dependent:

bynney lhiam	I loved
Cha bynney lhiam eh	I wouldn't love it
Bynney lhiam çheet	I should love to come

with *s'laik* = 'like':

| *S'laik lhiam yn geurey* | I like the winter |

Cha laik lhiam goll dy lhie dy anmagh
I don't like going to bed late

| *Kys laik lhiu yn caffee?* | How do you like the coffee? |
| *Quoi jeu share laik lhiu?* | Which do you like best? |

Cha laik lesh my voir ny oashyn noa
My mother doesn't like the new fashions

Past and conditional: *b'laik*

| *B'laik lhiam niee my laueyn* | I'd like to wash my hands |
| *B'laik lhiu eeast?* | Would you like fish? |

B'laik lhiam briaght jiu c'red bare lhiu jannoo jiu
I'd like to ask you what you'd prefer to do today

with *mie* (good = I like):

s'mie lhiam ushtey, s'mie lhiam soo
I like water, I like juice
(literally: 'is good with me water', etc.)

with *share, nhare, niare* (prefer):

Present and future independent	Present and future dependent
share lhiam etc. I prefer	*nhare/niare lhiam*, etc.

Past and conditional, both independent and dependent:

> *bare lhiam, lhiat,* etc.

by vie lhiam	I should like
cha niare/nhare lhiat	you don't prefer
bare lhien	we should prefer
bare lhiam fuirraght ec y thie	I'd rather stay at home
share lhiam feeyn na lhune	I prefer wine to ale

(literally: 'is better with me wine than ale')

9.7.12 Other expressions with the copula and *lesh*, etc.
The copula + (adjective or noun) + the appropriate form of *lesh*, *da*, or other pronoun-preposition, replaces verbs in many other common expressions:
s' + *(f)eeu*, feeuid, (to be worth):

Sheeu *argid eh*	It is worth money
Sheeu *lhiam/s'feeu lhiam*	I think it worthwhile
Cha **neeu** *lhiam*	I don't think it worthwhile

B'eeu dhyt y yannoo eh?
Would it be worth your while to do it?

Cha **b'eeu** *shen monney*
That would not be worth much, it is good for nothing

Note that *feeu* is also found with *ve*:

Cha nel eh **feeu** *goll dy ynsaghey*
It is not worth going to learn   [John Tom Kaighin (1862–1954)]

s'mooar lhiam, lesh, etc. (care about):

S'mooar lesh *ny kirree*
He cares about, thinks highly of, the sheep

S'beg lhiam, lesh, etc. (despise):

S'beg lhiam *shen*   I despise that   [Fargher 1979: 231]

s'cummey lhiam, lesh, etc. (I don't care about):

S'cummey *yn Jouyl lhiam!*	I don't give a damn!
By **chummey** *lesh*	He didn't care
Nagh **gummey** *lhiam?*	What do I care?

(fer) **s'cummey** *lesh baase ny bea*
dare-devil
(literally: 'one who cares neither for death nor life')

s'cooin lhiam, lesh, etc. (remember):

Cha **gooin** lesh	He doesn't remember
by **chooinee** lhien	we remembered
S'cooin lhiam dy mie eh	I remember it well

Gooin *lhiu yn vlein va'n geurey creoi ain?*
Do you remember the year we had the severe winter?

s'leayr dou, da, etc. (perceive, it is obvious to):

Cha **b'leayr** da	He did not see

Nagh **leayr** *dhyt yn lhong foddey jeh?*
Can't you see the ship in the distance?

S'leayr dou	I see it
B'leayr dou eh	It was obvious to me
Choud's **s'leayr** dou	As far as I can perceive/see

s'mooar lhiam eh, lesh eh, etc. (begrudge):

By **vooar** lhiam eh	I begrudged it
Cha **mooar** lesh eh	He doesn't begrudge it
Cha **mooar** lhiam dhyts eh	I don't begrudge it to you

s'taittin lhiam, lesh, etc. (be pleased/delighted):

S'taittin lesh shen y yannoo	He enjoys doing that

s'doogh lhiam, s'olk lhiam, s'treih lhiam, lesh, etc. (be sorry, grieved, regret):

S'treih lhiam	I am sorry
S'treih lhiam gra eh	I am sorry to say it
Cha **dreih** lhiam	I am not sorry
By **hreih** lhiam	I was sorry

S'treih *lhiam dy row mee ayns Sostyn ec y traa*
I'm sorry that I was in England at the time   [WC]

s'lhoys (dare) and *s'lhiass* (need) usually function as auxiliaries with a verbnoun in constructions such as 'dare to go', 'need to see':

S'lhoys dou gra dy row shiu	I dare say you were
B'lhoys dhyt goll?	Dare you go?
Cha **lhoys** dou goll	I daren't go
Cha **b'lhoys** dou	I didn't dare, dared not
Cha **by-lhoys** da fer	No-one dared

Cha b'lhoys⁷ dhyt ennym kayt y ghra er boayrd y vaatey,
You dared not mention the name of a cat aboard the boat

s'lhiass (need = be obliged to):

s'lhiass *dou*	I need to (*lhiass*, need, benefit)
b'lhiass	was necessary, needed,
Cha **lhiass** *diu goll*	You need not go
Cha **b'lhiass** *dhyt jannoo shen*	You did not need to do that
my **s'lhiass**	if need be

s'cair (right) with *dou, da,* etc. (ought):

By chair *da jannoo eh*	He ought to have done it
S'cair *dhyt jannoo myr shen*	It's right that you should do so

9.7.13 The copula + *shimmey, nhimmey*

The copula is used with the emphasised adjectival predicates *shimmey* and *nhimmey* to express 'many a', 'not many a'. The noun that follows is always singular:

cha **nhimmey** *keayrt*	not many times
shimmey *oie*	many a night
cha **nhimmey** *oie*	not many a night

Shimmey *dooinney nagh vel maynrey*
Many a man is not happy

Nagh **nhimmey** *sharvaant failt t'ec my ayr!*
How many hired servants my father has!   [Luke xv.17]

Cha **nhimmey** *laa duirree ad ayns shen*
Not many a day did they stay there   [John ii.12]

shimmey *yn obbyr vie*   many the good work   [John x.32]

Shimmey *keayrt hyndaa eh e chorree ersooyl*
Many a time he turned away his wrath   [Psalm 78.39]

---

⁷ *Lhoys* is originally the relative of the verb but now functions as an adjective and combines with the copula and the preposition *da*.

9.8   Defective verbs

9.8.1   *foddym*
foddym often means 'can', 'be able to', but usually means 'may', 'might'.
foddym is said to be 'defective' because it has no imperative, verbnoun
or participle.

Present and future:

Independent		Dependent
foddym	I can	*voddym, noddym*
fodmayd	we can	*vodmayd, nodmayd*
foddee eh	[all others] can	*vod/nod eh*, etc.

Relative: *oddym, oddys*

Past independent and dependent: *dod mee, oo*, etc. I was able, etc.

Conditional independent		Conditional dependent
oddin	I should be able	*voddin, noddin*
oddagh	[all others] sh/would be able	*voddagh, noddagh*

Oddins *er ve caillt*   I might have been lost
Cha **nod** *eh lhaih ny screeu*   He can neither read not write
Foddym *toiggal shen*   I can understand that

Foddee *dy jig eh*
It could be (= perhaps) (that) he will come

Foddee *dy jeanym eh*   I might do it
Noddym *goll?*   May I go?
Dy **voddym** *y ghoaill reesht eh*   So that I may take it again
                                                          [John x.17]

Oddagh *oo v'er gionnaghey eh ny s'neugheyr*
You might have bought it cheaper

liorishyn dy **voddagh** *dy chooilley ghooinney credjal*
so that by means of him every man might (be able to) believe
                                                          [John i.7]

Quoi oo? Dy **vod mayd**[8] *ansoor y choyrt dauesyn t'er choyrt shin*
Who art thou? So that we may give an answer to them who have
sent us
                                                          [John i.22]

---

[8] *mayd* may be written separately, hyphenated, or joined to the verbal stem.

*Dy **vod** chammah yn correyder as y beaynee boggey y ghoaill cooidjagh*
So that both the sower and the reaper may rejoice together
[John iv.36] (*chammah*, see 6.21.1)

9.8.2 *lhisagh* (ought)
lhisagh is found in the conditional only (in the first and last examples
'have to' is expressed by *ve* + *er*):

lhisagh *ee ve maynrey* she ought to be happy

*Cre v'orrym dy ghra, as cre **lhisin** loayrt*
What I had to/should say and what I ought to/should speak

*Son **lhisagh** soilshey ennagh jeh'n leigh shoh er ve currit ayns y lioar*
Some explanation of this law should have been given in the book
[Clague 1911: 110–111]

*ta'n boayl raad **lhisagh** sleih ooashlaghey*
the place where people should worship [John iv.20]

***V'eh orrym** dy lhieeney yn chrock roish va mee goll dys scoill*
I had to fill the crock before I went to school [WC]

9.8.3 *hioll, hiollee* and *dobbyr*
hioll, hiollee and *dobbyr* have only these forms. They express what might
have happened and almost did:

Haghyr eh ny share na hiollee eh
It turned out better than it might have done

hioll mee	I nearly did
dobbyr dou tuittym	I nearly fell
dobbyr dou ve marrooit	I was nearly killed

This last example can also be expressed with *bunnys* (nearly):

V'eh bunnys er ny varroo He nearly got killed

9.8.4 *strooys, stroo-hene* means 'I imagine', 'it seems to me'

Strooys shen That is my opinion

9.9 Impersonal verbs
Impersonal verbs are very often rendered by the phrase *ta … ayn*:

ta fliaghey ayn it is raining
t'eh ceau fliaghey
(literally: 'it throws rain')

ta sniaghtey ayn	it is snowing
t'eh ceau snaightey	
(literally: 'it throws snow')	

ta taarnagh ayn	there is thunder
t'eh taarnaghey	
(literally: 'there is thunder')	

ta tendreil ayn	there is lightning
t'eh tendreilagh	
(literally: 'there is lightning')	

ta keeiragh ayn	it is twilight, *t'eh keeiraghey*
ta rio ayn	it is freezing/frosty/icy, *t'eh riojey*
t'eh bodjaley	it is clouding over
t'eh curthoollaghey	it is lowering – threatening rain

9.10 The past participle

9.10.1 The inflected Manx past participle usually ends in *-t* or *-it*, (and occasionally in fixed expressions *-jey*) added to the stem or base form of the verb

tayrn	(draw)	*tayrnit*	drawn
jarrood	(forget)	*jarroodit*	forgotten
tayr	(catch)	*tayrit*	caught

It is used in such constructions as:

son te scruit	for it is written	[Matthew iv.6]

Note that the stem of the verb usually resembles the imperative:

goaill	(take)	*Gow!* Take!	Past participle *goit* (= *gow* + *it*) taken
jannoo	(do)	*Jean!* Do!	Past participle *jeant*, done

Ny buird nish **troggit**
The tables now (having been) set up

[*Pargys Caillit* 247]

t'eh **soilshit** *magh dooin ec y cheayn …*
It's demonstrated to us by the sea …

Ta'n slyst **aachummit** *lesh e phooar …*
The coastline is reshaped by its power …

Ta'n thalloo shoh **caghlaait** *dagh laa* This land is changed each day
[R. C. Carswell, 'Slyst ny marrey', *Shelg yn Drane* 1994]

9.10.2   Verbnoun suffixes such as *-aghey*, and the verbnoun stem
ending *-ee*, are removed before the participial ending (*-t*, *-it* or
sometimes *-jey*) is added

eignaghey → *eignit*	force, compel, forced, compelled
lhieggey → *lhieggit*	fell, felled
faagail → *faagit*	leave, left
foshley/fosh(i)l → *foshlit*	open, opened
ynsaghey → *ynsit*	teach, taught
kionnaghey → *kionnit*	buy, bought
smooinee → *smooinit*	think, thought

9.10.3   Preceding consonants may double

cur, currit (put, give/given); *enmys, enmy[s]sit* (name, named)

9.10.4   After vowels, and after *-l*, *-s*, *-sh*, or nasals, sometimes only *-t*
is added, in which case a preceding double consonant is
usually made single

dooney, doo[i]nt	close, closed
kiangley, kianglt	bind, bound
lhieeney, lhieent	fill, filled
sheeaney, sheeant	bless, blessed
skeayley, skeaylt	scatter, scattered
reill, reilt	rule, ruled
reih, reiht	choose, chosen
poosey, poost	marry, married
brishey, brisht	break, broken
freayll, freillit/freilt	preserve, keep, reserve, preserved, kept, reserved
cassey, cast	twist, twisted

9.10.5   In other cases where a verbnoun sufix has been removed the
past participle ends in *-it*

trullaghey, trullit   sully, sullied

Sometimes, as with *caillt, caillit, cail[l]jey*, lost, from *coayl*, lose, and *ceaut,
ceauit*, from *ceau*, throw, these alternative forms of the past participle
co-exist with no apparent difference of meaning.

9.11   The passive
The passive is usually formed in one of three ways:

9.11.1 *ve* + past participle
The passive with *ve* (be) + past participle, ending in *-t*, *-it*, e.g. *jeant*, done, *scruit*, written. This form is also used adjectivally to describe the state which is the result of an action:

> *va **chyndait** gys feeyn*   (that) was turned into wine
> [John ii.9]

> *va shin **caillt***   we were ruined

> *Bee oo **enmyssit** Cephas, ta shen dy ghra, Peddyr*
> Thou shalt be named Cephas, that is to say, Peter   [John i.42]

> *Va ny mraane obbee **grait goit** seose hug yn clieau as **currit** ayns stoandey, as treinaghyn **eiyrit** ayns yn stoandey, as v'ad **rollit** gys y vun. Va ooilley cooishyn **reaghit** ec yn Whaiyl shen ...*
> Witches were said to be taken to the mountain and placed in a barrel and nails driven into the barrel, and they were rolled to the bottom. All cases were settled at that Court ...
> [Clague 1911: 56/7]

> *Va'n moghrey **ceaut** shooyl trooid yn aasagh feayn*
> (literally) The morning was spent walking through the wide desert   [Thomas Parnell, The Hermit, trans. anon. l43]

> *V'eh   slane   **jarroodit**   aym   dy   row   eh   **poost**!*
> It was   quite   forgotten   at-me   that   was   he   married
> I had quite forgotten he was married   [WC]

Note that this form is also used adjectivally to describe a state which has come about as the result of an action:

> *t'eh **scruit***   it is written
> *Va ny dorryssyn **dooint***   the doors were shut
> (stative: ie the doors had been closed and remained so)

9.11.2 *ve* + *er* + possessive (*ny, nyn*, etc.) agreeing with the subject,[9] + verbnoun

> *as va'n seihll **er ny yannoo** liorish*
> and the world was made by him   [John i.10]

---

[9] Already in Biblical Manx there was a tendency to use only the third person singular masculine form *ny*. See *Lessoonyn Sodjey*, commentary on John i.3.

Shegin diu v'er nyn ruggey reesht
You must be born again   [John iii.7]

*T'eh er **ny screeu***	it is written
Va shin er nyn goayl	we were ruined
V'eh bunnys er ny varroo	he nearly got killed

as v'adsyn v'er nyn goyrt jeh ny Phariseeyn
and they who were sent were of the Pharisees   [John i.24]

dy beagh eh er ny hoilshaghey da Israel
so that he should be shown to Israel   [John i.31]

agh v'eh er ny choyrt dy ymmyrkey feanish jeh'n toilshey shen
but he was sent to bear witness of that light   [John i.8]

Often the phrase is fixed in the third person singular masculine, that is *er ny* + lenited verbnoun:

*Ta'n thie **er ny hoiaghey** rish tannyssyn*
The house is let to tenants (*soiaghey*, to rent out, let)

9.11.3   *goll* (go) + *er* + verbnoun (without mutation)

hie** shin **er coayl	we were ruined
hed** ad **er coayl	they will be ruined
hem er coayl	I shall be ruined
*t'eh **goll er coayl***	he is ruined

***Hie** Messina **er stroie** liorish craa-hallooin*
Messina was destroyed by an earthquake

*Cha **jagh** yn Raue **er troggal** ayns laa*
Rome was not built in a day

Hed** oo **er bannaghey   Thou shalt be blessed

*lurg da ny cayrnyn **goll er shellym***
after the horns were (= had been) blown

*ayn nagh **jagh** rieau dooinney **er coyrt***
in which no-one was ever placed   [John ix.41]

*Ta ymmodee thieyn noa **goll er troggal** ayns Doolish nish*
There are many new houses being built in Douglas now

9.11.4   *ve* + *dy* + infinitive
This is a rare alternative:

Va'n thie dy hroggal   The house was being built

dy agrees with the subject:

> *va shin dyn (dy + nyn) vakin*   we were being seen

Note: *ruggyr* (is born) is the only inflected passive form to survive in
Manx. The preterite active form *rug* (bore, gave birth to) is found.
Later, the verbnoun *ruggey* was formed:

Va mee ruggit ayns shen	I was born there
raad ruggyr David	where David was born
	[John vii.42]

9.11.5   The passive infinitive

Passive infinitives in Manx are formed with *ve* + *er* + *ny* + verbnoun, or
with past participle. The 'infinitive marker' is *'dy'*:

> *e lheid dy **ve er ny claghey***
> her like (= women such as she) to be stoned   [John viii.5]

> *son nagh **bee** leigh Voses **er ny vrishey***
> so that the law of Moses may not be broken   [John vii.23]

> *bee fys eu cre share **dy ve jeant***
> you will know what is best to be done
> > [John Kneen, 'The Gaaue' (c.1852–1958)]

> *cha nhegin da danjeyr **ve shirrit** ny **shaghnit***
> danger is to be neither sought nor shunned

> *as dooyrt eh, lhisagh yn thalloo shen **ve er ny chur** er-ash*
> and he said, let that land be given back   [JC]

> *lhisagh soilshey ennagh jeh'n leigh shoh **er ve currit** ayns y lioar*
> some explanation of this law should have been given in the book
> > [Clague 1911: 110]

> *Eisht va Yeesey er ny leeideil liorish Spyrryd Yee gys yn aasagh, **dy
> v'er ny violaghey** liorish y drogh-spyrryd ... as tra v'eh er drostey da-
> eed laa ...*
> Then was Jesus led up of the spirit into the wilderness to be
> tempted of the devil. And when he had fasted forty days ...
> > [Matthew iv.1–2]

> *Ta feme aym's **dy ve er my vashtey** liort's*
> I have need to be baptized of thee   [Matthew iii.14]

Sometimes Manx passive infinitives are formed with *ry-*:

Cha nel eh ry-akin	It's not to be seen
(literally: 'it's not for seeing')	[Fargher 1979: 381]

10   Phrasal verbs
Breearyn yl-ocklagh

The handful of Manx irregular verbs forms a great number of phrasal verbs. Often these correspond to a one-word verb in English. Here are some of the most common, just to give an idea of the range and ingenuity of the constructions.

There are many more to be found in the dictionary.

10.1   With *ÇHEET* (come)

çheet er-ash (return):

> **Hig** *ee er-ash Jesarn*   She will return on Saturday

çheet lesh/er y hoshiaght (prosper, succeed):

> *Cha **daink** mee er my hoshiaght ayns Nerin*
> I did not prosper in Ireland

> | *Ta reddyn **çheet** lhiam* | I am prospering |
> | **Haink** *eh lhiam* | I succeeded in it |
> | **Haink** *eh lesh* | He managed to do it |

çheet rish (appear):

> **Haink** *eh **rish** ayns ashlish*   he appeared in a vision

çheet ny whaiyl (meet, see 11.7.7):

> | *my-whaiyl* | towards me |
> | *dty whaiyl* | towards you |
> | *ny whaiyl* | towards him |
> | *ny quaiyl* | towards her |
> | *nyn guaiyl* | towards us/you/them |

> *Yn nah laa honnick Ean Yeesey çheet **ny-whaiyl***
> The next day John saw Jesus coming towards him   [John i.29]

Note: This is the same word as '*quaiyl*', 'court', which originally meant 'meeting', and is also the basis of the expression '*quaaltagh*', or 'first foot'. Unlike most others, this expression is not based on a simple preposition.

Higym dty whaiyl *ec jees er y chlag*
I'll meet you at 2 o'clock

Tar my whaiyl *ayns shen*   Meet me there

Ta mee **goll ny quaiyl** *dagh moghrey as t'ee* **çheet my whaiyl**
I meet her every morning and she meets me

Haink *mee nyn* **guaiyl**   I met them

10.2   With *CUR* (give, put)

cur da (thrash – popular):

Cur *da!*   Thrash him!

cur er (compel, oblige):

Cur *urree goll*   Make her go

cur er-ash (return, restore):

Cur er-ash *dooin bannaghtyn ny marrey*
Restore to us the blessings of the sea

cur er bun (establish):

Va'n Çheshaght **currit er bun** *'sy vlein 1899*
The Society was founded in the year 1899

tra va shin **cur** *Banglane Twoaie* **er-bun**
when we were setting up the Northern Branch   [JC]

cur er-shaghryn (lead astray):

Hug *ee* **er-shaghryn** *eh*   She led him astray

cur enn er (recognise):

Dug *oo* **enn** *urree?*   Did you recognize her?

cur ersooyl (dismiss):

V'ee **currit ersooyl** *ass-laue*   She was immediately dismissed

cur fo smaght (conquer):

Hug *mee tudjeenyn* **fo smaght**   I conquered cigarettes

cur fys er, huggey (to send for, summon, inform, send a message to, call to):

Hug *ad* **fys er** *yn 'er lhee*   They sent for the doctor

*My **dug** Karmane er e Obbyr kione*
***Hug** Jee **fys** er as hooar eh baase*

Before German finished his work
God sent for him and death came

[Traditional Ballad 15]

***Hug** ny shuyraghyn **fys** huggey* The sisters sent a message to him
[John xi.3]

cur geill da (heed, pay attention):

> *Cur geill dou!*   Pay attention!

cur haa(y)rt (vanquish, conquer, overthrow):

> *Va nyn noidyn **currit haart***   Our enemies were vanquished

cur jeh (undress):

> ***Cur jeed!***   Undress yourself!

cur leagh da (reward):

> *Ta fys echey kys dy **chur leagh** da treanid e hidooryn*
> He knows how to reward his soldiers' valour

cur lesh (bring, carry):

> ***Cur lhiat** arran hym!*   Bring me bread!

cur magh (publish):

> ***Vermayd magh** y slane skeeal*   We shall publish the whole story

cur mow (destroy):

> ***Hug** eh **mow** yn balley*   He destroyed the town

cur mysh (don, put on – of clothing):

> ***Hug** ee **moee** e cooat*   She put on her coat
> ***Hug** eh **mysh***   He got dressed

> *T'ee **cur moee** 'syn oash Rangagh*
> She dresses in the French fashion

cur rish (practise, commit):

> *V'eh **cur rish** fer lheeys*   He was practising as a doctor
> *Ny **cur rish** peccah!*   Commit no sin!

cur roish (propose, intend, advise):

> ***Hug** eh slaynt ny ben poosee **roish***
> He proposed the health of the bride   [Fargher 1979: 598]

cur (or *goll lesh*) *shilley er* (to visit, go to see):

> **Vermayd shilley** *er y çhenn pheiagh*
> We will visit the old one
>
> [Ned Maddrell (1877–1974)]

> *Va mish* **goll lesh shilley** *er Brian Stowell ayns shen*
> I was going to visit Brian Stowell there   [BC]

cur y lane fo defy, challenge (popular):

> *ta mee* **cur y lane feue** *ooilley dy yannoo y chooid smessey*
> I defy you all to do your worst

> *hug eh y lane fo*   he challenged him

cur taitnys da (please):

> *goaill er* **cur taitnys** *da ooilley*   trying to please all

10.3   With *GEDDYN, FEDDYN* (find, get)

geddyn baase (die):

> **Hooar** *ee* **baase** *yn laa lurg e poosey*
> She died the day after her wedding

> **Hooar** *adsyn* **baase** *lesh y jough*
> They died of the drink   [LQ]

> *Enmyn ooilley yn sleih* **hooar baase** *ayns y chaggey*
> The names of all the people who died in the war   [JC]

geddyn magh (discover):

> *yn fer ren* **feddyn magh** *Yn America*
> the discoverer of America

geddyn rey (rish) (rid … of, get rid of):

> **Hooar** *mee* **rey** *r'ee*   I got rid of her

10.4   With *GOAILL* (take)

goaill aaght (lodge, stay):

> *Ta mee* **goaill aaght** *maroo*   I lodge with them
> **Gowyms aaght** *'sy thie-oast*   I'll stay at the hotel

goaill aggle (roish) (fear, be afraid of):

> *Ny* **gow aggle** *roym*   Don't be afraid of me
> *Ta mee* **goaill aggle** *roish*   I am afraid of him

goaill arrane (sing):

> **Ghow** shin **arrane** dy creeoil   We sang heartily
>
> V'ee **goaill arrane** mychione yn ushag reaisht as y lhondoo
> She would sing about the plover and the blackbird   [JC]

goaill ayns laue (undertake, take in hand):

> **Goweemayds ayns laue** eh   We'll attend to it

goaill boggey (be glad):

> Ta mee **goaill boggey** clashtyn shen
> I am glad to hear it

goaill er (lament, make a fuss, fret):

> Ny **gow ort**!   Don't fret!

goaill fea, aash (rest):

> Soie sheese as **gow fea**   Sit down and take it easy

goaill foddeeaght ny yei (long for):

> Ta mee er ve **goaill foddeeaght ny yei'n** arragh
> I have been longing for the spring
>
> V'ee **goaill foddeeaght my yei** She was longing for me

goaill jeh (doff, take off, remove) e.g. *edd* (hat):

> **Gow** dty eaddagh **jeed**!   Take off your clothes!

goaill leshtal (excuse):

> **Gow** my **leshtal**!   I'm sorry!
> (literally: 'take my excuse')
>
> **Gow** my **leshtal**, my sailt   Excuse me, please
> Ta mee **goaill** dty **leshtal**   I excuse you

goaill padjer (pray):

> Lhig dooin **padjer** y **ghoaill**   Let us pray
> **Gow padjer** er nyn son!   Pray for us!
> dy **ghoaill padjer** gys Jee   to pray to God

goaill rish (confess, acknowledge):

> **ghow** eh **rish** jannoo eh   he confessed to having done it
>
> my ta shin **goaill rish** nyn beccaghyn
> if we confess our sins

Ren ad **goaill rish** *eh myr Eaghytrane*
They acknowledged him as President

goaill soylley (jeh) (enjoy):

Ghow *mee* **soylley** *jeh'n jinnair aym*
I enjoyed my dinner

V'eh **goaill soylley** *marish e phaitçhyn*
He was amusing himself with his children

Ta shiu **goaill soylley** *jeh reddyn millish, nagh vel?*
You enjoy sweet things, don't you?

goaill taitnys ayns (take delight in, be delighted, be interested in):

Ghow *mee* **taitnys** *dy yeeaghyn er yn Ghailck er y chlagh-oaie shoh
ayns y Ghermaain*
I was delighted to see Manx on this gravestone in Germany   [JC]

goaill toshiaght (er) (start, begin, make a start on):

Ghow *eh* **toshiaght** *daa laa er dy henney*
It started two days ago

Ta'n çhirveish **goaill toshiaght** *ec shey*
The service begins at six

Cha **gowyms toshiaght er** *gys y voghrey*
I shall not begin until the morning

goaill yindys (er) (to wonder, be surprised at):

Ghow *mee* **yindys** *mooar er*
I was greatly surprised at him/it

Ta mee **goaill yindys** *my hig eh ny dyn*
I wonder if he will come   [Fargher 1979: 877]

Note also: *Va yindys orrym* etc., I was surprised:

Va yindys mooar orrym tra honnick mee ...
I was very surprised when I saw ...   [WC]

Psalm xxii.17 has the contraction '*gindys*'

foddym ooilley my chraueyn y choontey; t'ad shassoo **gindys** *as
jeeaghyn orrym*
I may tell all my bones; they look and stare upon me

10.5   With *GOLL* (go)

goll dy lhie (retire = go to bed):

 *Te traa **goll dy lhie***   It's time to go to bed

goll roish (depart):

 Immee royd!   Away with you!

goll shaghey, pass:

 *Ta carriadsyn yn ree er **n'gholl shaghey***
 The king's carriages have just passed

 *Kys ta'n traa **goll shaghey**!* How time passes!
 T'ad goll shaghey   They are passing by

10.6   With *JANNOO* (make, do)

jannoo ass y noa (renew, repeat):

 *Va dy chooilley nhee **jeant ass-y-noa***
 Everything was repeated

jannoo er (trouble, worry):

 *Cre ta **jannoo ort**?*   What is troubling you?
 *Ta'n aacheoid **jannoo orrym*** I am troubled with rheumatism
 (literally: 'rheumatism is doing on me')

jannoo magh (satisfy, please):

 *Cha nel eh **jeant magh** foast* He has not had enough yet
 *Ta mee slane **jeant magh*** I am quite satisfied

 *V'ee **jeant magh** dy row shin çheet*
 She was delighted we were coming   [BC]

 *Ta mee lane **jeant magh** lesh!* I am very excited about it [JC]

jannoo mooar jeh (esteem, cherish, think well/much of):

 ***Ren** eh **mooar** jeh'n voddey* He thought a lot of the dog

 ***Ren** ny Galileanee **mooar** jeh*
 The Galileans made much of him   [John iv.45]

jannoo myghin er (to have mercy on):

 *Hiarn, **jean myghin orrin*** Lord have mercy upon us

jannoo soiagh jeh (esteem, value, accept):

 ***nee'm soiagh jeh** lesh taitnys* I will accept with pleasure

jannoo ymmyd (make use of, use):

Jean ymmyd *jeh ushtey feayr*   Use cold water

Vel oo **jannoo ymmyd** *jeh'n skynn ayd?*
Are you using your knife?

Cha lhisagh eh jannoo ymmyd jeh fockle myr shen
He should not use a word like that   [BC]

jannoo soo dy vie jeh (make (good) use of):

Ren *eh* **soo dy vie jeh'n** *lioar*   He made good use of the book

11 The verb in use

11.1 Uses of the tenses

11.1.1 Future and future perfect

Manx often uses a future where English uses a present. This is actually quite logical, because either the action has not yet taken place, or else the time referred to is indeterminate, and therefore has an element of the hypothetical about it, which in other circumstances might warrant a subjunctive:

> *tra* **higmayd**   when we come
> (future independent of *çheet*)

> *roish my* **vow** *my lhiannoo baase* before my child dies   [John iv.49]
> (*Vow*, future dependent of *geddyn* after *roish my*, before)

> *mannagh* **vaik** *shiu cowraghyn*   unless you see signs   [John iv.48]
> (*vaik*, future dependent of *fakin*, see after *mannagh*, unless)

> *neeym kionnaghey ooilley dty eayin, my* **yiowmayd** *lesh prios beg*
> I'll buy all your lambs, if we can (will be able to) get them for a
> small price   [Joseph Woodworth (1854–1931)]
> (*Yiowmayd*, future independent of *geddyn*, get)

Because most irregular verbs lack the future relative endings, they use the future independent:

> *cre-erbee* **jir** *eh*   whatever he says   [John ii.5]
> (future of *gra* (say))

Similarly, Manx has future perfect where English has present or future in sentences such as:

> *Tra* **vees** *Fer-ny-gherjagh* **er jeet**, *eh ver-yms hiu*
> When the Comforter has come, I will send him to you [John xv.26]
> (literally: 'when the Comforter will have come, I will send him to you'. The first future in this example, *vees*, is relative, after *tra*)

11.1.2   Future relative
Those verbs which possess a distinct future relative form use this instead
of the future tense in certain circumstances:
in relative clauses where the subject precedes the verb:

> *yn dooinney* **ghoys** *ayns laue yn obbyr shen*
> the man who will undertake that work

> *Nee'm cooney leshyn* **chooinys** *lhiams*
> I shall help the person who helps me

in future relative clauses where the direct object precedes the verb:

> *Mie lhiat y gioot* **chionneeys** *ee?*
> Do you like the gift she's going to buy?

after copula *s'* or *she* in future clauses, either expressed, as in the
following examples:

> *s'atçhimagh* **vees** *yn sterrym nogh*   the storm tonight will be terrible
> *she eshyn* **eiyrys** *orroo*   it is he who will follow them
> *s'maynrey* **vees** *shiu*   happy shall ye be   [John xiii.17]

or implicit:

> *Eshyn* **freillys** *ny annaghyn, t'eh freayll yn annym hene*
> He who keeps the commandments keeps his own soul

> *mairagh* **vees** *feailley'n eayst-noa*
> tomorrow will be the feast of the new moon
>
> [1 Samuel xx.5]

After interrogative pronouns or adverbs:

cre? c'red?	what?	*c'raad?*	where?
cuin?	when?	*caid?*	how long?
kys?	how?	*c'ren aght/fa/oyr?*	how, why?
quoi?	who?		

> *Quoi* **oddys** *y chlashtyn eh?*   Who can hear it?   [John vi.60]
> *Cuin* **roshys** *ad y charrick?*   When will they reach the rock?
> *Kys* **inshys** *ee da?*   How will she tell him?
> *Cre* **hirrym**?   What shall I be looking for?

> *Eshyn smoo* **hayrys** *smoo vees echey*
> He who catches most will have most

> *Cre-voish* **oddys** *mayd arran y chionnaghey?*
> Whence can we buy bread?   [John vi.5]

> *Liorish shoh* **vees** *fys ec dy chooilley ghooinney*
> by this every man will know   [John xiii.35]

Tra **scuirrys** *y laue dy choyrt,* **scuirrys** *y veeal dy voylley*
When the hand ceases to give, the mouth ceases to praise

In a subordinate clause introduced by: *tra* (when), *chamoo* (nor, neither), *cho ... as* (as ... as), *derrey* (till, until), *-erbee* (-ever), *choud's* (as long as), *my* (if):

my **oddym**	if I can
my **chreckys** *eh e hie-troailt*	if he sells his caravan
tra **chaillym** *yn stiurtys*	when I lose my stewardship
	[Luke xiv.4]

My **vees** *uss guilley mie as my nee uss fuirraghtyn aynshoh son sheshaght dooys, yiow oo yn thie shoh*
If you are (literally: 'will be') a good boy and you (literally: 'will') stay here as company for me, you will get this house (*geddyn*)
[Ned Maddrell (1877–1974)]

derrey **vees** *y jymmoose er ny chooilleeney*
until the anger is avenged   [Daniel xi.36]

choud's **vees** *y drogh-earish ayn*	as long as the bad weather is here
cho tappee as **oddysmayd**	as quickly as we can
chouds **veeym** *bio*	as long as I live
	[Fargher 1979: 465]

Verym freggyrt da dooinney erbee **vrieys** *jee'm, quoi erbee* **scarrys** *rish e ven, as* **phoosys** *ben elley, t'eh brishey poosey*
I will answer any man who asks me, whoever divorces his wife and marries another woman, commits adultery   [Luke xi.18]

Quoi-erbee **iuys** *jeh'n ushtey shoh bee eh paagh reesht*
Whoever (will drink) drinks of this water he shall be thirsty
again   [John iv.13]

The relative is not used after: *cha, nagh, mannagh, dy* or anywhere where the dependent form of the future would be required:

    mannagh **bee** *yn caa ayd*   if you don't get a chance (not *vees*)

    foddee dy **vod** *eh feddyn magh*
    perhaps he will be able to discover (not *oddys*)

    tra nagh **gooinee** *shiu er arragh*
    when you will no longer remember (not *chooineeys*)

    choud's nagh **vaag** *ad eh*
    as long as they will not leave him (not *aagys*)

The future may also function as a subjunctive (see 9.1.5).

11.1.3 The past tenses: the preterite
The irregular preterites often look as if they came from a different verb:

> *honnick mee*   I saw
> (independent *vaik mee*, preterite dependent of *fakin* (see))
>
> *vaik oo?*   did you see (Interrogative)
> *cha vaik mee*   I did not see

This tense corresponds to English simple past.
Manx preterite may also be used where English might prefer to use the perfect:

> *Marish y cappan* **chaill** *eh'n cliaghtey moal*
> Has with the cup the graceless custom lost
>   [Thomas Parnell, The Hermit, trans. anon. Mx l. 254, Eng. 212]

11.1.4 Past tenses: periphrastic or compound past tenses
English forms these perfect and pluperfect tenses with auxiliary 'have'. But Manx lacks a verb 'to have'. It usually expresses possession with *ta + ec* (see 4):

> *ta lioar aym*   I have a book
> (literally: 'there's a book at me')

The perfect and pluperfect tenses of transitive verbs are frequently replaced by *ta/va* + direct object + past participle + [*ec* + noun or a form of *ec*]:

> *T'eh er vrishey yn uinnag, Ta'n uinnag brisht echey*
> He has broken the window
>
> *V'eh er vrishey yn stoyl, va'n stoyl brisht echey*
> He had broken the chair
>
> *Va mee er screeu yn lettyr, va'n lettyr scruit aym*
> I had written the letter

A perfect or pluperfect passive without an animate agent can also be expressed using this construction:

> *Va'n uinnag er ve brisht (lesh clagh)*
> The window had been broken (by a stone)

11.1.5 Aspect in past tenses
Aspect concerns the manner in which the verbal action is experienced or regarded, for example, either as having been completed, or else as on-going or in progress, or iterative, that is, often repeated. To express

actions in the past, in addition to the perfect and pluperfect, Manx has a range of options:

In general, it may be said that the 'periphrastic imperfect/habitual' which is formed with the auxiliary *va*, the preterite of *ve*, + verbnoun, expresses habitual or incomplete actions and continuous states in the past. The periphrastic past tense formed with auxiliary *ren* (the preterite of *jannoo*), like the simple preterite or inflected tense of the verb, expresses individual events in the past.

The wide range of options means that Manx can handle nuances of aspect with considerable subtlety:

> *Va mee **my lhie** ayns my lhiabbee cur booise da Yee, as **haink** eh hym as **ren** eh **leih** dou ooilley*
> I was lying in my bed giving thanks to God, and he came to me and forgave (= did forgive) me all
>
> > [Thomas Christian (1851–1930)]

> *Va ben Juan v'ee ben feer chrauee, as **va** shin **kiaulleeagh** carvalyn … **ren** ben Juan **jeeaghyn** dooin yn voayl va'n luss gaase, as **ren** ee **scrapey** yn ooir voish yn luss*
> John's wife was a very religious woman, and we were singing carols … John's wife showed us where the herb was growing and she scraped the mould from the herb   [Clague 1911: 2]

> *As **yeeagh** eh er Yeesey, myr **v'eh shooyl**, as **dooyrt** eh*
> And he looked at Jesus, as he was walking, and he said
>
> > [John i.36]

> *Eisht **loayr** yn ainle; dy chlashtyn e choraa*
> *Va eunyssagh, as shoh myr **ren** eh gra*
> (literally: 'then spoke the angel; to hear his voice was blissful, and this he did say')
>
> > [Thomas Parnell, The Hermit, trans. anon. 226–7]

> ***Daink** shiu veih Nerin? Cha **daink**, quoi **va gra** shen?*
> Did you come from Ireland? No I did not, (literally: 'did not come') who was saying that?   [John Gell 1977]

> *Va'n moddey **toiggal** y Ghailck eisht? **Va**, dy jarroo, cha **geayll** eh rieau yn ghlare Vaarlagh*
> Did the dog understand Manx, then? (literally: 'was the dog understanding') Indeed he did (was), he never heard (i.e., never once) the English language   [ibid]

To express habitual or repeated actions in the past, Manx has several other options. These involve using an extra element that means 'used to', 'accustomed to':

va + *cliaghtey* + verbnoun, *cliaghtit rish* + noun (was accustomed):

> *Ta mee dy mie cliaghtit rish*   I am well used to it
> > [Fargher 1979: 835]

> *V'ad cliaghtey ve goll dy Rhumsaa*
> They used to be going to Ramsey
> > [John Tom Kaighin (1862–1954)]

> *Shen yn bwaane va mish cliaghtey fakin*
> That's the cottage I used to see   [Mrs Sage Kinvig (1870–1962)]

> *V'ad cliaghtey cur greesagh voan er yn chiollagh*
> They used to put turf ashes on the hearth   [Clague 1911: 8]

> *Va guillyn aegey cliaghtey goll mygeayrt*
> Young boys used to go about   [Clague 1911: 14]

boallagh
boallagh, bollagh, b'oallagh, is made up from the past of the copula and
the adjective *oallagh* (familiar, acquainted with). The original adjective
oallagh has been given a first person ending. This later became used in
the sense of 'accustomed to':

> *boallin*   I was used to
> > [Judges xvi.20 cit. Fargher 834]

> *bollagh eh*   it used to be   [I Samuel xviii.10]

> *boallagh shin cloie ry-cheilley*   we used to play together

> *Nagh nee shoh eshyn boallagh soie shirrey jeirk?*
> Is not this he who was accustomed to sit seeking alms?
> > [John ix.8]

> *Boallagh Yeesey dy mennick taaghey yn voayl shen*
> Jesus was often accustomed to frequent that place   [John xviii.2]

> *Cha nel eh gobbragh myr boallagh eh*
> He does not work as much as he used to   [Fargher 1979: 835]

Sometimes even in quite early Manx you may find imperfect tenses
apparently formed with the past conditional:

> *Cha nee lesh e Chliwe ren eh ee reayll*
> Not with his sword did he defend it

> *Cha nee lesh e Hideyn, ny lesh e Vhow*
> Nor with his arrows nor his bow (shield?)

> *Agh tra aikagh eh Lhuingys troailt*
> But when he saw a fleet sailing

Oallagh eh mygeayrt lesh Keau.
He would hide it round with mist.

Yinnagh eh dooinney ny hassoo er Brooghe
He would set a man on the brooghs

Er-lhieu shen hene dy beagh ayn keead
So you would think there were a hundred there

[Manx Traditionary Ballad 4–5]

Nevertheless, this tense is really best reserved for subjunctive and conditional usage, like the *beagh* in the second part of the example. In the above example, there would anyway be a case for reading *aikagh* and *yinnagh* as subjunctive /conditional in the sense of:

'If he saw (were to see) ships approaching, he would place a man on the brooghs.'[10]

11.2   State verbs
The distinction between action and state can also be made with such verbs as 'sit', 'stand', 'lie', and also with some 'state' adjectives like *host* (silent) using the personal particles *my, dty, ny, nyn*:

Ta	*mee*	*my*	*hassoo*
am	I	my	standing

I am standing (sometimes interpreted as meaning 'I am-in-my-standing')

yn pobble va nyn shassoo
the people who were standing   [John vi.22]

V'eh ny host   He was silent
(literally: 'he was in his silence')

T'ad nyn daue   They are idle
(literally: 'they are in their rest')

V'eh ny veshtey   He was drunk
(literally: 'in drink, in a state of inebriation)

Va mee my chadley   I was asleep/sleeping

T'eh ny cadley
He has gone to sleep, is asleep/sleeping

Vel oo er dty ghoostey?   Are you awake?

---

[10] Thomson notes that in later Manx forms such as *harragh* 'would come' were only conditional, but earlier perhaps past subjunctive. [*Etudes celtiques* ix.1960: p. 543]

Ta mee er my ghoostey   I am awake

Cha nel mee er ve my lhie daa oor
I haven't been in bed two hours

Ta shiu er ve nyn lhie bunnys jeih!
You've been in bed nearly ten! (see 3.2.2)

11.3   Infinitives with *dy, y, ry-*
dy, y, ry- (to) may precede the verbnoun to form an infinitive:
dy is the usual preposition preceding a verbnoun to form an infinitive,
especially where the object also precedes the verbnoun:

*Cha nel aym agh yn enmys **dy screeu** nish*
Now I've only the address to write

[John Kneen (c. 1852–1958)]

*Ghuee mee er eh **dy heet** stiagh*   I begged him to come in

*V'eh kiarit cre **dy yannoo***
He himself was resolved what to do   [John vi.6]

*Ta mee guee erriu **dy chur** da'n chooish geill shallid*
I beg you to give the subject a moment's consideration

*Ta mee geamagh erriu ooilley **dy ymmyrkey feanish***
I call upon you all to witness

11.3.1   *dy* of purpose (in order to, so as to)

dy cheau yn traa	to pass the time	[Clague 1911: 2]
dy yannoo magh ad shoh	to satisfy these	[John vi.5]

haink eh son feanish, dy ymmyrkey feanish jeh'n toilshey
he came for a witness, to bear witness of the light   [John i.7]

tra hug ny Hewnyn saggyrtyn dy ênaght jeh
when the Jews sent priests ... to enquire of him   [John i.19]

Note that *dy* with verbnoun is also found on the English model 'is to',
with future reference and some notion of destiny or necessity:

eshyn eh va dy vrah eh
he (is) he (i.e. the one) who was to betray him   [John vi.71]

cre'n baase v'eh dy surranse
what death he was to suffer   [John xviii.32]

11.3.2 *y* before *ve* etc.

y, sometimes for *e*, occurs regularly before *ve*, and quite frequently with other infinitives, especially where the object precedes the verb:

yn	*arran*	*neem*	*'s*	*y*	*choyrt*
the	bread	I shall	EMP		give

the bread which I will give (you)   [John vi.51

naight y chlashtyn   to hear a piece of news

[Fargher 1979: 38]

Kys oddys enney y ve ain er y raad?
How may we know the way?   [John xiv.5]

Lhig dooin padjer y ghoaill   Let us pray

Ren ad eh y haglym   They gathered them together

[John vi.13]

Cre-voish oddys mayd arran y chionnaghey?
Whence can we buy bread?   [John vi.5]

Nee eh dy gerrit eh y ghloyraghey
He will shortly glorify him   [John xiii.32]

quoi yinnagh eh y vrah   who would betray him

[John vi.64]

Nee yn irriney shiu y heyrey   The truth shall make you free

[John viii.32]

roish clashtyn y choyrt da   before giving him a hearing

[John vii.51]

Kys oddys ny reddyn shoh y ve   How may these things be

[John iii.9]

dy vod shee y ve eu   that peace may be to you

[John xvi.33]

Quoi oddys y chlashtyn eh?   Who can hear it?   [John vi.60]

V'ad shirrey eh y choyrt gy-baase
They were seeking to put him to death

dy row ny Hewnyn shirrey eh y varroo
that the Jews were seeking to kill him   [John vii.1]

Cha voddym jee'm pene nhee erbee y yannoo
I can of mine own self do nothing   [John v.30]

mannagh jean shiu feill yn Mac dooinney y ee, as e uill y iu
except ye eat the flesh of the Son of Man, and drink His blood
[John vi.53]

dy vod dagh unnane oc kuse y ghoaill
that each one of them may take a little   [John vi.7]

eshyn ... cha jeanym ... y yiooldey voym
him ... I will not ... reject (literally: 'spurn from me') [John vi.37]

jean-jee yn vrooillagh ... y haglym
gather up the fragments (*çhaglym*, to collect, gather) [John vi.12]

er-gerrey da'n boayl (sic*) ren ad arran y ee ayn
nigh unto the place where they did eat bread   [John vi.23]

* *'voayl'* would be expected after the article *y*

11.3.3   Verbnoun with *y* functioning as a noun
Sometimes the verbnoun preceded by *y* is really functioning as a noun
rather than as a verb:

yn coirrey y charraghey   to repairing boiler
(*karraghey* to repair)

S'taittin lesh shen y yannoo   He enjoys doing that
                                   [Fargher 1979: 281]

11.3.4   *y* embedded in a Manx phrasal verb
A phrasal verb may include within it the infinitive marker *y*:

peccah y yannoo   to sin (also: *jannoo peccah*)
tranlaase y yannoo er   to oppress, tyrannize
(literally: 'to do oppression upon': also found as *tranlaasey*)

11.3.5   Infinitives formed with *ry* and verbnoun
Ry + verbnoun may form infinitives (usually passive, 9.11.5), especially
these common ones:

ry-akin	to be seen	*ry-gheddyn*	to be got, obtained
ry-clashtyn	to be heard	*ry-ennaghtyn*	to be felt
ry-ghra, ry-loayrt	to be said/spoken	*ry-heet*	to come

Cha row veg ry-chlashtyn jeu rieau arragh
Nothing was (to be) heard of them again

[Fargher 1979: 381]

cha nel eh ry-akin	it's not to be seen

[Fargher 1979: 670]

Cha jinnagh dooinney ta coyrt de ve ry-akin dy bragh jeirk 'sy dorraghys
A man who gives in order to be seen, would never do alms in the dark

[Cregeen 1984: 158]

t'eh ry-gheddyn	it is to be had [Fargher 1979: 369]
t'eh ry ghra	it is said
thie ry-chreck	house for sale
daa ghooinney ry-chroghey	two men to be hanged
cre ta ry-yannoo ayns shoh?	what's to be done here?

*ta fockle aym ry-loayrt	I have a word to say
(literally: 'to be spoken')	

*bee raad liauyr ayd ry-gholl
you will have a long road to travel   [Fargher 1979: 641]

sheeloghyn ry-heet, eeashyn ry-heet
ages to come

traa ry-heet, laghyn ry-heet	times/days to come

dooyrt eh dy row ram enmyn ry-gheddyn
he said there were many names to be got   [JC]

* The equivalent English sentence here prefers an active infinitive. But the Manx adopts the logical view that the word 'is spoken', the road 'is travelled', hence the passive infinitive marker *ry*.

Note that 'seen', 'visible' may be expressed with *ayns akin*, 'within sight'
[Adrian Pilgrim, *Oardagh Noa yn Erin* 2006]

11.3.6 Negative infinitives
Negative infinitives are marked by *gyn, dyn* (not):

*dy ve ny **gyn dy ve***	to be or not to be
*abbyr rish **dyn goll***	tell him not to go

*T'eh ny share dooin **gyn ve** er yn aarkey noght*
It is better for us not to be at sea tonight

*Abbyr rish Illiam **dyn traaue** y magher*
Tell William not to plough the field

*Gow eh, veagh eh ommidjagh **gyn goaill** eh!*
Take it, it would be foolish not to take it!

> *Choyrlee shin ny joarreeyn* **gyn** *ad* **dy hannaghtyn** *ny sodjey*
> We advised the strangers not to stay any longer

Classical Manx usually had '*dy*' before the verbnoun in the negative infinitive as well as *gyn*: *abbyr rish gyn dy gholl* (*goll* lenites here because of the *dy*, like *tannaghtyn* in the last example).

11.4 Verbs requiring prepositions

Some verbs may require prepositions to be used after them.

verbs + *da*

bannaghey (salute)	*bentyn* (touch, belong to)
coyrlaghey (advise)	*cur* (give)
eeck (pay)	*freggyrt rish* (answer)
gialdyn (promise)	*insh* (relate, tell)
jeeaghyn (show)	*leih* (forgive)
lhiggey (allow)	*oltaghey* (welcome)
ynsaghey (teach)	

> *leih* **dooin** *nyn loghtyn myr ta shinyn leih* **dauesyn** ...
> forgive us our sins as we forgive them who ...

verbs + *er*

berraghtyn (overtake)	*çhionney* (oblige to do)
cooinaghtyn (remember)	*cur* (oblige to do)
feaysley (relieve)	*greimmey* (seize)
guee (beseech, pray for)	*smooinaghtyn* (remember)
troggal (rise)	*yeearree* (request)
cur fys (inform)	*jeeaghyn* (look at)
yllagh (call for)	*shirrey* (ask for)
yeearree (ask, desire, seek)	*fuirraghtyn (er/rish)* (await, wait for)

> *cur-jee* **er** *ny deiney soie sheese*   make the men sit down
> [John vi.10]

> *shirrey argid* **er** *yn charrey eu*   ask your friend for money

> *shir* **er** *Jee ny grayseyn shen y choyrt dou*
> ask God for those graces

verbs + *jeh*

briaght (ask, inquire):

> *brie* **jeh** *cre'n traa te*   ask him what time it is

fênaght (ask, demand):

> *D'ênee eh* **jeh** *cre'n oyr nagh row shoh jeant echey*
> He asked him why he had not done this

verbs + *huggey*

cur (send):

Cur hym eh	Send it [to] me
	[Fargher] (see 4.1.8)

cur fys huggey (send for):

*Hug ee fys **gys** e leighder*	She sent for her advocate

verbs + *lesh*

cooney (help):

as dooyrt mish dy jinnagh mee [sic] *jannoo my share son dy **cooney lhee***
and I said that I'd do my best to help her
[Ned Maddrell (1877–1974)]

cur (bring):

*As **hug** eh **lesh** eh gys Yeesey*
And he (Andrew) brought him (Peter) to Jesus   [John i.42]

verbs + *mysh*

craid (make fun of)

verbs + *noi*

coyrlaghey (dissuade, advise against)

verbs + *rish*

gra (tell)	*caggey* (fight)	*cur* (practise)
eaishtagh (listen to)	*fuirraghtyn* (wait for)	*loayrt* (speak to)

scarrey (separate from)	*lhiantyn* (adhere to)
sniemmey (affix to)	*freggyrt* (reply, respond to)
festal (fasten)	

*Ta mee **scarrey rish** my vioys*
I part with my life (literally: 'separate from')   [John x.15]

verbs + *roish*

goaill aggle (fear):

*Ta aggle aym **roish***	I am afraid of him

goll (depart):

***Jed** shiuish myrgeddin **reue**?*	Will you also go away?
	[John vi.67]

Some of these elements may not, in reality, be prepositions at all, but adverbs bound to the verb and therefore not declinable (this just means they don't have to change their endings for different persons, as pronoun-prepositions do).

Others relate to the English object, e.g. *cur er*, make someone do something, and others again to the subject, e.g. *goll roish* (go away), *cur lesh* (bring). Manx has large numbers of phrasal verbs, i.e., verbs which are formed from a verb combined with another element or elements to give a new meaning (see 10).

Manx examples of phrasal verbs include *goaill aggle*, fear (literally: 'to take fright'), above.

11.5 Manx equivalents for English -ing forms

These are generally indistinguishable from the verbnoun, with *g-* being prefixed to verbs which begin with vowels. This form is generally used with *jannoo*, *ve*, *foddym*, in place of the verbnoun.

English -ing forms are used in the following ways and in most cases correspond to a verbnoun in Manx:

11.5.1 Gerunds

*Hie ee roee dyn **jeeaghyn** peiagh erbee*
She left without **seeing** anyone

*Chum yn taarnagh mee veih **cadley***
The thunder kept me from **sleeping**

*Son gyn **jannoo** shoh bee shiu kerrit*
For not **doing** this you will be punished

*Ghow eh rish **jannoo** eh*
He confessed to **having done** (doing) it

*Cre hon ghow oo eh dyn **insh** mee?*
Why did you take it without **telling** me?

*Ta lane eddyr **raa** as **jannoo***
There is much between **saying** and **doing**

*dy freayll y baareyder veih **giarrey** ad jeh*
to keep the barber from **cutting** them off
[Thomas Christian (1851–1930)]

*Cha jeanym cumrail oo veih **ymmyrkey magh** dty yeearree*
I shan't prevent you from **carrying out** your project

*Va'n moghrey ceaut **shooyl** trooid yn aasagh feayn*
The morning was spent **walking** (= in walking) through the wide desert   [Thomas Parnell, The Hermit, trans anon. 43]

T'ee dy kinjagh taggloo ayns ynnyd jeh **ynsaghey** *e lessoonyn*
She's always talking instead of **learning** her lessons

T'eh shooyl er oirr eaynin fegooish **ennaghtyn** *tollaneagh*
He walks on the brink of a precipice without **feeling** giddy

Va ny Hewnyn wheesh shen smoo shleeuit er **cur dy baase** *eh*
The Jews were that much more keen on **putting him to death**
[John v.18]

In the following examples, the English -ing form gerund replaces a finite verb:

Lurg **raipey** *eh, stamp eh er*
after **tearing** it up, he stamped on it
(= after he had torn it up)

Erreish cur seose yn chrooin, hie eh stiagh ayns manishter
After relinquishing the crown, (after he had ...) he entered a monastery

And here, a passive infinitive:

Ta my vraagyn laccal kerraghey
My shoes want/need mending (= to be mended)

11.5.2 Present participles
The English -ing form acts as a present participle. These have many functions. They may:

a) correspond to an infinitive:

As cheayll yn daa ynseydagh eh **loayrt**
And the two disciples heard him speak(ing)   [John i.37]

V'eh dooinney beg giare lesh skeoghyn liauyr **tuittym sheese** *er toshiaght yn eddin echey ... Ta mee er n'akin eh* **goaill** *lieh-keead punt as shey er e vair veg.*
He was a small short man with long curls falling over the front of his face ... I have seen him taking 56 pounds (weight) on his little finger.   [Thomas Christian (1851–1930)]

b) introduce a phrase:

Dyn **fakin** *peiagh erbee çheu-sthie, daag mee yn çhamyr*
Not seeing anyone within, I left the room

fakin *dy vel eh red cairagh ...*
seeing it is a righteous thing with God   [Thessalonians II i.6]

fakin dy vel shiu er chasherickey nyn anmeenyn …
seeing ye have purified your souls … [Peter I i.22]

Note that in the case of the verb 'be' the verbnoun/present participle is often omitted altogether [R. L. Thomson, *Pargys Caillt*, Introduction, p. 6]:

Surranse foddey, […] lane mieys firrinagh, freayll myghin cour thousaneyn, lhiggey sheese mooad kerragh toillit
Suffering long, **being** full of genuine goodness, keeping mercy for thousands, remitting the amount of deserved punishment
[*Pargys Caillt* 44–6]

Yn fastyr er   It **being** evening
[*Pargys Caillt* 251]

Or a finite verb is substituted for 'being':

*Myr **ta shiu ruggit** reesht, cha nee jeh rass hed naardey …*
Being born again, not of corruptible seed … [Peter I i.23]
(= as you [are] born again)

c) function as an adjective (often in the genitival verbnoun form):

*clagh **rolley***   a rolling stone
(although Manx often expresses this differently):

*Ayns aile **loshtee** cooilleeney kerraghey … Vees er nyn gerraghey lesh toyrt-mow dy bragh farraghtyn (loshtee, see 2.4.3.e)*
In flaming fire taking vengeance … who shall be punished with everlasting destruction [Thessalonians II i.8–9]

In general, in most cases where English has an -ing form, Manx would use a verbnoun:

***Jannoo** eh-hene corrym rish Jee* making himself equal to God
[John v.18]

*Immee dy-jeeragh royd, dy-kinjagh **geiyrt** er y raad*
Go straight on, always following the road

*C'red ta shen ta **croghey** noi yn voalley?*
What's that (that's) hanging against the wall?

*Va e voir as e vraaraghyn nyn shassoo mooie **shirrey** loayrt rish*
His mother and his brethren stood without, desiring to speak to him [Matthew xii.46]

liehbageyn … ta follit, **goaill** *fastee fo grineyn geinnee … t'ad bransey roue ersooyl,* **faagail** *nyn gooyl bodjallyn … ta ein varrey gooillian … shelg eeastyn*
… the flatfish … that are hidden, taking shelter beneath the … sand … they dash all before them away, leaving behind them clouds … seabirds are soaring … , hunting fish
[R. C. Carswell, 'Bun as Baare', *Shelg yn Drane* 1994]

Note that *ve er-mayrn, er mayrn* (remain), now corresponds to an adjective or present participle, 'remaining', or past participle 'left':

ny Manninee foast **er mayrn**	the surviving Manx
cha row veg **er mayrn**	nothing remained/was left

Ny Stanleghyn ta nish eck kione
As **ermaarn** *jeusyn cha vel money*
The Stanleys now are at an end
There remains of them no trace   [Manx Traditionary Ballad 58]

… er-y-fa nagh row agh beggan jeh ny sampleyryn va prentit 'sy vlein 1947 foast **er-mayrn**
… because only a few of the copies printed in the year 1947 remained   [R. L. Thomson, *Gys y Lhaihder*, First Lessons in Manx, third revised edition 1965]

Compare:

Ayns Rama va eam treih er ny chlashtyn, yllaghey as keayney, as dobberan hrimshagh, Rachel keayney son e cloan, as gobbal dy ve er ny gherjaghey, er-yn-oyr nagh row ad **er-mayrn**
In Rama was there a voice heard, lamentation and weeping, and great mourning, Rachel weeping for her children, and would not be comforted, because they were not   [Matthew ii.18]

11.5.3 Verbal force
Where the English -ing form has verbal force, that is, it functions as a verb, Manx often expresses this differently:

a) sometimes by using finite verbs:

Ga dy vel ad **fakin**, *cha vel ad cur-my-ner: as* **clashtyn**, *cha vel ad cur geill*
Because they seeing (Manx: although they see) see not, and hearing (Manx: although they hear) they hear not   [Matthew xiii.13]
As **yeeagh** *Paul dy gyere er y choonceil as dooyrt eh …*
And Paul, earnestly beholding the council, said: [Acts xxiii.1]
(Manx: And Paul beheld … and he said …)

As haink earrooyn mooarey dy leih huggey, as nyn mast'oc va croobee ...
And great multitudes came unto him, having with them those that were lame ...   [Matthew xv.30]
(Manx: ... and among them there were the lame ...)

Ersyn ta shiu graihagh, ga nagh vel shiu er vakin eh; ayn, ga nagh vel shiu nish fakin eh, ny-yei credjal, ta shiu goaill boggey lesh boggey erskyn insh ... Cosney jerrey nyn gredjue, ...
Whom, having not seen, ye love, in whom, though now ye see him not, yet believing, ye rejoice ... Receiving the end of your faith ...   [Peter I i.8–9]
(Manx: Whom you love, though you have not seen him; in whom, though now you do not see him, yet you believe ... you receive the end of your faith)

b) sometimes with a verbnoun expressing a state, such as *shassoo* (stand), *soie* (sit), used with the appropriate personal pronouns:

As honnick yn assyl ainle y Çhiarn ny hassoo ayns y raad
And the ass saw the angel of the Lord standing in the way
                                    [Numbers xxii.23]

Va daa ghooinney doal nyn soie rish oirr yn raad, as tra cheayll ad
Two blind men sitting by the wayside, when they heard ...
                                    [Matthew xx.30]
(Two blind men were [in their state of] sitting ...)

cha der-ym ad ersooyl nyn drostey
I will not send them away fasting   [Matthew xv.32]

c) sometimes with an infinitive:

Haink ny Phariseeyn huggey myrgeddin dy phrowal eh, as dooyrt ad rish ...
The Pharisees also came unto him, tempting him, and saying ...
                                    [Matthew xix.3]
(infinitive *dy phrowal*, to tempt, and active verb *dooyrt*, said)

d) sometimes with a prepositional phrase:

As cre erbee nee shiu geearree ayns padjer, lesh credjue, yiow shiu eh
Whatsoever ye shall ask in prayer, believing, ye shall receive
                                    [Matthew xxi.22]

(*lesh credjue* = with faith)

11.4   Emphatic forms of the verb
In the future and conditional, both independent and dependent, the first person singular may be given an emphatic form by adding *s* or *'s*:

Tilgey (throw):

Future:	independent	*tilgym*	emphatic	*tilgym's*
	dependent	*dilgym*	emphatic	*dilgyms*
Conditional:	independent	*hilgin*	emphatic	*hilgins*
	dependent	*dilgin*	emphatic	*dilgin's*

The first person plural of the future, both independent and dependent, may have the emphatic form *tilgmayds*, in Northern dialects, *tilgmainyn*.

11.5   English verbs expressed differently in Manx, as phrases (see 10)
Sometimes the phrasal verb is an alternative option to a one-word verb:

11.5.1   Have: there is no verb 'to have' in Manx
The usual equivalent to express possession is the verb *ve* (to be) + preposition *ec*, at:

*Ta cabbyl **ec** Juan*	Juan has a horse
*Vel thie **ayd**?*	Have you a house?
*Va aigney mooar **aym** dy gholl*	I had a great mind to go
*Cha row thie **oc***	They had no house
*Nagh row thie **echey**?*	Did he not have a house?
*C'red **t'ain** 'sy thie?*	What have we in the house?

*C'red vees **eu** son jinnair jiu?*
What will you have for dinner today?

*Ta lhesh-eill-vart saillt **ain***   We have a round of salt beef

*Lhig stegyn-feill-vart as glassan ve **ain***
Let's have steak and salad

The same construction, with the preposition *ec*, is often used to form the perfect of transitive verbs with a direct object where English has auxiliary 'have':

*T'eh jeant **aym***	I have done it
*Cha row shoh scruit **aym***	I did not write this

Compare the alternative construction:

Cha nel ee er n'eeck yn coontey	She hasn't paid the bill,
Vel eh er choayl e lauenyn?	Has he lost his gloves?

11.5.2   Own: *ve + lesh*

*Ta'n lioar **echey** nish, agh cha nel ee **lesh-hene***
He has the book now, but he doesn't own it

*Nagh vel ny lioaryn shen **lhiu**? Nagh **lhiu** ny lioaryn shen?*
Aren't those books yours?

11.5.3   Know: *ve + fys* (knowledge) + *ec*

*Ta **fys eu** cre voish mee*   You know whence I came
*Vel **fys ayd** er yn ennym echey?* Do you know his name?

*Cha **s'ayms**, va mee ro aeg, agh va **fys echey** er dy chooilley nhee
ayns Gailck*
I don't know, I was too young, but he knew everything in Manx
[WC]

*My ta **fys ayd**, cre hon t'ou fênaght jeem?*
If you know it, why are you asking me?

*Cha noddym gra veg nagh vel **fys** hannah **ayd** [er]*
I can't say anything you don't already know

*Myr sloo yn **fys t'ec** fer, smoo corvian t'**echey***
The less a man knows, the greater his conceit

fys may be contracted to *s'*:

*Cha **s'eu** cre*   You do not know what
*Cha **s'ayd** eer shen?*   You don't even know that?
*Cha **s'aym***   I do not know   [John ix.14]

*Cha **s'aym**'s dy nee drogh-ghooinney eh*
I do not know whether he is a sinner   [John ix.25]

ve + enney + ec (know a person, recognise):

*er-yn-oyr dy row **enney echey** er dy chooilley dooinney*
because he knew every man   [John ii.24]

*Ta fer shassoo nyn mast'eu, nagh vel **enney eu** er*
One is standing amongst you whom you do not know [John i.26]

*as cha row **enney aym**'s er*
and I did not recognise him   [John i.31]

*Cre'n **enney t'ayd** orrym's?*
What (is the) acquaintance that thou hast with me?   [John i.48]

cur + enney + er (recognise):

*cha dug mee **enney er***   I did not know him

*as y seihll cha dug **enney er***
and the world did not recognise him   [John i.10]

*as cha dug mish **enney er***
and I did not recognise him   [John i.33]

cur + er + enney + da (introduce):

*Lhig dou cur **er enney diu** my inneen*
May I introduce my daughter

*Cur mee **er enney j'ee** my sailliu!*
Do introduce me to her!

*Cur **er enney daue** mee*   Introduce me to them

11.5.4   Need, have need of: *ve + feme + ec + er*

*Kionnee ny **vees mayd feme** cour y feailley*
Buy what we shall need for the festival   [John xiii.29]

*Ta **feme ain** er ushtey*   We need water
*Ta **feme echey** er kiarail*   He needs care

*... agh **row feme echey** er unnane erbee*
... he needed no-one   [John ii. 25]

11.5.5   Think (an opinion): *er + lesh*

Er-lhiam dy re shen eh!   I think that's it (*re* see 9.7)
*Cre **er-lhiat?***   What do you think?

Er-lhiam dy vel oo red beg scoorit
I think you're a bit drunk   [Joseph Woodworth (1854–1931)]

Er-lhiam dy lhisagh eh jannoo eh
I think he should do it   [Thomas Christian (1851–1930)]

*Un vlein, **er-lhiam**, ny shinney na mish*
One year, I think, older than myself   [LQ]

Compare other ways of saying 'think' using *smooinaghtyn, sheiltyn, credjal*:

*Cha **smooinee** mee dy row eh cho anmagh*
I didn't think it was so late

***Smooinee** mee dy row ee er ve ec y chonsert*
I thought she'd been at the concert

*Vel shiu **smooinaghtyn** dy vel shin eeckit dy mie?*
Do you think we're well paid?

T'eh ny s'anmagh na **heill** *mee*   It is later than I thought

Heill *mee dy row shiu ny shinney*
I thought you were older

Cha noddym **sheiltyn** *kys oddys eh reih cullyr cho graney*
I can't think (imagine) how he can choose such an ugly colour

Cha nel mee **credjal** *dy jig reddyn lesh*
I don't think (believe) he will succeed

Ta mee **credjal** *nagh dooyrt ee eh agh myr spotch*
I think she only said it as a joke

11.5.6   Owe
'Owe' is usually translated *ta mee ayns (fo) lhiastynys* (I am in/under debt), or with the pronoun preposition *er*:

Ta punt er	He owes a pound
Ta skillin erriu	You owe a shilling

Yn mayll d'eeck dagh unnane ass e heer
Va bart leagher ghlass dagh blein:
As va shen **orroo** *d'eeck myr keesh*
Trooid magh ny çheerey dagh Oeil-Eoin
The rent each one paid out of his land
Was a bundle of green rushes each year
And that was on them to pay as tax
Throughout the country each St. John's Eve
[Manx Traditionary Ballad 6]

When the creditor is mentioned as well as the debtor, two pronoun prepositions are used:

Ta punt **aym er**   He owes me a pound

Er hoh yn dooinney ta'n argid **echey ort**
Here's the man you owe the money (to)

11.5.7   Meet
As well as the verb *meeiteil*, 'meet' is usually translated by *goll/çheet ny whaiyl*, with the appropriate form of the possessive:

Haink mee ny whaiyl dooinney	I met a man
Haink ee my whaiyl	She met me
Higym dty whaiyl	I shall meet you

Ta mee **goll ny quaiyl** *dagh moghrey as t'ee* **çheet my whaiyl**
I meet her every morning and she meets me

Meeiteil is normally bound to a preposition:

> **veeit Philip **rish** Nathanael*   Philip met Nathanael   [John i.45]

* *veeit* is the preterite of *meeiteil*. Elsewhere in Biblical Manx *meeiteil* occurs without a preposition.

11.5.8 Help
The English idiom 'I can't help it' is translated by:

> *Cha vel **niart** aym er shen*   I have no strength on that

> *Va graih aym urree – cha row **niart** aym er*
> I loved her – I couldn't help myself
> > [R. C. Carswell, 'Ushag y Tappee', *Shelg yn Drane* 1994]

> *Cha **noddym jannoo rish** cha **jargym jannoo rish***
> I can't help (do to) it

fegooish (without) with a verbnoun is also used to express 'couldn't help':

> *cha row mee jargal dy yannoo **fegooish garaghtee***
> I couldn't help laughing

11.5.9 *jargym* (I can, am able) is rare, and occurs most often in negative constructions

> *Cha **yarg** ad eh y lheihys*   They could not heal him
> *Cha **jarg** fer erbee y ghoaill ad*   No-one can take them   [John x.29]

12 Word order and sentence structure; word building
Troggal ny raaghyn as ny focklyn

12.1 Sentence structure

Manx prefers a simple sentence structure following one of these patterns:

a) a one-clause sentence with the verb usually first

> **Va** Leslie aitt imlee caarjoil
> Leslie was funny modest kindly

b) a string of main clauses linked by the co-ordinating conjunctions

> *as* and   *agh* but   *ny* or

c) one main clause plus a single subordinate clause. For example in Manx a structure with two co-ordinate main clauses corresponds to a structure with a subordinate relative clause in English

(*va*)	Leslie	*as*	*y*	*vraar*	*bunnys*	*yn*	*chied*
(were)	L.	and	the	brother	almost	the	first

sleih	*as*	*bainney*	*TT*	*ocsyn*
people	and	milk	TT	at-them

> Leslie and his brother were almost the first people [who] had TT (tuberculin tested) milk   [BC]

> *Honnick mee Juan as eh çheet dy-valley*
> I saw John when he was coming home

> *Bione dou eh as mish my ghuilley*
> I knew him when I was a boy

> *Woaill yn clag as eh çheet stiagh*
> The clock struck just as he came in

12.2   Omission of the relative pronoun
Manx does not need a relative pronoun even where it is required in English:

> *Enmyn   jeh   ooilley   yn   sleih   hooar   baase*
> Names   of   all   the   people   found   death
> The names of all the people [who] died (in the war)   [JC]

> *Yn   red   smoo agglagh   va   rieau   jeant   ayns   Doolish*
> The   thing most dreadful   was   ever   done   in   Douglas
> The most dreadful thing [that] ever was done in Douglas   [BC]

The relative possessive pronoun 'whose' may be expressed with the emphatic form of the pronoun preposition *ec*:

> *fegooish   y   chooney   echeysyn*
> without   the   help   at himself
> without whose help

12.3   The usual order of elements
The usual order of elements in the simple affirmative sentence and within the clauses of a complex sentence is:
Verb + subject + direct object/complement + indirect object/prepositional phrase:

> *T'   eh   agglagh*
> Is   it   awful
> It's awful

> *T'   eh   ayns   y   thie-oast*
> Is   he   in   the   pub
> He's in the pub

> *ta   mee   dy kinjagh   faagail   y moddey   ec y thie*
> am   I   always   leaving   the dog   at the house
> I always leave the dog at home

Note: In Classical Manx the direct object was normally at the end of the sentence or phrase but in modern Manx the word order is the same as in English. Either is acceptable:

'I saw him on the street':

Classical Manx: *Honnick mee er y traid eh*
Modern Manx: *Honnick mee eh er y traid*

12.4   Position of the object
Noun objects and sometimes pronoun objects also take the normal position after the verb-noun.

> | *t'* | *eh* | *clashtyn* | *my* | *choraa* |
> |---|---|---|---|---|
> | is | he | hearing | my | voice |
>
> he hears my voice

> | *t'* | *eh* | *clashtyn* | *mee* |
> |---|---|---|---|
> | is | he | hearing | me |
>
> he hears me

12.5   The older order of elements
This is the older order of elements where the particle *y* (or *dy* when the auxiliary verb *ve* is used) is inserted before the verb noun (causing lenition) with a preceding direct object:

> | *jean-jee* | *coyrle* | *y* | | *dooinney* | *creeney* | *y* | *chlashtyn* |
> |---|---|---|---|---|---|---|---|
> | do | advice | (of) the | man | | wise | PART | hear |
>
> Hear the advice of the wise man!

> | *jean-jee* | *eshyn* | *y* | *chlashtyn* |
> |---|---|---|---|
> | do | him | PART | hear |
>
> Hear him!

This is now often expressed more simply with the object taking its place at the end of the phrase:

> | *jean shiu* | *clashtyn* | *coyrle* | *y* | | *dooinney* | *creeney* |
> |---|---|---|---|---|---|---|
> | do you | hear | advice | (of) the | man | | wise |
>
> hear the wise man's advice

> | *jean shiu* | *clashtyn* | *eh* |
> |---|---|---|
> | do you | hear | him |
>
> Hear him!

12.6   Negative conjunctive or interrogative particles precede the verb, which then takes the dependent form

Hem
(first person singular future independent *goll* go)
I'll go

Cha jem
Negative + first person singular future dependent *goll* go
I shan't go

Dy jem
Conjunction + first person singular future dependent *goll* go
That I (shall) go

Nagh jem
Negative conjunction + first person singular future dependent
goll go
That I shan't go

(zero) Jem?
(interrogative) + first person singular future dependent *goll* go
Shall I go?

Nagh jem?
Negative interrogative + first person singular future dependent
goll go
Shall I not go/shan't I go?

12.7   Interrogative elements precede the verb, which then takes the
       independent or relative form

Quoi   hed   er-nyn-son?
Who   will go for us?
Who will go for us?

Cre   'n fa   ta   shiu   farkiaght   ayns shoh?
What   the reason are   you   waiting   here?
Why are you waiting here?

12.8   Conjunctions with the conditional

a) The conjunction *dy*, 'so that', with the conditional dependent of
foddym expresses 'may, might'. *Dy* cannot be separated from the verb
by any intervening word.

Liorishyn   dy   voddagh   dy chooilley   ghooinney   credjal
By-himself   so that   may   every   man   believe
So that by means of him every man might believe   [John i.7]

b) Unfulfilled conditions are expressed with the conditional acting as
imperfect/pluperfect subjunctive with *dy* 'if'. Generally Manx like
English has the conditional or subjunctive in both clauses.

***dy beagh** fys ayd's er gioot Yee*
if you knew the gift of God (but you don't)

***veagh** oo er hirrey ... veagh eh er chur*
you would have sought ... he would have given   [John iv.10]

Dy beagh *shiu er chredjal ...* **veagh** *shiu er chredjal*
If you had believed ... you would have believed   [John v.46]
(here Manx has conditional in both clauses, the first functioning
as a pluperfect)

Dy beagh *eh er aght elley* **veign** *er n'insh diu*
If it had been otherwise I should have told you   [John xiv.2]

Simple conditional followed by past conditional simplifies the above
construction, which could just as easily been:

Dy beagh *eh* **er ve** *er aght elley* **veign** *er n'insh diu*

as in [John xxiv.7]:

Dy beagh *enney er ve eu orrym's* **veagh** *enney eu er my Ayr*
If you had known me you would have known my Father

c) Open fulfillable conditions are introduced by *my*

my **ta** *fys ayd*
if you know (and perhaps you do; actual present)

my **vees** *fys ayd*
(and perhaps you may, hypothetical present or future)

12.9   Manx often avoids the subjunctive

bare		*lhiam*	*eh*	*dy*	*ve*	*ayns*	*shen*	*na*	*mish*
would be better		with-me	he	to	be	here		than	me

I'd prefer that he should be here rather than myself

Nagh	*nhare*	*dooin*	*gyn*		*ad*	*shoh*	*dy*	*ve*	*ayns*	*y*	*vaatey?*
Is it not better	for us		without	these		to	be	in		the boat?

Is it not better for us that these should not be in the boat?

12.10   Periphrastic constructions
When the verb is complex i.e. formed using the primary auxiliaries *ve*
be or *jannoo* do or a modal auxiliary such as *foddym* 'I can', some variations appear:

a) Sentences formed with auxiliary *ve*, be
Pronoun objects in the first, second and sometimes third person singular
may be included in the verbal complex after *dy* in present tenses, after
er in past tenses:

T'	*eh*	*dy*	*my*	*chlashtyn*
is	he	to	my	hear(ing)

He hears me

> *V'   ad   dy dty woalley*
> Were they to thy beat(ing)
> They were beating you

> *V'   ou   dyn   dilgey   (ad)   'syn   aile*
> wert thou to-their throw(ing) (them) in the fire
> You were throwing them in the fire

> *Ta   mee er   dt' akin*
> am I   after thy see(ing)
> I've seen you

b) Sentences formed with auxiliary *jannoo*, do
Both pronominal objects (in the possessive form) and nominal objects
are included in the verbal phrase:

> *Cha jean   eh   my chlashtyn*
> not fut.dep. 'do' he   my hear(ing)
> He won't hear me

> *Ren ad   my choraa y   chlashtyn*
> did they my voice PART   hear
> They heard my voice

12.11   Word order in copula sentences (see 9.7)
'Be' may be expressed either with the substantive verb *ve* or with the
copula. The traditional order of elements in copula sentences is:

> copula + predicate + subject

> *s'   feer   eh*
> COP PRES true   it
> It's true

12.12   Statements of existence
Statements of mere existence (often with impersonal 'it' or 'there is' –
compare French 'c'est' 'il y a') employ the substantive verb *ve* and fill
the predicate position, i.e., that part of the sentence which is neither the
subject nor the main verb, by the pronominal preposition *ayn*, in:

> *ve* + subject + *ayn*:

> *Bee   fliaghey ayn*
> will be rain   in
> There will be rain

> *Va   kiuney vooar ayn*
> Was calm   great   in
> There was a great calm

12.13   Subordinate clauses

Subordinate clauses are introduced by conjunctions such as *my*, if; *tra*, when; *derrey*, until; *dy*, that; *nagh*, that not, or by phrasal conjunctions such as *er-yn-oyr, er-y-fa dy/nagh*, because/because not (see 7)

12.13.1 Reported speech and verbs of asking, fearing, thinking

In reported speech and after verbs of asking, fearing, thinking, etc., the subordinate clause is introduced by *dy*, that; *nagh*, that not; or 'zero' i.e., without any conjunction but with the meaning 'whether' (see the third example, below).

All these are followed by dependent verb forms.

T'	*ad*	*gra*	*dy*	*vel*	*mooarane*	*skeddan*	*ayn*
Are	they	say(ing)	that	is	much	herring	in

They say [that] there's a lot of herring

Dinsh	*eh*	*dou*	*nagh*	*row*	*veg*	*yn*	*argid*	*echey*
Told	he	to-me	that not	was	little	the	money	at-him

He told me [that] he had no money

Dênee	*ad*	*j'ee*	*row*	*ee*	*rieau*	*ayns*	*shen*
Asked	they	of-her	was	she	ever	there	

They asked her [whether] she was ever there

12.13.2 Verbs of requesting, advising, commanding

With verbs of requesting, advising, commanding, etc., the construction used is:

subject + *dy* + verb-noun

Ghuee	*mee*	*er*	*eh*	*dy*	*heet*	*stiagh*
Beseeched	I	on-him	he	to	come	in

I begged him to come in

Choyrlee	*shin*	*da*	*ny*	*joarreeyn*	*gyn*	*ad*	*dy hannaghtyn*	*ny sodjey*
Advised	we	to	the	strangers	without	they	to stay	longer

We advised the strangers not to stay any longer.

12.13.3 Relative clauses

Relative clauses may be direct or indirect; either type may be affirmative or negative:

a) In direct relative clauses the relative refers to the subject or direct object: Relative pronouns such as 'who' can in many cases be omitted in English (the man [whom, that] I saw) etc., and Manx hardly ever needs them even when they would be needed in English

Shinyn [...] *va ruggit tra ren sheel nyn ayrey snaue*
Dy gholl stiagh ayns ooh.

We [who] were born when the seed of our fathers swam
To enter into an egg.
[R. C. Carswell, 'Kione Vaghal', *Shelg yn Drane* 1994]

b) Affirmative relative clauses in Manx are no longer introduced by a particle but are attached directly to their antecedent, i.e., the noun or pronoun to which they refer. If the antecedent is a pronoun it is usually in the emphatic form. If it is a possessive the periphrastic form with *ec* is employed.

*Eshyn	*yn*	*dooinney*	*ren*	*jannoo eh*
He	the	man	did	do(ing) it

He is the man (who) did it

*Eshyn	*dooinney*	*yn*	*phoosee*	*ta ben y phoosee*	*echey*
Himself	man	the	bridegroom	is the bride	at-him

He who has the bride is the bridegroom   [John iii.29]

rishyn v'er ny lheihys   unto him that was cured
[John v.10]

Eshyn va mayrt ... *t'eshyn bashtey*
He who was with thee ... he is baptizing   [John iii.26]

The verb is in the independent or relative form:

*Shoh	*yn*	*thie*	**hrog**	*mee*
This	the	house	raised	I

This is the house I built

* In modern Manx sentences like these often begin with *ta*.

c) Negative relative clauses are introduced by *nagh* followed by dependent verb forms

shen	*clagh*	*nagh*	**drog**	*oo*
that	stone	not	FUT DEP	thou

That's a stone you won't lift

Eshyn	*yn*	*dooinney*	*nagh*	*ren*	*jannoo*	*eh*
Himself	the	man	not	did	do(ing) it	

He's the man who didn't do it

Hug	*eh*	*booise*	*dauesyn*	*v'*	*er*	*ghellal*	*dy*	*dooie*	*rish*
Gave	he	thanks	to-them	were	after	deal(ing)	PART	kind	to him

He thanked all those who had dealt kindly with him

Y   chooid   ocsyn   hug   nyn   marrant da
The property at-them gave   their trust   to-him
The property of those who trusted him

Cur-my-ner Israelite firrinagh ayn nagh vel molteyrys erbee
Behold a true Israelite in whom there is no deceit   [John i.47]

d) Indirect relative clauses are 'governed' by a preposition

Eng: 'the barge **in which** she sat':

The appropriate personal form of the prepositional pronoun is used
either before the dependent form of the verb in the relative clause in
unusual constructions such as the first example below, or at the end of
the relative clause with 'zero' affirmative relative particle, i.e., without
including a relative particle, with the independent form of verb or the
negative *nagh*.

*yn baatey **ayn** row mee*   the boat in which I was

Or:

*yn baatey va mee **ayn***   the boat I was in

Shoh   'n   thie   ta shin   baghey   ayn
This   the   house   is we   liv(ing)   in it
This is the house we live in

e) With the genitive of a relative such as 'whose' the appropriate
possessive appears in the relative clause

Shen   y   dooinney ta   'n   mac **echey**   çhing
That   the   man   is   the   son   at-him   sick
That's the man **whose** son is sick

f) Relative *ny*
When the antecedent has the meaning 'that', 'which', 'what', or when
it follows *ooilley*, 'all', the relative used in Manx is *ny*

Ta mish loayrt shen ny ta mee er n'akin
I speak that which I have seen   [John viii.38]

Cha   dod   mee   clashtyn (shen)   ny   dooyrt   eh
Not   could   I   hear (that)   REL   said   he
I couldn't hear what he said

g) Relative dy
With an antecedent qualified by 'each' 'all' 'every' 'any' or a superlative adjective, the affirmative relative was traditionally *dy* (of those that) followed by a dependent verb form:

Thie	**erbee**	*dy*	*jed*	*shiu stiagh*	*ayn*
House	**any**	REL	FUT DEP	you into	in+it

Any house you enter

Note: *dy or y?* When the relative was accusative (for a direct object) and the verb in the relative clause was formed with auxiliary *ve*, the particle *dy* was used. When the auxiliary verb used was *jannoo*, the particle *y* was used:

Shen	*y*	*thie*	*t' eh*	*dy*	*hroggal*
That	the	house	is he	at-its	raising

That's the house he's building

shen	*y*	*thie*	*ren*	*eh*	*y*	*hroggal*
That	the	house	did	he	its	raising

That's the house he has built

This is less common in modern speech.

12.14   Nominal phrases
A nominal phrase in Manx may contain any or all of the following elements in the sequence indicated:

a) preposition (*son, fo* etc.)

b) definite article/possessive particle/*gagh* = each /*dy chooilley* = every

c) numeral (ordinal or cardinal numerals may be split, see 8.6)

d) prefixed adjective (these are few in number in Manx, see 6)

e) noun

f) modifier of following adjective (also few in number: *feer* very; *bunnys* almost; *ro* too; *lane* quite)

g) adjective(s)

h) demonstrative (requiring article at b, above, e.g. *y ven shoh*)

i) alternative possessive (also requiring article at b) or clarification of ambiguous possessive *nyn* being used for our/your/their (b). e.g. *y thie aym*, my house; *y thie ain/eu/oc*, our/your/their house: compare *nyn dhie*, our/your/their house.

It is rare to find more than a few of these elements in combination and some of them are mutually exclusive. The following is an example of a sentence with most of the elements in the right order:

(a)	(b)	(c)	(d)	(e)	(f)	(g)	(h)
ayns	*ny*	*three*	*shenn*	*tholtanyn*	*feer*	*ghraney*	*shoh*
in	the	three	old	ruins		very ugly	these

In these three very ugly old ruins

12.15   Verbal phrases

12.15.1 Simple verbal phrases

When the verb is formed by inflection (in which case it must be either an imperative or a future, conditional or preterite tense) the verbal phrase may be simple. In that case the usual order of elements is as follows:

a) interrogative/ negative/ relative particle or subordinating conjunction

b) verb

c) subject (noun inflection or pronoun)

d) object pronoun

Imperative:	b + c	+ d
	trog-jee	*ad*
	lift you	them

Lift them!

Future:	a	+ b + c
	tra	*higmayd*
	CONJ	we shall come

When we come

Conditional:	a	+ b	+ c	+ d
	Dy	*vaikagh*	*shiu*	*ee*
	CONJ	would see	you (pl)	she

If you saw (= were to see) her

Preterite:	a	+ b	+ c	+ d
	Nagh	*dug*	*oo*	*ad?*
	INTER-NEG	sent	you (sg)	them

Didn't you send them?

12.15.2 Complex verbal phrases
The complex verbal phrase is the only means of forming all tenses in Manx other than the preterite, the conditional, and the future.

Complex sentences in Manx are usually constructed with the various elements in the following order, which is somewhat different from English:

a) any one of these if required: interrogative/negative/relative particle or subordinating conjunction

b) Auxiliary verb (*ve/jannoo* etc.)

c) Subject (noun inflection or pronoun)

d) (with auxiliary *ve* 'be' only) 'zero' (*g-* before initial vowels) for present tenses or *er* (*n-*) for perfect tenses

e) pronoun objects where appropriate. With auxiliary *jannoo* 'do' or *lhisin/agh*, *foddym* and copula phrases, noun objects: *Ren ad my choraa y chlashtyn*, They heard my voice

f) Verbnoun

>   a   b   c   e   f
>   *cha jean eh   my* chlashtyn*
>   He will not hear me

>   a   b   c   d   e   f
>   *cha row   eh   er   my* chlashtyn*
>   He had not heard me

* *my* is not, strictly speaking, a pronoun object in Manx but a possessive adjective. In English 'me' would be a pronoun object. These terminological labels don't make any difference to the way the elements are used though!
Note: Noun objects follow the verbnoun:

> *V'eh er vakin yn **ogher** ayns y glass*
> He had seen the **key** in the lock

Pronoun objects may either:

a) follow the verbnoun

> *Ta mee er n'ghoaill **eh***   I have taken it
> *V'ad er vakin **mee** er y traid*   they had seen me in the street

b) be included in the verbal group between *er* and the verbnoun

> *V'ad er **my** (or **m'**) akin*   They had seen me

*T'eh er **dty** chlashtyn* He has heard you

This construction is usual only when the pronoun object is first or second person singular, to avoid confusion with the passive.

12.15.3 Position of adverbial elements

a) An adverbial element may be placed first in the sentence for emphasis

Fastyr	*Jecrean*	*haink*	*ad*	*dy*	*chur*	*shilley*	*orrin*
Evening	Wednesday	came	they	to	put	sight	on-us

(It was) Wednesday evening they came to see us (see 13)

b) The usual position for adverbs with a periphrastic verb is between subject and participle

*cha row Ean **foast** tilgit*
for John was not yet cast into prison [John iii.24]

*tra v'eh **eisht** er jeet gys Galilee*
then when he was come to Galilee [John iv.45]

*gys y boayl raad ren Ean **hoshiaght** bashtey*
to the place where John first baptized [John x.40]
(*hoshiaght* is an adverb meaning 'at first' formed from the noun *toshiaght*, beginning, see 6)

12.16 Word building with affixes
Common prefixes with or without hyphens include the following:

12.16.1 *aa-*
The prefix *aa-* (which causes lenition see 1) may be:

a) iterative (repetition):

bioghey	enliven	*aavioghey*	revive
caarjaghey	make friends	*aachaarjaghey*	reconcile
tuittym	fall	*aahuittym*	relapse
rheynn	divide	*aarheynn*	subdivide
irree	arise	*aa-irree*	resurrection

b) intensifying:

gaer	pain	*aaghaer*	agony
glenney	clean	*aaghlenney*	purify

c) negative:

dowin	deep	*aaghowin*	shallow

Note: *an-* can be both negative and intensifying:

aash	ease	*anaash*	anxiety
caarjagh	friendly	*anchaarjagh*	unfriendly
mian	desire	*anvian*	craving

12.16.2 *co-* = with

co-eirey	joint heir	*co-aigney*	concord
co-akin	interview	*co-heean*	harmonic

12.16.3 *lieh* = half, semi

cruinney	sphere	*lieh-chruinney*	hemisphere

12.16.4 *myn* = small

brishey	break	*mynvrishey*	shatter
clagh	a stone	*mynchlagh*	a pebble
taggloo	talk	*myn-haggloo*	mutter

12.16.5 *ooilley-* = all

ooilley-fakin	all-seeing
ooilley-varrialtagh	all-conquering

12.16.6 *do-*, difficult and *so-*, easy*

geddyn	find		
do-gheddyn	hard to find rare	*so-gheddyn*	easy to find
fakin	see		
do-akin	invisible	*so-akin*	easy to see, visible
brishey	break		
do-vrishey	unbreakable	*so-vrishey*	brittle, friable
donnys	bad luck	*sonnys*	good luck

12.16.7 *ym-*, *yl-* many ('poly')*

daah	colour	*ym-daahagh*	multicoloured
mooad	a quantity	*ymmodee*	many
çhengey	tongue, language	*ym-hengagh*	polyglot
yl-cheirdee	jack-of-all-trades		
yl-lioar	a book of many volumes		

12.16.8 *yn-* fit, worthy*

yn-laih	readable, worth reading
yn-ee	fit to eat
yn-cowree	worthy of note

12.16.9 Negatives may be formed with

aa-	*aaghowin* (*dowin*, deep)	shallow
an-	*anvennick* (*mennick*, frequent, often)	infrequent, seldom
do-	*do-lostey* (*lostey*, burn)	inflammable, fire-proof*
mee-	*mee-chrauee* (*crauee*, religious)	irreligious
neu-	*neu-chadjin* (*cadjin*, common)	uncommon

Note: *Neu-* is generally merely negative whereas *mee-* often has a note of disapproval as well.

* Recently borrowed from Irish.

For ways in which Manx forms nouns from other word classes see 2.5.

13 Dates and seasons
Laghyn as imbaghyn

Manx possesses specific expressions and alternative expressions for certain times and dates. For telling the time see 8.11

1st *yn chied laa*
2nd *yn nah laa* the second (day).
    This can also mean 'the next day'.
31st *yn chied laa jeig as feed*

13.1 Seasons

arragh (m)	spring	*sourey* (m)	summer
fouyr (f)	autumn harvest	*geurey* (m)	winter

13.2 The months

Manx has several names for the months. Most of them are listed here but a dictionary might supply one or two alternatives as well. Some of the expressions are rather like English, while others mean the start, middle or end of one of the four seasons:

Jerrey Geuree/Mee s'jerree yn Gheuree   January
(the end of winter)

Yn chied vee jeh'n arragh/Toshiaght Arree   February
(the start of spring)

Mart/Mayrnt/Mee Vayrnt/Mean Arree/Mee Veanagh
yn Arree/yn gha Mean Arree/Mee ny Mannan   March
(mid-spring; month of the kids)

(Mee) Averil/Jerrey Arree/Mee s'jerree yn Arree   April
(the end of spring)

(Mee) Boaldyn/yn chied vee jeh'n touree/Mee ny Cooagyn
/Toshiaght Souree/ Mee ny Boaldyn   May
(the start of summer; month of the cuckoos)

Mean Souree/Mee Veanagh y Touree (mid-summer)	June
Jerrey Souree/Mee s'jerree yn Touree/Mee Vuigh (the end of summer; the yellow month)	July
Yn chied vee jeh'n ouyir/Luanistyn/ *Mee Luainistyn Mooar/Toshiaght Fouyir* (the start of autumn)	August
Mean Fouyir/Mee Veanagh yn Ouyir (mid-autumn)	September
Jerrey Fouyir/Mee s'jerree yn Ouyir (the end of autumn)	October
Yn chied vee jeh'n gheurey/Mee Houney/Sauin/ *Sounaghyn/Souney/Toshiaght Gheurey* (the start of winter; Hollantide)	November
Mee Veanagh y Gheuree/Mee ny Nollick (mid-winter; the Christmas month)	December

13.3 Days of the week

Jedoonee	Sunday
Jelhune/Jelhein/Jeluain	Monday
Jemayrt	Tuesday
Jecrean	Wednesday
Jerdein/Jerdune	Thursday
Jeheiney	Friday
Jesarn	Saturday

Note: All the days of the week with the possible exception of *Jerdein*, Thursday, can be found with alternative spelling *jy-* instead of *je-*.

13.4 Expressions about days and nights

jiu	today
jea	yesterday
mairagh	tomorrow
noght/oie noght	tonight
riyr	last night
oie ny vairagh	tomorrow night
arroo-y-jea	the day before yesterday
arroo-y-riyr	the night before last
nuyr	the day after tomorrow
laa ny vairagh	on the morrow

13.5   Times of day

munlaa	noon
moghrey	morning
fastyr	afternoon evening
oie	night
mean-oie	midnight

13.6   Periods of time

shiaghtin (f)	week	*kegeesh* (f)	fortnight
mee (f)	month	*raiee* (f)	quarter

blein (f) year:

genitive	*bleeaney*
plural without numeral	*bleeantyn*
plural with numeral	*bleeaney*

tree bleeaney	three years

But: *daa vlein*   2 years
(singular noun after *daa*, see 8.2.2)

nurree	last year

yn çhiaghtin s'jerree/yn çhiaghtin shoh chaie
last week

Jedoonee chaie	last Sunday
kerroo s'jerree ny heayst	last quarter (of the moon)
yn çhiaghtin shoh çheet	next week

yn vlein ry-heet/yn vlein shoh çheet
next year

13.7   Festivals

Caisht (f)	Easter
Nollick (f)	Christmas
Kingeesh (f)	Whitsuntide
Sauin	Hollantide, Hallowe'en
Oie'll Verrey/Oie'll Vayree/Oie'll Voirrey	Christmas Eve
Oie Nollick	Christmas night
Oie Nollick veg	New Year's Eve
Oie Voaldyn	May Eve
Oie Innyd	Shrove Tuesday/Mardi gras
Oie yn nah laa jeig/oie yn Ghiense	12th night
Oie'll Eoin	St John's Eve
Oie Hop-tu-naa	Hogmanay

Oie Houney	Halloween/All Hallows/ Hollantide

Note: Manx also has expressions for other phenomena:

Rehollys vooar ny Gabbil/ *Rehollys vooar Cooyl Cleigh/* *Rehollys vooar yn Ouyr*	October moon
Raad Mooar Ree Gorree *Bow Ghorree*	Milky Way

14   Emphasis
Trimmid

Manx has a large array of options for adding emphasis or for stressing one element in particular. These include the following:

14.1   Word order
An element may be stressed by placing it at the beginning of the clause or sentence:

> **yn   skynn** *hug   eh   da   'n   dooinney*
> the   knife   gave   he   to   the   man
> **the knife** he gave to the man

> **da 'n   dooinney** *hug   eh   yn   skynn*
> to   the   man   gave   he   the   knife
> **to the man** he gave the knife

> **s'   tappee** *hug   eh   yn   skynn da   'n   dooinney*
> COP   quick(ly)   gave   he   the   knife   to   the   man
> (**how**) **quickly** he gave the man the knife

> *hug   eh   dy tappee   yn   skynn   da 'n   dooinney*
> gave   he   quickly   the   knife   to   the   man
> he gave the knife to the man quickly

> **fastyr Jecrean**   *haink   ad   dy   chur shilley orrin*
> evening Wednesday   came   they   to   put   sight   on-us
> (It was) **Wednesday evening** they came to see us

> *Mish   t'   ayn*
> I-EMPH   am   in-it
> It is I

> *Shen   gow*
> This   take-IMPERATIVE
> This take   [Matthew xvii.27 (1745)]

14.2 Copula (see 9.7)

For more explicit emphasis the copula, in present tense form only, is used irrespective of other tenses in the sentence:

> Cha nee mish dooyrt shen
> NEG COP-PRES-DEP- I-EMPH said that
> It was not I that said that

> Ta mee credjal dy re ayns y gharey
> Am I believing that COP-PRES-DEP in the garden
>
> hooar ad eh
> found they it
>
> I think it was in the garden they found it

14.3 Emphatic elements may be added

14.3.1 Personal pronouns

The reflexive -*hene*, self, selves, (-*pene* after first person -*m*) may stand in apposition to a personal pronoun, a pronominal preposition or a noun:

mee-hene	I myself
rhym pene (p- after *m*-)	to myself, to me
y dooinney hene	the man himself
ad-hene	they themselves (the fairies)
er-my-hon-hene	I for my part

> Cha voddym **jeem pene** nhee erbee y yannoo
> Of myself I can do nothing   [John v.30]

> Quoi oo **hene**?   Who are you?   [John i.19]

> Cre t'ou gra my-dty-chione **hene**?
> What dost thou say about thyself?   [John i.22]

> Cha hreisht Yeesey **eh-hene** orroo
> Jesus did not trust himself to them   [John ii.24]

> Cha vod dooinney nhee erbee y ghoaill er **hene**
> No man can take anything upon himself   [John iii.27]

> Yeesey **hene**   Jesus himself   [John iv.2]

> Ta shin **hene** er chlashtyn eh
> We ourselves have heard him   [John iv.42]

> Chamoo ren e vraaraghyn **hene** credjal ayn
> His brothers themselves did not believe in him   [John vii.5]

Chamoo ta shiu goaill eu **hene** *kys dy vel eh ymmyrçhagh er nyn son ain*
Nor consider that is is expedient for us   [John xi.50]

*Er-lhiam-**pene** dy row*   I (myself) think so   [JC]

Note: Following a possessive, *hene* means 'own':

my hie **hene**   my own house

Haink eh gys e vooinjer **hene**
He came to his own people   [John i.11]

Hooar eshyn hoshiaght e vraar **hene***, Simon*
He first found his own brother, Simon   [John i.42]

14.3.2   Verbal inflections
An emphatic ending may be added to an inflected verb:
first person singular in the future and conditional tenses may add *'s*:

kionneeym's I will buy   *hem's*   I will go
yinnins   I would do

O dy beign's my vriw ayns y çheer ... as yinnins cairys da!
O that I were made judge in the land ... and I would do him
justice!   [2 Samuel xv.4]

first person plural future adds -*mayd* which becomes -*mainyn* in Classical
Manx, -*mayds* in Late Manx.

Cre nee mainyn?   What shall we do?   [John vi.28]

14.3.3   Pronoun-prepositions may add emphatic endings

	Singular	Plural
first person	-*s*	-*yn*
second person	-*s*	-*ish*
third person (m)	*'syn*	-*syn*
third person (f)	-*ish*	

For example, *da*, to:

	Singular	Plural
first person	*dooys*	*dooinyn*
second person	*dhyts*	*diuish*
third person (m)	*dasyn*	*dauesyn*
third person (f)	*jeeish*	

S'mie lhiams *shen*   I like **that**   (*lesh*)
row **ish mayrts**?   was **she** with **you**?   (*marish*)
Yn thie **euish** *as* **ayms**   **your** house and **mine** (*ec*)

*Vel shoh yn kayt **echeysyn**?*   Is this **his** cat?   (*ec*)
*Vel shen y thie **ocsyn**?*   Is that **their** house?   (*ec*)
*Dooyrt mee **rishyn***   I said **to him**   (*rish*)   [JC]

*As ghow mee ram skeealyn **voishyn***
And I got a lot of stories **from him**   (*veih, voish*) [JC]

*Yn beaghey **aym's** eh*   It is my food that it is (*ec*) [John iv.34]

Note: the -*'s* of the first and second person singular of the simple
   pronoun-preposition may be used for emphasis with the phrasal
   preposition *er-my-hon = er-my-hons*, and may also be added to
   other nouns following the possessive: *my yishig's*, my father

*Kionneeym's ny lioaryn shid **er-dty-hon's***
I'll buy those books for you[11]   [JC]

14.3.4   Emphatic adverbs
Certain adverbs may add the suffix -*agh* for emphasis:

reesht → *reeshtagh*   again, yet again
eisht → *eishtagh*   then, even then
nish → *nishtagh*   now, right now
foast → *foastagh*   still

*Doort Yeesey rishyn, **eishtagh**, cha vel veg er y chloan dy eeck*
Jesus saith unto him, then are the children free
   [Matthew xvii.26 (1748)]

***Reeshtagh** ta mee gra riu*
Again I say unto you   [Matthew xviii.19 (1748)]

14.4   Emphatic personal pronouns (see 3.4)

	Singular	Plural
first person	*mish*	*shinyn*
second person	*uss*	*shiuish*
third person (m)	*eshyn*	*adsyn*
third person (f)	*ish*	

These are typically used:

14.4.1   For emphasis

***Mish** t'ayn*   It is I

---

[11] Emphatics were over-used in Late Manx and became commonplace, so much of the
emphatic impact has been lost in cases like this example.

*as dooyrt **eshyn** dy row eh ruggit as troggit ayns Formby*
and he said he himself was born and brought up in Formby [JC]

14.4.2 For contrast

*Ta **mish** bashtey lesh ushtey: agh ta fer shassoo nyn mast'eu ...*
I baptize with water: but there is one standing amongst you ...
[John i.26]

*Ta **shiuish** er gholl stiagh er y laboragh oc*
You (in contrast to *deiney elley* other people) have entered upon
(the results of) their labour
[John iv.38]

*Cha nione **diuish** eh; agh shione **dooys** eh*
You do not know him; but I know him   [John viii.55]

14.4.3 As the antecedent of a relative clause

*Ta shin er gheddyn **eshyn**, jeh ren Moses ayns y leigh, as ny
phadeyryn scrieu*
We have found him, of whom Moses in the law, and the
prophets, wrote   [John i.45]

*yn aigney **echeysyn** t'er my choyrt*
the will of him that has sent me   [John iv.34]
(emphatic of pronominal preposition introducing relative clause)

14.4.4 Emphatic imperative
The emphatic pronouns of the second person singular or plural may be
added to the imperative for emphasis:

jean-jee shiuish	do	[John ii.5]
immee-jee shiuish	do ye go	[John vii.8]
jean uss eh	you do it	

15 Spelling and pronunciation
Lettraghey as fockley magh

15.1 The spelling system

The spelling system of Manx differs markedly from that of Irish and Scots Gaelic. The system itself is riddled with exceptions and some inconsistencies.

The alphabet used resembles that of English, but lacks both x and z.

A final 'e' is usually silent (*lane, bane, close*), just as it is in English words such as 'lane', 'sane', 'game', but, as in English, the -e ending lengthens the preceding vowel or diphthong (compare the vowel sounds in English 'Sam' and 'same' 'man' and 'mane', 'kit' and 'kite', etc.)

The use of hyphens and apostrophes is erratic. The same word may appear written with or without hyphens, for example:

er yn oyr/er-yn-oyr   because

A few Manx words have more than one spelling in common use (some English words have alternative spellings, too, both of which are considered correct: compare English dis/despatch, judg(e)ment, etc.) The commonest variations in Manx are *l/ll*, *i/y*:

meil/meill   lip
emshir/emshyr   weather

The consonants do not present a major problem for the learner, generally speaking. The simple vowels, also, are relatively consistent.

It is when we come to diphthongs that we find the system is most full of inconsistencies.

Homophones often have different spellings:

lieh, lheh	=	[lʹjeː]
olley, ollay	=	[ɔlə]
leigh, leih	=	a sound between 'lay' and 'lie' [lɛi]

Manx does its best to avoid homographs.

15.2   Pronunciation
This chapter shows some of the options. The stressed syllable (see 15.5) is in **bold** in the IPA phonetic transcription, in cases where the stress falls on any syllable other than the first:

leeideil	[lɪd´jɛːl´]	lead
coraa	[kərɛː]	voice

Regional variation
There are slight variations in pronunciation between Northern and Southern Manx, but these rarely cause misunderstandings. The Northern variety was spoken in Bride, Andreas, Jurby, Ballaugh, Michael, Lezayre, Maughold and Lonan. There is evidence that the Northern dialect included German and stretched to the southern reaches of Patrick (Dalby).

The Southern variety was spoken in Rushen, Arbory, Malew, Marown, Santan, Braddan and Onchan. Peel speech was slightly different again. For more technical information about phonetics, refer to the work of Robert Thomson, J. J. Kneen, Adrian Pilgrim.

15.2.1   Vowels: general
Most Manx vowels may be either short or long. The long vowels are usually just a drawn-out version of the short vowels. The comparisons with English given here are approximate, and are loosely based on Standard English pronunciation except where it is relevant to state 'Northern English' or 'Southern English'. Even the pronunciation of one and the same native speaker may display variations, dependent upon many factors. The same examples have been used for different spelling variations of the same sound.

A sounds:

'cat':	[a]	short in *lhiannoo, cass*	G. Katze, Fr. canne
'father'	[aː]	(Northern English): long in *nah, fakin, clashtyn* Fr. lâche, It. casa	

E sounds:
open:

'then'	[ɛ]	short in *ben*	G. wenn, Fr. <u>est</u>-ce-que
'there'	[ɛː]	long in *baase, ayr, aeg*	Fr. mère

close:

'fate'	[eː]	long in *she, breh*	G. Geh!, Fr. été, It. av<u>ete</u>

I sounds:

'kit'	[ɪ]	short in *bing, kiyt*	G. hin
'clean'	[i:]	long in *Jee, creeney*	G. sieht, Fr. Gîte

Note: Different symbols are used here as this is not really a simple case of lengthening.

O sounds:
open:

'not'	[ɔ]	short in *son, crosh, honnick*	Fr. homme, G. Gott
'nought'	[ɔ:]	long in *shoh, ro, boght*	

close:

'no'	[o:]	'Côte d'Azur', in *bio, foast, trome*	Fr. eau, G. Sohn

U sounds:
open:

[ʊ̩]	N. Eng. 'luck': short in *hug, muc*

close:

[ʊ]	'book': short in *aarloo, shelloo*	G. Mund, It. frutto
[u:]	'rude': long in *oo, ashoon, poosey*	G. Schuh, It. ciascuno

Y sounds:
Like the second, unstressed vowel 'a' in English 'Tina' or 'sofa', or the first unstressed vowel in 'about' [ə] short in *yn, my*

Neutral vowel:
-y following other vowels is often silent:

kiyt ('kit')	[kɪt']	cats

But when 'i' follows one or more written vowels, as in *'eei', 'ooi', 'ai'*, it may serve to show that the following consonant is palatalised:

leeideil	[lɪdˈjɛːlʲ]	lead

When 'y' follows one or more written vowels, it may show that the following consonant is not palatalised:

eeym	[i:m]	butter

In the first example below, 'l' is broad, in the second, slender (see 3, below, for broad and slender consonants):

ooyl	[u:l]	apple
ooil	[u:lʲ]	oil

| keeayll | [ki:l] | sense, wit |
| keeill | [ki:l′] | church, chapel |

Similarly, where usually final -*ey*, *y* is pronounced like the final -*a* in 'sofa':

Breeshey = 'Breesha', *dubbey*, dub, pond = [dʊbə], the presence of 'i' may indicate a change in pronunciation:

fanney	[fanə]	flaying
fainey	[fɛ:n′jə]	ring
bainney	[ba:n′jə]	milk
billey	[bɪl′jə] ('bill-ya')	tree
guilley	[gɪl′jə] ('gill-ya')	boy

Note: *Ny eeanlee*, the birds, and *ny eeastyn*, the fishes, are pronounced as if they started with a consonantal 'y' and are often written with y-:

ny yeeanlee, ny yeeastyn

15.2.2 Pronouncing vowels and diphthongs

Adding extra length to a double vowel by adding another *e*, *i*, *h*, *y*, etc., does not usually change the pronunciation of the vowel:

aaie	[ɛi]	kiln
caaig	[kɛ:g]	jay
caays	[kɛ:s]	convenience
eairk	[e:ʳk]	horn
leeid	[l′i:d]	lead, conduct
meeyl	[mi:l]	louse
coayl	[kɔ:l]	lose
foayr	[fɔ:r]	favour

A: short [a] 'cat' mac son

A: long [a:] 'father' fakin see
This sound may be written -*a*-, -*aah*-, -*ah*-:

-a-:	dy valley	[ðə va:l′jə]	home
-aah-:	raah	[ra:]	report, prosperity
	daah	[da:]	dye, singe
-ah-:	gah	[ga:]	a sting

Note: 'a' is pronounced [ɔ] before -*ll*- in:

jalloo	[dʒɔlʊ] ('jolloo')	image, picture
thalloo	[tɔlʊ] ('tolloo')	earth, ground
balloo	[bɔlʊ] ('bolloo')	mute, dumb

(Compare -*a*- in English 'swallow', 'wallow').

A: long 'fair' [ε] may also be written -a-, -ae-, -aa-, -ai-:

-a-	*marym*		with me
	rollage	[rəlɛ:g]	star
	cre'n fa?	[krɛn **fɛ:**]	why?
-ae-	*aeg*	[ε:g]	young
-aa-	*aalin*	[ε:lin]	beautiful
	faagail	[fəgɛ:l′]	leave
	faasaag	[fəzɛ:g]	beard
-ai-	*mairagh*	[mε:rax]	tomorrow

Aew: (diphthong) [æʊ]

braew	[bræʊ]	good

Ai: short [a]

caill	[kal′]	lose
faik!	[fak]	see!
Gaelg, Gailck	[gɪl′g, gɪl′k]	Gaelic

long: [ε:]

faill	[fε:l′]	hire, wages

Ai: [ai]

aile	[ail]	fire
ain	[ain]	our

Au: [ɔ:]

giau	[g′jɔ:]	creek

Ay: short [ε]

kayt	[kɛt]	cat
ayd	[ɛd]	at you

Ay: long [e:]

kay	[ke:]	fog

-ar-, -ayr-, -aar- are often pronounced [ö:, ö] ('er' as in 'her')

ard	[örd, ö:d]	high, chief

| *jemayrt* | [d͡ʒəmöːrt] | Tuesday |
| *aarloo* | [örlʊ] | ready |

E: [e], [ɛ], short, may be written -*e*-, -*ea*-

| *ben* | [bɛᵈn] 'ben' | woman |
| *tead* | [tɛd] | rope |

Note: *red*, thing, is pronounced 'rud'. *'shenn'*, old, is pronounced 'shan' in Northern Manx.

-*ê*-, -*ea*-, -*ei*-, *eh*, -*ey* may be pronounced [eː] like the Scottish 'say':

fênaght	[feːnax]	asking
bea	[beː]	life/lifetime
rea	[reː]	ram
keim	[keːm]	amble
ben-rein	[bɛᵈn **reːn**]	queen
key	[keː]	cream
tey	[teː]	tea
fey	[feː]	fathom

Note: *Eh*, he, may also be pronounced [a] when as object pronoun it means 'it, him':

| *Varr eh **eh*** | [vaːrea] | He killed him |

Ee, eea, is usually long [iː]

feed	[fiːd]	twenty
peesh	[piːʃ]	piece
ree	[riː]	king
sheeabin	[ʃiːbən]	soap
eean*	[jiːən]	chicken

Ee may be pronounced [ɪ] as in 'fit':

| *çheet* | [tʃɪt] | come |
| *bee'm* | [bɪm] | I shall be |

* Ee initially is preceded by 'y' sound:

| *eeast* | [jiːst] | fish |

Ei may be pronounced [ɛi] ('say') or [ai] ('eye'):

| *treigeil* | [trəgɛːlʲ] | forsake |
| *Jerdein* | [d͡ʒərdain] | Thursday |

Oe: [o:] long:

coe	[ko:]	weep
dhone	[do:n]	brown
croe	[kro:]	coop

Oie may be pronounced [ɛi] ('aee'):

cloie	[klɛi]	play
roie	N. [rɛi] S.[ri:]	run

Oi: often [ɛi] ('aee'):

thoin	[to^dn, tai:^dn]	backside
quoi?	[kwɛ:]	who?

Oo: short [u]:

tooilleil	[tul jɛ:l']	labouring, toiling
thalloo	[tɔlu]	earth

Oo: long:

dooin	[du:n´, dun´]	to us
rooin	[ru:n]	to us
ooir	[u:r]	earth
pooar	[pu:ər]	power
noo		saint
loo		oath
doon		close
booiagh	[b^wuiax]	thankful

Oh: short:

stoht, poht		pot, creel

U: short [o̞]

muc		pig
hug		gave

U: diphthong ['j] ('yoo': English 'dew')

lhune	[l'ju:n]	ale

Ui: short

guilley	[gɪl'jə] ('gill-ya')	boy
fuill	[fuɪl']	blood

Uy: 'oo'

    shuyr   [ʃuːr]   sister

Y: short [ə] pronounced like the vowel in the second syllable of 'London':

    dys   [dəs]   to
    emshyr   [ɛmʃər]   weather
    dorrys   [dɔrəs]   door

Y: short [ɪ] like 'i' in 'gill':

    ynsagh   teach

ai, ea, eh, ei: usually pronounced like the first vowel in French été, German geben.

15.2.3   Writing vowels and diphthongs

In different words, the diphthong [ai] heard in English 'height', 'eye', may be represented in several ways in Manx:

-ai	*aile*	fire
-aih	*graih*	love
-ie	*mie*	good
-iy	*siyn*	plate
	riyr	last night
-i	*drine*	thorn
-eiy	*feiyr*	wild
-oi	*noi*	against

[au] as in 'bough', 'house' may be written *-au-, -aw-, ou-, -ow-, -oau-, -oauy-*:

-au-	*niau*	heaven
-aw-	*awin*	river
-ou-	*dou*	to me
-ow-	*yiow*	you will get
-oau-	*coau*	chaffer
-oauy-	*roauyr*	fat

[ɛi] as in 'grey' may be written *-aaie, -aie, -eih, -eiy, -oih, -oie, -eïe, -uy, -eoaie*:

-aaie	*traaiet*	[trɛi]	shore
-aie	*baie*	[bɛi]	bay
-eih	*leih*	[lɛi]	pardon
-eiy	*seiy*		thrust

	lheiy		calf
-oih	*roih*		arm
-oie	*oie**		evening
-eïe	*feïe*	[fɛi]	wild
	greïe	[grɛi]	engine
-uy	*ruy**	[rɛi]	red
-eoaie	*freoaie*	[frɛɪ]	heather

† In Northern Manx. Southern Manx pronounces this 'try'.
* In Northern Manx. Southern Manx pronounces these 'ee' and 'ree'.

E: [e], [ɛ], short, may be written *-e-, -ea-*

ben 'ben' woman

Note: *red*, thing, is pronounced 'rud'.
'*shenn*', old, is pronounced 'shan' in Northern Manx.

[e:] long (Scottish i.e. pure 'say') may be written *-ê-, -ea-, -ei-, eh, -ey*

fênaght		asking
bea		life/lifetime
rea	[re:]	ram
keim	[ke:m]	amble
ben-rein	[bɛᵈn **re:n**]	queen
key	[ke:]	cream
tey	[te:]	tea
fey	[fe:]	fathom

[au, ɛu] may be written *-aue, -eau, -ow*

-aue	*traaue*	[trɛu]	plough
*-eau**	*ceau*	[k'jau, k'jɛu]	throw
-ow	*çhiow*		warm up

* pronounced 'ow' in the North.

[ju] as in 'dew' may be written *-eeu, -iu, -eiau, -ioo*

-eeu	*screeu*	[skrju:, skru:]	write
-iu	*diu*	[d'ju]	to you
-eiau	*fieau*	[fju:]	wait
	slieau	[sl'ju:]	mountain
-ioo	*gioot*		present, gift

O: short [ɔ] may be written *-o-* or *-oi-*:

son	[ɔn]	for
sock	[sɔk]	ploughshare
Nollick	[nɔlik]	Christmas
goll	[gɔl]	go
croi(t)t	[krɔt] ('crot')	croft

O: [ɔ:] long = 'or', may be written *-o-*, *-oa-*, *-oe-*, *-oi-*, *-oai-*, *-oh*, *-oy-*, *-oay-*, *-eo*

moddey	[mɔːð ə]	dog
doal	[dɔːl]	blind
moal	[mɔːl]	slow
noa	[nɔ]	new
goaill	[gɔːil]	take
shoh	[ʃɔː]	this
boayrd	[bɔːrd]	table
ben-treoghe	[bɛn ˈtrɔːx]	

O: [oː] long = 'oh' may be written *-o-*, *-oe-*, *-oi-*, *-oa-*, *-oai-*, *-ow*, *-oy-*, *-oay-*, *-io-*, *-eo*:

dhone	[doːn]	brown
croe	[kroː]	coop
cro	[kroː]	nut
slayntoil	[slɛntoːlʹ]	healthy
coan	[koːən]	ravine
oanluckey	[oːnləkə]	burying
kione	[kʹjoːn]	head (Peel prn.)
heose	[hoːs]	up
towl	[toːl]	hole
boyn	[boːn]	heel
foayr	[foːr]	favour

[uːi] may be written *-ooie*:

dooie	[duːi]	true-born, patriotic

'Öi', 'ö' as in French 'meure', German 'Goethe', may be written *-eay*, *-ei-*, *-ey-*, *-oy-*, *-ar-*, *-er-*, *-uir*:

-eay	*geayl*	[göːlʹ, gɪːl]	coal
-ei-	*seihll*	[söːl]	world
-ey-	*keyl*	[köːl]	thin
-oy-	*voym*	[vöm]	from me

-ar-	*ard*	high
	argid	money
-er-	*merg*	woe
-uir	*guirr*	hatch

'i' accompanying other vowels often sounds [j] as in English 'yet', 'dew':

kione	head
stiagh	in, into
liooar	enough
miu	about you

[u] may be written -*oy*:

Lerphoyll	Liverpool [lörful] ('Ler-ful')

Note: *feer*, very, is pronounced 'fee' [fi:] before a consonant.

jannoo, do = 'jinnoo', also 'junnoo', Northern 'jennoo'.

Note: 'Secondary lengthening': Some speakers lengthen a short stressed vowel, so that, for instance, *hoght*, eight, becomes 'hawkh':

aittin	[a:ʒən] ('aa-zhin')	gorse
cabbyl	[ka:vəl] ('ka-vul')	horse

Exception: *feayr*, cold, is pronounced 'foo-rr' in the South, 'fear' in the North.

15.3   Consonants

The pronunciation of many consonants corresponds well to that of their English counterparts.

These include: *b, f, j, k, m, p, q, v, w*.

15.3.1   Broad and slender consonants

Originally, Manx had two distinct types of consonant, 'broad' and 'slender'.

Former 'slender' consonants may now be followed by a 'y' or 'j' sound (palatalisation). For example, in final position, or when they follow slender vowels (*i, e*) *t, d*, and *l* have palatalisation, as in English 'Tuesday' 'dew' 'new', 'Britannia' 'lute', 'million'.

aitt	[at´]	funny
heemayd	[hi:məd´]	we will see
niart	[n´ja:rt]	strength
keeill	[ki:l´]	church
bwilleen	[bwɪ l´ji:n] ('bwil-yeen')	loaf

çhengey	[tʃɪnˈjə] ('chin-ya')	language, tongue
mwyllin	[molˈjən] ('mull-yin')	mill
dooinney	[donˈjə] ('dun-yer')	man
clashtyn	[klaʃtˈən] ('clasht'yin')	hear
dy liooar	[ð əlˈjuːr] ('the lyooer')	enough
inneen	[ɪnˈjiːn] ('in-yeen')	girl, Miss

Tip: If you say 'had you' in English and stop short of pronouncing the '-ou' you will hear a whispered 'y' or 'j' sound. This sound corresponds to the Manx slender 'd'.

'*c*', '*ck*' may sound like 'g' in medial position:

fockle	[fɔːgəl] ('faw-gul')	word
fakin	[faːgɪn] ('fahggin')	see

Note: '*c*' is also pronounced 'g' in final position in *ec*, at [ɛg] ('egg')

15.3.2 Pronunciation of consonants

çh = ch as in 'cherry, church' but pronounced without pushing the lips forward, e.g. *çhiamble*, temple. This sound occurs medially and initially, i.e., in the middle of words or at the beginning. Medially, it is often preceded by -*t*-

bwoailtçhyn folds	*paitçhyn* children

In modern Manx it is often written with the cedilla (ç) to distinguish it from '*ch*', below, which is a different sound.

'*ch*' is the aspirated form of '*c, k*'. It usually occurs initially, but also in verbnoun endings *aghey*/-*aghtyn* and in the adjectival ending -*agh*.
   It is pronounced 'ch' as in the Scottish word 'loch': *chayt*, cat

gh is often silent when it occurs medially between two vowels:

magher	[maːr]	field
staghyl	[staːl] ('stah-ul')	an awkward person
fliaghey	N. [flˈjaː] ('fl'yah'), S. [flˈjaːxa]	rain

The '*gh*' serves to lengthen the vowel. When this sound occurs medially or finally, it is written '*gh*' or '*ght*':

boght		poor
*boghtnid**	[bɔːxnəd]	poor, foolishness

* The medial 't' is silent.

Initially and medially, *gh* is [ɣ], a continuous 'g' sound heard when gargling:

| *ghow* | [ɣau] | take |
| *baghey* | [be:ɣə] | live |

c, k are pronounced 'hard' as in English 'case, cat'. They are never silent in Manx, as in 'knee', and only rarely sibilant, as in 'city'. 'c' is written before a broad vowel, 'k' before a slender one:

| *cappan* | cup | *kione* | head |

Medially, 'c' may be elided (see below):

| *laccal* | [la:l] | want |

or it may be pronounced like 'g':

| *gaccan* | [ga:gən] | grumble |

d often sounds like 'd+th' as in the English phrase 'he ha**d the** book', especially before or after 'broad' vowels *a, o, u, y*, e.g. *daa*, and also in some monosyllables such as *dy*.
A 'y' or 'j' sound, as in English 'dew' may be heard:

| *noid* | [no:d´] ('nohd(j)') | enemy |
| *mayd* | [məd´] ('madj') | we |

Medially 'slender' 'd' may be pronounced like 'dg' in 'edge' or 'g' in 'pigeon', but more often as in leisure [ʒ]:

troiddey	[trɔʒə]	scold
sheidey	[ʃe:ʒə]	blow
sheeidey	[ʃi:ʒə]	silk

For words such as *credjal*, see Elision, below.

f occurs initially only: *fer*, man
or in connection with 't': *riftan*, hooligan

h is pronounced as in 'heel' (never silent as in 'honest'):

| *hoght* | | eight |

hi as in 'hue' (hyew):

| *hiar* | | east |

This is also the pronunciation when '*h*' is a mutation of '*sh*' or '*çh*':

hooill	[hˈjuːlˈ]	walked	(from *shooyl*)
haglym	[hˈjaːgləm]	gathered	(from *çhaglym*)

j occurs medially and initially, never finally. Medially it is usually written with preceding '*d*': *maidjey*, stick. *Lajer* is written without the '*d*' but is pronounced [ʒ] ('zh').

n accompanied by slender vowels is often palatalised:

shinyn	[ʃɪŋən]	we
ainyn	[ɪŋən] ('ing-un')	at us
dooinyn	[dɪŋən]	to us
uinnag	[onˈjag] ('un-yag')	window

ph: [f] as in 'Philip':

phadeyr	[fadɛːr]	prophet

qu: [kw] as in 'quick', never [k] as in 'pique':

queig	[kwɛg]	five

s is pronounced more or less as in English, but with more of a lisp, when it occurs initially: *sap*, wisp, or when doubled (*cass*, foot): medially it is pronounced '*z*', or '*zh*':

ynsaghey	teaching

Medially, double '*s*' may also be pronounced [ð] ('th'):

shassoo	[ʃaːðʊ]	standing
assyl	[aːðəl]	donkey

Finally, single '*s*' is pronounced '*z*' in *as*, and.

sh medially is pronounced [ʒ] ('zh', rather like French *je*):

aashag	[ɛːʒag] ('airzhag')	sofa
ushag	[oʒag] ('uzhag')	bird
foshil	[fɔːʒɪlˈ] ('fawzhil')	open

or sometimes as [j] ('-y-'):

caashey	[kɛːjə] ('cair-yer')	cheese (Northern Manx)

t

'Broad' 't' medially is pronounced 'th' (see elision, below):

| *baatey* | [bɛ:ð ə] | boat |
| *lhiattee* | [l'ja:ð i] | side |

'Slender' 't' medially is pronounced 'j' (French je):

| *aittin* | [a:ʒən] ('aa-zhin') | gorse |

Final slender 't' is pronounced like the first 't' in English 'tutor'

| *caillt* | [kal't'] | lost |

Medial 't' immediately following 'n' or 'l' is generally pronounced 'd':

| *molteyragh* | [mɔldɛ:rax] | fraudulent |
| *coontey* | [ku:ndə] | account |

Final 't' is often silent:

| *boght* | [bɔ:x] ('bawkh') | poor |

(and always in *-aght*):

| *cruinnaght* | [krun'jax] ('krunyakh') meeting/gathering |

'wh' as in 'when' (Scots):

| *whing* | [hwɪŋ] | yoke |

The '*c*' of '*cha*' (negation) is silent: thus *cha ren*, did not = 'ha ren', etc.

Note: 'r' medially is occasionally pronounced almost like 'z':

| *poanrey* | [pɔ:nr'ə] ('pawnz-ra') | beans |
| *ynrick* | [ɪnr'ɪk] ('inzrik') | upright |

Remember, the list is not exhaustive and there are many exceptions!

15.3.3 'Intrusive' consonants

Sometimes an unexpected consonant sound sneaks into Manx words when they are spoken aloud: these 'intrusive consonants' are heard but not usually written.

In words where a stressed syllable contains a vowel followed by a nasal consonant (-*m*, -*n* or -*ng*[ŋ]), a so-called 'intrusive' consonant, usually 'b' or 'd', may be introduced after the vowel. When this happens, a long vowel becomes shortened.

Thus *bane* may become	[bɛᵈn] ('bedn')	white
lane →	[lɛᵈn] ('ledn')	full
lheim →	[lˈjɪᵇ m] ('l-yibm')	leap
ben/ven →	[bɛᵈn] ('bedn')/('vedn')	woman
lhong →	[loŋ] ('lug-ng')	ship
Tom →	[tɔᵇm] ('Thobm')	Tom

Other common examples include *shenn*, old; *shen*, this; *cam*, crooked
    Similarly with 'rn' and 'rl' where the 'r' sound is lost or not heard:

oarn	[ɔːᵈn]('awdn')	barley
Baarle	[bɛːᵈl] ('baedl')	the English language

In the spoken language, 'l' may be introduced between a labial (*b, p, f*) and the following vowel:

bio	[blˈjo] ('b-lyo')	alive

15.4   Stress

Usually the stress falls on the long vowel of the first syllable: '*thalloo*', earth.

Verbnouns ending in -*eil*, -*ail*, have palatal -l and the stress falls on the last syllable:

sauail	[sawɛːlˈ]	save
treigeil	[trɛgeːlˈ]	abandon

Nouns ending in -*ane*, -*age*, -*aig*, -*eyr*, -*eein*, -*oge* have the stress on the last syllable:

farrane	[farɛːn]	spring
rollage	[rəlɛːg]	star
molteyr	[mɔldɛːr]	deceiver
brilleein	[brɪlˈjiːn]	sheet
graynoge	[grɛnoːg]	hedgehog

15.4.1 Numbers

When pronouncing the **cardinal numbers** between 11–19, the stress falls on the first element of the compound number: *kiare-jeig*, fourteen, etc.

When pronouncing numerals from 21 onwards, the stress falls on the final element *'feed'*: *kiare-as-**feed***, twenty-four, etc.

15.4.2 Diminutives

Manx has three sets of suffixes which form diminutives:

> *-in/-een*   *-an/-ane*   *-ag/-age, -eig*

Words formed with the first of each pair (i.e., *-in*, *-an*, *-ag*) have the accent on the first syllable:

blebbin	[blɛbɪn]	a simpleton	(*bleb*, a fool)
treoghan	[trɔːxan]	an orphan	(*treogh*, widowed)
broddag	[brɔðag]	a bodkin	(*brod*, a prick or stab)

Words formed with the second of each pair (*-een*, *-ane*, *-age*) have the accent on the suffix. A long vowel in the first syllable is shortened when the suffix is added:

dooinneen	[donˊjiːn]	a pygmy	(*dooinney*, man)
creggeen	[krɛgiːn]	a little rock	(*creg*, a rock)
croagane	[krɔgɛːn]	a hook	(*croag*, a claw)
cuilleig	[kʊlˊjɛːg]	a nook	(*cuill/cooill*, a corner).

15.5 Elision

Medial consonants, especially double consonants, may be softened or completely elided with the surrounding vowels:

cappan	→	[kaːvan] ('cah-van')	cup
magher	→	[maːr] ('ma-r')	field
tuittym	→	[toʒəm] ('tuzhum')	fall
laccal	→	[laːl] ('la-l')	want
baatey	→	[bɛːðə] ('bay-ther')	boat
roddan	→	[rɔðan] ('raw-than')	rat
lhiabbee	→	[lˊjaːvi] ('l-ya-vee')	bed
cabbyl	→	[kaːvəl] ('ca-vul')	horse
tappee	→	[taːvi] ('ta-vee')	quick
credjal	→	[krɛːl] ('krair-l')	believe

Note: *shassoo*, stand, often sounds like 'shazoo' or 'shathoo': [ʃaːzʊ, ʃaːðʊ]

15.6 Intonation

Intonation includes the following elements which all combine to make the unique 'melody' of a language:

> phrasing
> pitch (rising, falling)
> tempo
> rhythm
> accent/stress

Intonation is perhaps the most characteristic aspect of spoken Manx, and at the same time the least well researched, the most elusive and difficult to describe. Also, clearly, all speakers of any language have personal mannerisms and traits which make up their individual idiolect.

The best advice that can be offered to people who want to speak Manx is a study of the speech of native and near-native speakers, and also the Manx English of (especially older rural) ethnic Manx people. The recorded material available on the website which accompanies this book is an example of this. A new nucleus of speakers, especially those connected with the Manx Medium primary school at St John's, is moving the language on, as all languages must move on, or wither and die, (and the rumours of the death of Manx have been very much exaggerated!)

In very general terms, it may be stated that the tempo of traditional spoken Manx was neither hasty nor staccato, gabbled nor discordant, but 'rolling', musical and with a measured rhythm, avoiding sharp extremes of pitch. The syntactic preference of Manx speakers for stringing main clauses together with '*as*' rather than the ponderous complexity of a series of subordinate clauses lent Manx a spontaneity and immediacy.

It is the intonation which most uniquely distinguishes the 'spirit of Manx speech', what used to be known as the 'rale sof' oul Manx', an ancient language which is now proving itself more than capable of adapting to the demands of a new generation of speakers.

Gist English translations of recorded Manx conversations

The recordings were made during the late summer and autumn of 2004. They are available at http://www.practicalmanx.com

B = Mr Bernard Caine

W = the late Mr Walter Clarke

J = Mr Juan Crellin

L = the late Mr Leslie Quirk

1   How Breagagh acquired his nickname

W: Liar (Breagagh[12]) – Douglas Fargher, he was first, and one time we were speaking with the Gaaue[13] – John Kneen – and John Kneen said: 'Who's himself? Who's himself?' and I said, 'His name's Fargher'.

'Oh. Where's he from?'

I said, 'Well, now he lives in Douglas, but he used to be in Ramsey.'

'Fargher, Fargher – he's a big fellow, a big fellow – with big feet', he said, 'with big feet.' And then he said (now what did he say?) 'Your father's brother was living in Kirk Andreas!' and Breagagh said 'He was, he was, for a while.'

'Chalse Fargher,' the Gaaue said.

'Yes,' Breagagh said 'that's right enough.'

'Chalse! Chalse Breagagh!'

---

[12] Douglas Fargher, Manx speaker, lexicographer and recorder of Manx speech.
[13] John Kneen the Smith, a fluent native speaker.

Douglas laughed and I laughed, and I said, 'Why did he have that nickname?'

'Oh, that was no nickname, he told lies every day, every day', he said, 'and you're a relation of his?' the Gaaue said.

Douglas said, 'Yes, I'm his relation,' and after that Breagagh said: 'My name is Breagagh!' That's how he got the nickname 'Breagagh'. From the Gaaue – from the old Gaaue!

2   On speaking Manx

W: Thomas Karran in Douglas – all his Manx came back within a fortnight. I hadn't the faintest idea that he had Manx.

L: Really?

W: And he used to say – what was it he used to say now, Tom Karran? 'That's right', he'd say, 'that's right!' And he would think and think and then he was getting better and better each time you saw him.

L: He was right out of practice, that man!

W: He was.

L: Right out of practice. He'd forgotten the words and they were coming back and coming back each time.

W: He told me a tale of the time he was a boy, he was a cook-boy going to the fishing, going for the herring, and he was something like eleven or twelve years of age at that times, he was cook on board a nickey, and there was an old man – the old man spoke Manx, but nobody else in the crew had Manx except for the boy and the old man, and they spoke together and war almost broke out on the boat, and he wasn't allowed to speak Manx again because nobody else in the crew – they couldn't understand Manx.

L: Yes.

W: He wasn't allowed to speak it. The skipper said 'Don't speak Manx again, the crew are against it!'

L: Aye!

W: And he said: 'All right. I'll forget it then', and he did.

J: It was all like that, man, at that time.

W: 'That's the way,' he said, he didn't use Manx for …

L: The Manx themselves are against the Manx language.

W: Yes.

L: Not – aye – if you …

W: They think you're talking about them – it was awful!

L: There were better things to talk about than that.

J: John Corlett told me that his grandfather and grandmother lived in a little house near Ballacorey and both of them had Manx and they often spoke Manx alone, and John went to that place in his holidays and he came out with Manx now and again without thinking, and he did it in school once, and the head-teacher (Walker was his name) came and boxed his ears and said: 'We speak English here, man!'
  He boxed his ears! *'We speak English here, young man!'*

W: Well, when I went to school, at that time I was living with my grand-father in the Big Glen and when I spoke English I had an accent ...

J: Accent, aye!

W: ... a strong Manx accent, and they laughed at me, and the teacher – he made me stand on the table!

L: Aye!

W: And read aloud out of the book and all the other children and he himself all laughed at me because I spoke with ...

J: a Manx accent!

W: A Manx accent in English!

J: Aye!

W: I'll never forget that!

J: Aye!

W: I never did forget it!

L: It's shameful and more than shameful!

J: Aye, they were making mock ...

L: Very bad!

J: Aye!

W: Oh, and I met that fellow many years after when I was working at the Museum and he came and spoke to me and I said: 'Get away from me!'

J: Aye!

W: I was so angry!

L: Aye, right enough, oh, aye!

W: I said 'You laughed at me – now I'm laughing at you!'

L: ... [laughing] 'at you!' Because he was stupid and ignorant!

W: That's right! That's right!

L: Aye!

W: Oh, I was – I was furious!

L: If you don't understand something, well, that's ignorant!

J: And nowadays it's something else, man, isn't it? They're all looking for Manx nowadays!

L: Mrs Clague from Dalby was speaking of her son and he spoke wonderful Manx – very fluent because it was their [first] language. When his father and his mother – when the two of them were alive they always spoke Manx, and anyway when he went to school they impressed upon him: 'It's English that's spoken here,' they said, 'not Manx. If you want to speak Manx at home, well, that's another thing but not …' and he protested … well, anyway, a man came from Manchester, a very learned man, and he was looking for Manx, and the schoolteacher told him to go to see Mrs Clague's son, but he would not speak: He said: 'If you don't want me to speak it I won't'.

W: God bless me!

J: When Manx Radio were making recordings the first time, there were lots of farmers and seamen and other people making recordings, telling tales of this and that in the Isle of Man, and they had wonderful accents. And I asked them if all those recordings were kept for posterity, and they said they weren't, they were all destroyed.

W: Really?

J: They kept nothing, and all those old people are dead now, and their accent is lost forever. I'm sorry, aye! They didn't know at that time that those recordings were so precious, that's the trouble, and they're lost forever!

W: Yes!

J: Well, that's the way! They thought the like was going to be around forever, but it wasn't so.

W: It was like the Manx Language Society – when we were going about there was a tape recorder at the Museum to record birds …

J: Aye!

W: … singing and things like that, and I said to Megaw:[14] 'There are old men and old women with good Manx. We ought to record them.' And he said 'Oh, you can't – that recorder is for the birds!' And we had to buy one ourselves. And we got the money from John Gell.

J: We did.

W: John Gell bought the tape-recorder, and we paid him back over something like six months or maybe years, something like that,

---

[14] Basil Megaw, 1913–2002, former Director of the Manx Museum

because we didn't have the money. But they said at the Museum 'Oh, Manx, it's not ... it doesn't matter!' But I said: 'The birds will be singing that song in a hundred years from now but the old Manx speakers won't be alive!

L: They'll be singing! [In heaven]

W: There'll be no Manx to be had. But he said 'Go away!' And then after a little while the Irish came.

L: Yes!

W: They were standing down and the realisation came to him 'Oh, there's something in this, we must do it!' But it was too late!

L: Almost too late –

W: Almost too late.

L: It was late, almost too late!

W: Almost too late, because all the Manx had gone up in the air! People like Mrs Kinvig ...

L: Aye!

W: ... from Ronague. I was in Mrs Kinvig's house at Ronague and the old contractor himself ...

L: Was he?

W: ... was there, and he was terribly deaf, man!

L: Oh, very, very deaf!

W: Terribly deaf, and he was by the fireside ...

L: Even worse than me!

W: ... and he had a pipe and he was (spits) in the fire. And Breagagh and myself had come to take the old lady to Kitty Tommy Howe's house ...

L: Aye, you had!

W: ... because she had electricity.

L: Yes ...

W: There wasn't such a thing in the Kinvig house. Anyway, we got the old man's permission to take the lady to record her and the contractor said – he looked at her and he looked at us and she was putting her coat on, and he said 'Where are they going now?' I said: 'They're going to make a recording.' 'Where?' I bawled into his ear then 'We're going to make a recording!' 'Who?' 'We and this lady!' He said: 'She'll make a mess of it!'

L: That's right! 'She'll make a mess of it!' I remember! But she didn't – thank God, she didn't! She certainly didn't!

W: But he was so deaf, it was terrible! He had wonderful Manx, oh wonderful, incredible – but the lady – the old lady was in awe of him!

L: She was. I expect she was!

W: She didn't speak Manx when he was there.

J: Did she not?

W: When he was gone away out into the fields somewhere plenty of Manx flowed from her mouth!

L: When the old man died she herself came to be very fluent and loved it too, then.

W: Oh, yes.

L: Yes.

W: She was a wonderful woman.

L: She always said: 'These people saying "going and grumbling!" Go and rejoice! "Going and grumbling?" Go and rejoice!'

W: She told me a story about the time she was courting somewhere, she said, another fellow in the parish near Ronague, she said 'A foreigner he was, a foreigner, he was from a different parish!' A foreigner! Anyway, she was from – I don't know whether she was from Peel or where it was – she had to walk home and it was growing dark 'and it was getting dark and I was walking and walking and I was looking about, looking about, and it was very dark, ' she said, 'and a dog followed me', she said, 'and the dog was barking, making a terrible noise, and I ran down the road,' she said 'I was scared out of my wits!'

L: Scared out of her wits!

W: Out of her wits!

L: This is a story from the old days in Foxdale, and there was a man – he was a preacher – and he was a bit of a sissy, and he was scared stiff of the dark. He was going down the road one time and the boys and some of the girls were there too, and they had a white sheet over their heads, and they were standing on the hedge and they were 'Ooah!' and all sorts of noises, and this man ran, and he was saying – he had very good Manx – 'don't harm me and I won't harm you!'

3   Youth

W: Anyway, when I was young and – you remember, probably, and I remember when I was young – I was a young lad – in the summer when school was over we used to go down to the shore after breakfast, without shoes, no shirt, almost naked, running about all summer on the shore, playing and doing that and on the rocks looking for crabs and such things, playing around, but those days, man, they're gone now!

J: No longer seen now.

W: No.

L: Nobody does that sort of thing now, do they?

W & J: No!

L: They're all sitting at the ... sitting in front of the television and the *computer* ...

W: ... without shoes ...

L: ... computer ...

W: for six or seven weeks in the summer. No shoes, running on the stones, and everything, man!

L: How about sitting in front of the *telefís*, without a net?

W: Yes!

J: Albee Radcliffe told me when he was young they used to jump over the gorse bushes ...

W: That's right!

J: ... barefoot, and no worries! The soles of their feet were so hard ...

W: Yes, yes.

J: ... from running about all summer with no shoes at all!

W: And we used to go up Sulby River there to swim in the river stark naked ...

J: Stark naked! Aye, that's right!

W: Starkers!

L: Like the *red dub* at Peel.

W: Yes, yes!

L: They used to go ... all the lads ... swimming, well, they go now, but they all went quite naked ...

J: Aye, I guess so.

L: Oh, yes.

W: Well, we hadn't the money to buy such things.

J: Perhaps they didn't exist.

L: No, no, they didn't exist. For children ...

J: I don't know.

W: Well, when the visitors came, they stayed in the big houses by the Mooragh in Ramsey, they used to put all their clothes outside the window to dry and we used to go under the windows in the morning with a big stick and ...

J: Pinch them!

W: Pinch them, aye! Because we knew they were only there for a week or a fortnight and after that we'd wear them!

J: Aye, that's right enough!

W: Yes, yes.

J: And you got them for nothing!

W: And we did that many times!

J: Many times!

W: I'm ashamed now. I had to do it, we had no money.

4   Benefits of whiskey and treacle,
         and the *Gaaue*'s first recorded words

W: In the winter, when it's cold, at night before going to bed, I take a drop of whisky and a spoonful of honey in it.

L: That'd be very good!

W: With hot water.

J: Really?

L: Oh, that'll be good for you!

W: Wonderful!

J: And a piece of lemon – a slice of lemon, yes?

W: The honey and the whisky and hot water, mixed.

J: Mixed together.

W: Wonderful!

J: And a little honey in it?

W: Yes.

J: Oh, that'll help!

W: Wonderful!

J: A little, a little.

L: And then lots of vigour!

J: Aye, that's it! Anyway, you all appear to me to be very well, in very fine health, and the *treacle's* not too bad, anyway.

L: Well, I was speaking to the doctor and he said you should swallow about a full spoon of treacle to have much effect, he said, it couldn't help you much, but a little.

J: A little.

L: Yes.

J: That's right.

L: But it couldn't – it wouldn't make you rush wildly to the 'little house', either, just stroll to the 'little house'.

W: Stroll. The first word we recorded from the Gaaue, the first thing – I went to get the recorder and the Gaaue came to Ramsey, I took him to William Radcliffe's house in Ramsey, and the Gaaue, he was dressed up, dressed in brand new clothes, his Sunday coat …

J: Oh, that's right!

L: Yes!

W: I said, 'God bless me, you're got up like a king,' I said, and he said: 'This is my Sunday coat. And anyway,' he said, 'what were we talking about then?' Now and again he'd say: 'What were we talking around?' And I'd say 'about' 'Oh, yes, yes, yes, I clean forgot,' he'd say. And then I said: 'Right enough. It's on now,' and he said 'Is there someplace outside I can have a pee?'

L: The very first thing! I heard that!

5   Johnny's truss creates havoc at Ronaldsway airport

J: Anyway, I've got a good story about the hole in my stomach: once upon a time I was a farmer, and working a lot, and so on, and this is a really funny story, man. My wife and I were going to Malta on holiday once, nearly eight years ago, and we went to the airport at Ronaldsway, and that time they had a 'pinging' machine, because of the IRA, and I went through the machine, and it went 'ping', and the man said 'Hand over your change, man!', and I gave him my change, and he said: 'Go back through this machine', and I went back, and there was another 'ping'. And he said 'Have you got keys on you?' and I said 'I think so', and I gave him my keys, and he said 'Go round again,' and I went through again, and it 'pinged' again. And he asked, 'Well, how about your watch? Give us your watch!' And I gave him my watch, and he said 'Go back again!' and

I went through again and it 'pinged' again, and he said 'I don't know what's the matter with you!' and he went to the shelf and he had a Geiger counter and he came back – there were lots of people behind me, and they were grumbling, all waiting for the plane – and he ran the Geiger counter over me, and he started at my head, and it went 'peep-peep-peep-' and he went down with the thing 'peeppeeppeep' and when he reached the top of my stomach it went 'brrr' and the man said: 'I've never seen the like before! What's the matter with you?'

'Oh, I don't know,' I said. 'Have I got to drop my pants now in front of all these women?'

And he said 'Well, what's the matter with you?' And then the penny dropped, man, I had a special belt round me for the hole – the hernia – and I'd put new rivets of iron in it, and that iron was causing all the trouble! And I said 'Oh, I've got a special belt!' 'Then go away and don't come back!' he said. And the people behind me were furious. That's not all: when I was climbing up the steps to the aircraft a huge fat woman was coming behind me, man, and she said – I think she was a nurse, maybe a matron – and she said: 'Oh, you ought to get rid of that tiresome thing,' she said, 'you made an awful lot of trouble this morning!'

'Well, lady' I said, 'if there were rivets like that in your bra you'd cause a few "Pings!" and she was awfully cross!

6   Of herrings and tobacco

W: There are big herring in that loch, aren't there?

J: In Loch Ney, there are a special kind of herrings, but they're extremely rare now. They've been in that loch since Northern Britain was all frozen over.

L: Really?

J: Aye, and they came from the sea, man.

L: Indeed!

J: And they've remained there ever since ...

L: and grown accustomed to the water?

J: ... accustomed to fresh water, and they developed into a special kind of fish. And they're still to be had, they say.

L: Oh, aye! This is another thing: I was with Neddy and we were working from the Island and we went to Ballanahinsh, we were fishing and the boys were saying 'Swim, herring, swim,' and I said ' That's worth nothing in this kind of water. This is Gaelic water, we must say '*Snámh, scadán, snámh!*' And they said: '*Snámh, scadán, snámh!*' and then when we came to haul in the net, it wasn't very full, but it was better than it had been all the previous months. It was the best catch we had, and they all said, Oh it's *Snámh, scadán, snámh*, that's done it!

J: That's it! How did they eat them in the old days, man, and all the salt there was in them?

W: Everything was salted, wasn't it?

J: And nowadays they'd all die ...

L: Well, at that time they were working.

W: The doctors say 'You'll die if you eat too much salt'

L, J: Yes!

W: But the old people – look at the Gaaue – I don't know – and all the people like that – they were over ninety years of age ...

L: They weren't sitting in front of the *telefís*, they were working.

W: Oh, they weren't!

L: And if you had a pick or something and a shovel, and were working like that, salt wouldn't worry you at all ...

J: They needed it

L: Yes. They needed it, aye! They ate stuff, grease and the like ...

W: When I was a boy I ate salt herring and they came straight out of the pot!

J: That's right!

W: And put on the fire, then turned again from the fire, and – man – they were so – I don't know, I was sweating when I ate them!

J: And you're still alive?

W: Oh, yes.

J: And it's the same thing with tobacco.

L: That's the thing. The old people used to take this tobacco every day, through the night, for years and years, but they were working.

J: There was a man working for me called William Kennaugh and he used to chew tobacco, aye, twist, they said, and sometimes I used to go and get *silage* in town, and William said 'How about a *chew?*' he said, 'of this tobacco?' And I said 'Well, all right then, give it here!' And then I chewed all the way back, and when I got to the field, man, the whole sky was going round, aye, the whole world and I had to stop, man ...

W: Were you sick?

J: Well, I wasn't sick, everything was upside down and I lay on my back on the ground!

W: Indeed!

J: Yes, for almost a quarter of an hour!

L: At one time I was getting my breakfast at Ballacooil Dalby and I took a sandwich and it was good enough, very good, and then all the room was going round and round and I opened the sandwich and there was 'Craven A' – 'Craven A' on top of the brawn and that's why – there were foreigners – people and – what were they, 18B they called them, Internees, they were there and they called her 'Chain-Smokerloo' because she had Craven A in her mouth all day and all night perhaps!

W: I was speaking with the old Gaaue at Balley ny Loghey, Robby Kelly, and there was a little box in the forge. And there were shreds of tobacco in it, in the box, and I asked 'Why do you keep this stuff?' He said, 'Well, when a horse comes in, if the horse is noisy and leaps about, I'd give it a bit of tobacco and in two minutes it's calm and everything, and you could do anything with it,' he said! In two minutes! Eating the tobacco! After eating the tobacco!

7   Of age and vitality

J: … you were the warden[15] for almost ten years, weren't you?

L: Twelve!

W: Oh, were you?

L: I was there twelve years!

J: Were you?

L: Twelve years!

W: What age are you now?

L: Well, if I manage to get to the last day of next month I'll be 90.

W: 90?

L: Yes.

W: Really?

L: If I make it till the last day of next month!

W: 90!

L: This is August, well, it's next month!

W: 90!

[15] Leslie Quirk was warden at Thie ny Gaelgey, St. Judes.

L: Yes.

W: God bless me! How about yourself, John? How old are you?

J: I'm over 21, man. I am!

W: What age are you, then?

L: Nobody would think you were 21!

J: I'm 80 – 81 now!

W: 80? Are you really?

J: I am, yes, that's right.

L: Aye, that's right. If I'm 90, you're 81.

J: You're almost ten years older than me.

L: Almost ten!

W: I'm still a child, then.

L: You're only just out of your cradle.

W: I'm 76.

L: Still on your knees!

J: You should be wearing short pants, man!

L: Yes. You should be walking now, not crawling about on your knees!

W: I thought I was growing old – God bless me! Eighty …

L: We're 'elders'.

W: Indeed!

J: We're still young, man, aren't we? Aye!

W: Well, when the Gaaue was 97, he said to Harry Boyde 'Let's go to Ramsey and get ourselves a girl apiece!' and he was 97!

J: Oh, there was stamina in them in those days, wasn't there?

8   The bread cart comes to town

W: We were collecting carts of all types in the Museum and it was far – outside Ramsey. I was well aware that the cart was there. I went to speak to the old man. He was giving up work. He was a baker, he said to me: 'I'm too age – too old now, I'm giving up that work.' Quayle his name was, from Ormly. Anyway, he said, 'Here's the cart. If you want it, take it! Right away,' he said, 'because I'm getting out of the house in a week.' I said: 'Right enough!'

Anyway, I went to the station in Ramsey for the horse – the iron road, and it was the first iron horse going from Ramsey something like seven o'clock in the morning to Douglas. And I spoke to the station master there and I said: 'I'm bringing the cart there.' 'Oh', he said, 'right enough, and do it tomorrow, because I have to put it in the wagon like that'. I said: 'All right.' Anyway, at six o'clock I went up in the morning – walked to Ormly, on my own, and I said, 'Well, if a horse can do it, I will.' Anyway, I got it out of the shed, and I was in front of the cart and pulling it along, pulling it along, and there was a heap of stones directly in the road and a sandy hill on it, and I ran for the worst side and up the top of it and ... and I got it on top and then I was going down the hill. Well, we went quicker and faster and faster and when I was halfway down the hill I was running like the Devil, man, I couldn't let it go because it would have run me over!

J: That's it!

W: And I ran and I was almost on the ground when I reached that station: and there were two men walking to the *gasworks* in Ramsey and they were laughing at me and they were saying awful things to me when I ran past. 'I can't stop!' I said 'I can't stop!' I couldn't!

J: You could not!

W: Anyway, I got it very – I got it to the station and I was sweating terribly, I was wet, the sweat was running down me, and the station-master said: 'What's this?' 'I've brought the bloody thing from Ormly!'

J: Ormly!

W: 'You're mad!' he said, 'you're bloody mad!' Anyway, I got it onto the train and we went to Douglas and then I got it from the station in Douglas to the Museum but that was – man, was I frightened that day, that morning. Very heavy, that cart!

L: Couldn't you get a horse to pull it?

W: I couldn't.

J: It would be terribly heavy, that cart.

W: Oh, it was!

L: In Douglas it would be – Douglas was a hilly place – there's nowhere flat in Douglas. Apart from the *Prom* – there's no flat place in Douglas, it's all hills – a hilly place.

W: I saw the other men a few days after that, they were laughing at me and laughing at me and they said 'You're completely mad,' they said, 'you're completely mad!' I said 'We wanted that cart and now we've got it!'

J: Aye!

W: Oh, yes! Thank God it was seven – half past six in the morning;

there weren't people about. We went right over without people and everything.

J: If you did it now …

L: Now!

W: I couldn't do it now! I couldn't do it now!

9 The Polish pilot and his son

J: And this was just at the beginning of the last war, and I had an awful story about that. We were children and up on the roof of the house and we were using hammers and suchlike and there was a man living with us at the start of the war called Alex Maievsky, yes, he was from Poland, and his father was a pilot in Jurby at that time, and sometimes he was flying the Hawker Henley, towing targets, and that sort of thing and now and again he used to telephone my father and say 'Well, there'll be chocolate coming down tomorrow, go out into that field!' and sure enough Captain Maievsky comes in the Hawker Henley, terribly low, he was crawling over the hedges, man! At the side over the field …

W: God bless me!

J: … anyway, the parachute would come down almost as big as that, and there would be a bar or two of chocolate and we were very excited then. But this young man Alex Maievsky was living with us – he was slightly crazy – and he had red hair and was a wild fellow, and anyway we were on top of the house and there was Alex with the hammer and he dropped the hammer down the flue, and there was a light, and we saw the hammer lying on the bottom of the flue and he said 'I'm going to go in and grab it'. And I said, 'You can't do that, you'll never get out again,' and he said, 'Well, once you've gone, I'll do it,' and I said to myself, well, that'll be the end of him, and anyway I said to Alex, 'I'll put a rope round your legs and you could go into the flue and get hold of the hammer.' And he said 'Right enough, we'll do that.' He was right out of his mind, that boy! Anyway, he went in and I went and paid out the rope, and then there came a voice from the bowels of the house 'I have the hammer! Pull me out now!' And we started to pull him out of the flue, and all the mortar fell down into his britches, it was lost and collapsed around his legs and we couldn't get him out, and the rope went straight down the flue, and there was nothing to be seen but mortar and stones and Alex was in there upside down! And thank God there was a man on a table beside the house, and that was a stone-mason, what was his name, you will know him – a stone-mason at that time – he was always smoking, he had a pipe – didn't he build a house near the hospital? Anyway, never mind – his name will come back – and I went to his table – to the stage and I told him 'Alex is upside down behind this house, behind the wall here – and we have to –

W: Get him out!

J: Aye, rip out all the bricks!' And he said, 'You can't do that, the house will fall down! And then I said 'We'll have to!' And I took the hammer from him and I began to tear out all the bricks and anyway Alex – he was complaining terribly behind the wall and he was saying 'I can't breathe! I can't breathe!' and 'What are you doing? Pull me out!' and all this, and I said ' We can't!' And anyway, we pulled out all the bricks and we got to Alex at the bottom of the place, he was close to death, and then he could breathe – there was enough air – and we pulled out more bricks and we got down to his head and his face was like a beetroot, man!

W: Indeed!

J: I never saw a man as red as Alex!

W: God bless me!

J: And, anyway, he was breathing and we got him out of that hole to the table and he was still alive! And you can still see the hole in the house – there isn't a hole, but the place where the bricks were pulled out! But thank God the table and the stone-mason were there. That man. I've forgotten his name.

W: God bless me!

J: Aye. Constantly smoking, man, aye.

Anyway, that's not the end of the story. I went back out to the war, to the sea, and Alex went out after rabbits with a gun, a sixteen bore, and there were hammers on that gun, two hammers, double barrel, and he climbed up the hedge somewhere to get out of the field and into the next field and he took his sight over the barrels and pulled the gun through the thorns to the top of the field and he shot … Aye, and shot off most of his hand. And he went to a house near the place to an old woman and I think there was a boy in the house and the boy ran back to my mother at Ballachurry and said that Alex had been shot with his own gun. And she was a nurse in the first World War and very well up in that sort of thing, and anyway they brought Alex back to the house and then to the hospital and the doctor said, 'We'll have to save your thumb at least,' and they had to remove the first, second and third fingers, they cut them all off, but the last finger and the thumb were left …

W: That's all?

J: … And anyway the first time I was thankful that he was alive and the second time I was thankful that he was still alive! Even though many misfortunes befell him!

10   The wrong funeral

J: Do you remember when you came to me at *Thie ny Gaelgey* and you said someone told you William Corkish had died?

L: Oh, aye!

J: And you said I was to say the twenty-third psalm at his funeral tomorrow and I answered: 'Oh, William Corkish? Oh, that's too bad, he was a wonderful Manx speaker and a good friend of mine. I must go to the funeral tomorrow'. Well, in the morning – the next morning I was in Ramsey on the promenade, and I saw the face of a man like William Corkish coming along the promenade towards me. And I was terrified, man! And I said, 'Well, is this a ghost? Does he have a brother?' I was terrified! Anyway, he came up to me and said, 'Good morning, Juan!' And he said, 'You don't appear to me to be feeling too well!' and I replied 'I'm not very well, either. I was going to your funeral this afternoon!' And he said, 'Oh, now I understand!' and he laughed, and he said that another man called William Corkish had died and 'They're putting him under the earth this afternoon.'

L: I was at that funeral and I didn't know.

J: Didn't you?

L: I went in and I was sitting here and – I was amazed – I never knew he was a big man in the brass band and the like, perhaps he was, I was learning something, and I was at the funeral! And I was amazed that there was no mention of his love of Manx; there was no mention of it.

J: Well, did you say anything?

L: No, I didn't say anything

J: You didn't?

L: Oh, no, I wasn't going to do that at all.

J: William Corkish – do you know him? He had grey hair, didn't he? Oh, a wonderful man! That was a good joke.

L: And I was at the funeral.

J: You were, aye.

L: The wrong man!

W: John Tom Kaighin once told me a tale when I was there, about an old man; an old man lived in Kirk Bride and he was courting a woman a lot younger than himself, and she was much younger. Anyway, John Tom said, 'He went to Ramsey and bought new clothes for the wedding.' And I said 'Oh, really?' 'He did, he did,' he said, 'he was dressed in new clothes. Everything new for the wedding. ' Oh,' I said, 'that took a lot of money'. 'Oh, it cost a lot, it cost a lot. Anyway,' he said, 'he was out in the field doing something and suddenly he dropped dead.'

J: Just like that?

W: 'Really?' I said. 'Yes, yes'. And he said 'On the day he was going to get married he was getting buried!' He was laughing and laughing!

J: Aye!

W: 'On the day he was going to get married,' he said 'he was getting buried.' And I said, 'What about the new clothes?' 'I don't know, I don't know,' John Tom said.

11   Tobacco

W: Do you know an old man who lived in the big glen, Billy Christian? He lived in Sulby, up there – in the big glen.

J: Oh, did he?

W: He virtually ate tobacco – almost an ounce a day he would buy in the shop and it wasn't brown, it was black, it wasn't brown – 'pig tail' – it was black …

L: Oh, aye!

W: Very black, he would take a pinch …

L: Black as an egg!

W: That's it! He'd take a pinch and put it in his mouth and then he'd go round and spit out …

J: That's it!

W: … and I went to the house one day, and he was just about to have his dinner, and the old woman said, 'Come in, dinner's ready.' Billy went in and the old woman said: 'Would you like a bit of broth?' 'Oh, no, ' I said, 'a cup of tea will be fine. Right, ' I said. And Billy was there and he had a bowl of soup, and he said 'Hang on!' He removed the tobacco …

J: from his cheek …

W: … yes, from his mouth and he ate the broth, and when he'd done with the broth, he put it back and said, 'All right now!' and he was chewing again!

J: Was he? Aye! I don't know what ...

W: Oh, man, he was ... !

J: I've got a great tale of Alfie Allen. You know the Ginger pub, don't you?

W: Yes.

J: Well, Alfie was living in Narradale up in the mountains and he used to go to the Ginger and all the tobacco was on a shelf behind the bar, and he had a walking-stick and he put a pin on the top, and when the barmaid went into the other room at the back, to the back, Alfie used to put the walking stick over the bar and stick the pin in the tobacco and he did that for years!

W: Indeed?

J: Aye. But one time the woman came back directly, she was wondering where the tobacco had gone, man! And she came back immediately and poor Alfie was over the bar like that with his walking-stick and a piece of tobacco on the top ...

W: Really!

J: And that was the end of those tricks! And that was a true story!

12   Leslie's motorcycling mishaps

L: Anyway, I had a Maglighter and they're terrible – and I was up the mountains coming from Pt St Mary or Port Erin and coming down, near Dalby, and there was no light on, it was something like 9 or 10 o'clock or later than that in the winter and I hit my headlight. There wasn't any – you could hardly see anything – and I hit one side of the hedge, one side and then the other side and the other and the other and the other and then right in the middle of the road and I woke up and I let out a great shout: 'Where am I?' Or something like that. I remember I yelled aloud. And later the doctor said that that virtually saved my life, because there was a sort of pressure in my head – it was congested – I had a congestion of the blood and that loosened the congestion of the blood. Anyway, I got up. I left my bike – I wasn't thinking about it – and I saw Ballacooil house and I walked down and went into the house and the blood was running down my jacket and everything; anyway, Sheila wasn't worried. Her Mum was a bit worried. And they helped me. They staunched the flow of blood.

J: I heard an old story from you once, man, about an old woman who put oil from the lamp into the tank of the AJS or the Norton.

L: Oh, aye. It wasn't an AJS or a Norton, that was an Enfield.

J: Oh, Enfield.

L: Aye, it was an Enfield 600.

J: Oh, was it?

L: It was terribly heavy. To lift. Anyway, I ran out of petrol at Ballacraine and that woman – Mrs? Never mind – the woman came out with a lamp and she started the chimney and she poured the oil into the tank, and thank God the engine was good and warm and I got home on that paraffin!

J: Really!

W: I've heard of fishing boats running on paraffin but I've not heard of bikes running on it.

L: It wasn't great, but when they're hot they're all right – not all right, but they go. It spluttered terribly!

W: I'll just bet it did!

13   The tug-boat in Ramsey

W: It was a boat made of wood, I think – it was working with, oh God bless me! The new boat called the *Tarroo Ushtey* ...

B: *Tug boat* – tug – *dredger* –

J: Dredger.

W: Anyway there was a small boat with it and there was a man – the master – Moore his name was, he was in the House of Keys for a while, he was a large fat man and he was called Captain Moore by the old people in Douglas for a while when he was in the Keys, anyway they'd come to Ramsey in the *Mannin* and there was no telegraph in her ...

J: Wasn't there?

W: There was a closed bridge on her. And there was a fellow sitting on the – below the bridge and the Skipper was saying 'Go astern now!' and he was shouting through the window below again 'Astern' and so on, and that's how they were going on, anyway, he got to Ramsey and they were coming into harbour and Captain Moore said 'you can go astern if you like, and the fellow that was sitting below there said: 'You can go astern if you like!' And the fellow who was below said 'To heck with it, I don't want to go astern!' and they steered up into the side!

B: God bless me!

W: They were there for ten hours!

B: Oh, God bless me!

W: Aground.

J: Right below the bridge, almost?

W: Yes. They were in court in Ramsey ...

B: Were they?

W: ... and the question was – they asked 'What happened?' and the chap said 'the Skipper said, " You can go astern if you like", and I said to the man below, "You can go astern if you like", and he said "to heck with it!" Directly! [Ran her] aground!

B: Oh, that's awful!

W: Awfully funny, sometimes!

15   Puns and political correctness

B: But sometimes we used to go to St Matthew's Church – St Matthew's ... on a Sunday morning, and there'd be Leslie, and Breagagh, and myself and Brian. After the service we used to go to a little café and in those days people didn't think much of – especially the Wesleyans – they didn't think much of people who went to cafés on Sunday, you understand, and we used to go there, and as I said, Leslie often made puns and word-plays and so on, and we used to eat biscuits there that were called Penguins, and Leslie invented a new verb, he used to go in and say 'Let's Penguin!' That meant, let's eat Penguins! *Penguinamayd!*

J: Aye, he made 'let us' into lettuces, didn't he, *'let us*! Let us, aye, that's what he called them in Manx! But now we're joking about word-jokes, that reminds me of a story about a black man who came to see me at St Jude's, I think he was a minister of some kind, from Africa or India or somewhere, he was almost as black as tar, and a girl – my neighbour's daughter came with a puppy on a *lead* and she came to speak to us, and then the big black man asked the girl in English, 'Oh, that's a nice puppy, a lovely puppy, what's his name?' and the girl said: *'His name is nigger!'* And I nearly fell down the nearest rabbit hole, man! He didn't say anything.

B: Well, you have to be very careful, because I heard something on the radio the other day – I don't know where it was – it was in England someplace and they were paying for things – official things – and they were talking about money, and the man often said in English:

'*That was a niggardly amount of money!*' And [people] were furious because he said 'niggardly'. But that has nothing at all to do with black people, but they were furious and they said, he shouldn't use a word like that. That was '*political correctness*', as they would call it.

16   Remembering Leslie

B: And they were selling very little there [in the fruit shop in Douglas] and – for three people to be there. It was very full, and Brian Stowell and Leslie and Breagagh, and Breagagh and myself sometimes, would be there, and we used to talk about the old people who spoke Manx, and now and again we listened to the recordings ... because every one of them answered, whenever someone addressed them, they would answer, and they'd start off with 'Aaawww – I – I remember ...' every single one of them! And there was a door there and when you opened the door it went 'Aaawww' and we said 'That door's talking Manx!' And we were there often, and as you said Leslie was cheerful and he was constantly making puns and maybe there'd be Manx words, and English words, and French and so on in the word-plays he invented and he was funny like that.

J: Yes. When we were working on the *Dexion* in *Thie ny Gaelgey* for the books Leslie and I were working together and he'd say 'give me a hook, [*croag*] John!' 'Aye, right enough! Here's a hook or two for you,' and then after a while he'd go 'Give me a crow!' He'd go on like that – absolutely terrible!

B: Terrible puns!

J: One time we were working together there and I went out of the door and locked it, and Leslie was inside! And I didn't realise, and I went back [home] for my dinner, and in the evening I was riding past on my bicycle and I heard a yell from *Thie ny Gaelgey* and then I saw a man saluting me through the window and there was Leslie! Inside the building!

W: Yes, yes!

J: And he was complaining, man, and I had to unlock the door and let him out!

17   Remembering Leslie and his sister

J: Noreen [Leslie Quirk's sister] was married to a man called Frank.
Aye, he was an Englishman. He was in the Army during the War
and then they went to live in Weymouth in England, and they had
a boat, a *Volkboot* …

W: Oh, really?

J: They did, and they used to go sailing about the place for quite a
long while, and then Frank died and Noreen returned to the Island.
And for a while she was helping Leslie at the *Dhonnag*.[16]

W: Oh, she was, she was, I remember it well!

J: She was a short woman, and she ran around like a spinning top,
like a tomtit she ran about, almost, extremely quickly and she did
everything …

W: Nimble!

J: Oh, nimble, without a doubt! She was very good that way. And she
looked after Leslie.

W: Did she?

J: Oh, she did! She chucked all Leslie's rubbish out of the house – and
Leslie brought it back in again!

B: Women don't understand those things, man. No!

J: And there was a battle between the two of them and in the end she
went away.

B: Women don't understand things like that!

J: Aye, that's right! He was good at tough tasks, Leslie, but he didn't
know about what I'd call taking care. And he was bad at keeping
things in order, and he broke everything he laid hands on.

B: He was a powerful man, wasn't he?

J: Oh, he was, he was!

B: He had great strength!

J: Aye, rather rough and ready and he worked on the highways and
so on … but he was extremely cheerful!

W: Oh, he was always cheerful!

J: And always making jokes!

---

[16] The warden's cottage next to *Thie ny Gaelgey*.

18   The war grave

J: Talking of Manx, an interesting thing happened to me a week or two ago. We were going to mention the names, the names of all the people who died in the war, in both wars, in Kirk Andreas, and I was looking for more information about them, because it's no good just mentioning names; I was looking for information about where they lived in Kirk Andreas, so as to tell people where they were from, and what happened to them, in the war, and there was a man called Freddie Quine and he was in the RAF ...

W: He was a relation of mine, Freddie Quine ...

J: Well, probably, and he was a relation of the member of Tynwald ...

W: Edgar. That's right.

J: Aye, and I phoned Edgar about it and he said, you ought to phone a woman called Myrtle in Ramsey. Anyway, Myrtle told me, 'I've got a picture of the man's grave, he was shot down in the war and he was flying a Lancaster ...'

W: That's right!

J: '... a bomber, and he was shot down in Germany a long way over on the other side,' and anyway Myrtle said, 'I've got a picture of that man's grave in Germany, a man went to look for the name of a man – of another man and he saw the stone with "Quine" on, and he said, "that must be a Manxman," and no doubt he took a picture of it.' And when I looked at the picture of that head-stone I saw there was Manx on it!

B: Really!

J: Yes, there was Manx on it, and the Manx was:

> *Rest in peace*
> *My most valiant son*
> *Far from the shores and hills of Ellan Vannin*

W: Indeed!

J: On that stone in Germany!

W: Freddie!

J: Freddie Quine!

W: Really!

J: And I said to Myrtle 'What do you think about the Manx? I'm thrilled about it!' And she said: 'I thought it was German!'

Glossary

Where appropriate, examples are given in Manx. But don't expect a Manx example for everything, because Manx deals with some of these phenomena in a different way from English. For this reason, where a Manx example would only cause confusion, the examples are given in English only. Also, some of the terms, such as relative, rather inconveniently have more than one meaning, or else refer to something that doesn't happen in English; one example of this is the contrast between the independent and dependent forms of the verb.

A term which is underlined has its own entry in this glossary.

Note: the abbreviation *a.m.s.* stands for *as myr shen*, which is one way of writing 'etc.' in Manx.

Accusative
See case. The accusative is the case of the direct object.

Active and passive sentences
Many verbs can be active or passive, for example, 'bite': (a) The dog bit Joney (active); (b) Joney was (got) bitten by the dog (passive). In the active sentence (a) the subject (the dog) performs the action. So sentence (a) is mainly about what the dog did. In the passive sentence (b), the subject (Joney) is on the receiving end, and the sentence is mainly concerned with her. The two sentences give similar information, but there is a difference in focus.

Actor-noun
An actor-noun denotes a profession or occupation: *greasee*, cobbler; *ferynsee*, teacher; *dunver*, murderer.

Adjective
An adjective is a word which describes ('qualifies') someone or something: *jiarg*, red; *mooar*, big; *shenn*, old.
* Adjectives may be used attributively or predicatively.

- In English, adjectives used attributively precede the noun: the **big** house; my **old** chum; **dirty** boots; the teenager's **disgusting** room.

- Adjectives used <u>predicatively</u> are separated from the object they describe by a verb: the house looked **huge**; we all felt **horrified**; his boots were **filthy**; his room smelt **disgusting**.

The situation is different in Manx because the verb is typically the first word in a sentence, and also because most Manx adjectives, even attributive adjectives, always follow the <u>noun</u>: *y thie mooar*, the **big** house.

- There are some exceptions: a small number of adjectives always go in front of their <u>noun</u>. One of the commonest is *shenn*, old:

  shenn *charrey*   **old** friend

- Predicative adjectives follow the <u>noun</u> in both Manx and English in <u>equative</u> cases such as:

  *T'eh cho **shenn** as ny sleityn*
  He's as **old** as the hills

  (Manx also has other options to express this).

  But where English would have: Leslie was funny, modest, kindly Manx has the verb first: *Va Leslie aitt, imlee, caarjoil*

- Manx adjectives may change their form according to whether the <u>noun</u> they accompany is feminine or masculine <u>gender</u>, or (sometimes) plural:

  ben vooar   a big woman, big woman
  dooinney mooar   a big man, big man
  deiney mooarey   big men

Adverb

An adverb is a word which 'modifies' a <u>verb</u> by adding information. Adverbs may tell you such things as:

- When: *T'eh jannoo eh jiu*
  He is doing it **today**

- Where: *T'eh jannoo eh ayns shoh*
  He's doing it **here**

- How: *T'eh jannoo eh dy tappee*
  He's doing it **quickly**

- How often: *T'eh jannoo eh **dy mennick***
  He does it **often**

Adverbs may also intensify another adverb or adjective:

feer vooar	**very** big
lane tappee	**extremely** quickly

Often the Manx adverb follows the word it intensifies:

*graney **atçhimagh***	**horribly** ugly
*troggit **mirrilagh***	**miraculously** built

[*Pargys Caillit*: 226]

Note: *Pargys Caillit* often omits the *dy* in adverbs formed from adjectives. Poetry doesn't have to abide by the same rules as the rest of us.

Adverbial clause

An adverbial clause is a group of words clustered around a <u>verb</u>, which tell:

When: he visits *every Friday evening* (**fastyr Jeheiney**)
Where: they sit **in the garden** (**ayns y gharey**)
How: he speaks **in a low voice** (**ayns coraa dowin**)

Affirmative sentence

Positive statement, i.e. one that is neither a question (<u>interrogative</u>) nor negative.

Va mee ruggit as troggit ayns Ellan Vannin.
I was born and raised in Man.

Affix

An affix is a <u>morpheme</u> which is not itself a word, but is attached to a word. It may change the meaning of the word. This <u>morpheme</u> may be

- a <u>prefix</u>:

  aavlass, **after**taste; *neu-chiart*, **in**correct

- or a <u>suffix</u>:

  sheeoil, peace**ful**; *eeasteyr*, fisher**man**

Affixes often

- make a word mean the opposite:

  mee-arrey, reck**less**; *neuchreestee*, **un**christian

- make it feminine:

  ben-cloieder fillym, film act**ress**

- make an 'agent <u>noun</u>', i.e. someone who carries out the action of a <u>verb</u>:

  shelgeyr, hunt**er**

- make an <u>adjective</u> from a <u>noun</u>:

  sheeoil, peace**ful**

- create a <u>diminutive</u>:

  jesheen, trinket ('little fancy thing')

Agent

In a <u>passive sentence</u>, (see <u>active and passive sentences</u>) the person or thing responsible for the action of the <u>verb</u>, preceded in English by 'by', and often in Manx by '*ec*', is called the agent:

> *Va'n uinnag brisht ec **drogh guilley***
> The window was broken by **a wicked boy**

> *Grine er grine ta geidit voue, Skeabit **ec ny tonnyn mooarey***
> Grain on grain that's stolen from them, Swept by **the big waves**
> [R. C. Carswell, 'Slyst ny Marrey', *Shelg yn Drane*, 1994]

Antecedent

The word, phrase or clause to which a pronoun refers. In the sentence '**Solomon, who** built the temple, reigned for 40 years', 'Solomon' is the antecedent of the pronoun 'who'. Both refer to the same person. Relative pronouns such as 'who' and adverbs such as 'where' can in many cases, although not in the above example, be omitted in English (the man [**whom, that**] I saw; the place [**where**] I used to live), etc., and are usually not needed in Manx, even when they would be needed in English:

> *Shinyn [...] va ruggit tra ren sheel nyn ayrey snaue*
> *Dy gholl stiagh ayns ooh.*
> We **who** were born when the seed of our father swam
> To enter into an egg.
> [R. C. Carswell, 'Kione Vaghal', *Shelg yn Drane*, 1994]

Apposition

Two <u>nouns</u>, <u>pronouns</u> or noun phrases which both perform the same function in the sentence are placed side by side:

> *Va **Benainshter Kinvig, yn ven-loayreyder dooghyssagh jerrinagh**, 78 bleeaney d'eash.*
> **Mrs Kinvig, the last female Native Speaker**, was aged 78.

Here 'Mrs Kinvig' and 'the last female native speaker' both act as <u>subject</u> of the sentence. Either phrase could be left out and the sentence would still make sense, but the two phrases each express an additional detail about the lady in question, i.e., her name, and the fact that she was the last female speaker.

Nish va Philip veih **Bethsaida, ard-valley Andreays as Peddyr**
Now Philip was from **Bethsaida, the city of Andrew and Peter**
[John i.44]

In this example, too, the sentence would be complete without one of the phrases in apposition, but each adds a little more information.

Article

In English the definite article has only one form: 'the'
In Manx 'the' may be *y, yn, ny,* depending on the circumstances.
In English the indefinite article **a** becomes **an** before a word starting with a <u>vowel</u>. There is no plural indefinite article in English.
Manx, however, like some other languages, including Latin, Russian and several far Eastern languages, has no indefinite article, either singular or plural.
Thus *dooinney mooar* can mean either 'a big man' or 'big man'.

Aspect

Verbal aspect differentiates between actions that are:

* on the one hand, 'ongoing' or 'repeated'.

These forms use verbs with the <u>morpheme</u> '-ing' in English and the resultant tense is called by various rather vague names including the 'progressive', 'continuous', 'habitual':

I am writing, I was writing, I was drinking two bottles a day then

* on the other hand, the action is perfective, completed:

I've written that letter now.
I had drunk two bottles by ten o'clock in the morning.

Aspiration

Aspirated sounds are usually represented by 'h'. In English, 'p', 't', 'k' are automatically 'aspirated'. This means that when they are pronounced it is if the sound is accompanied by a small puff of air, even though 'h' is not written. 'b' is not aspirated in English. Compare the pronunciation of Standard English 'boy' with standard Irish English, often written , 'bhoy'.
In Manx, the term 'aspiration' is often used as a synonym for <u>lenition</u>.

Attenuated vowel

The so-called 'broad' vowels are **a, o, u**; the 'slender' vowels are **e** and **i**. When attenuation occurs, the effect is that a broad vowel becomes slender.

> *Share as fer **s'gilley** jeh mooinjey y vadran (**gial**)*
> Brightest and best of the sons of the morning

Attributive comparison

> *y thie **syrjey*** the **tallest** house

Auxiliary verb

A <u>verb</u> which helps to form the <u>tenses</u>, etc., of other <u>verbs</u>.

- In English the principal auxiliary verbs are:

  be, have, do, and <u>modals</u> such as **may, can, must.**
  I **have** eaten my dinner; She **is** going out now; she **may** do it later; He **might** lend me the money if you **can't** or **won't**; you **did**n't **have to** do that.

- In Manx the principal auxiliaries include:

  ve (to be); *jannoo* (to do); and modals like

  fod (be able)

***Ta** mee goll*	I am going
***Ren** mee fakin eh*	I saw him

  ***Foddee** oo geddyn ad fegooish poosey*
  You **can** get them [women] without marrying them
  [Ned Maddrell (1877–1974)]

Cardinal numbers

Numbers used for counting

> **one, two, three**, etc.
> *nane, jees, tree, a.m.s.*

Case

That aspect of a noun or pronoun which relates to its function in the sentence. The cases to which brief reference may be made in this book are the <u>nominative</u>, <u>vocative</u>, <u>accusative</u>, <u>genitive</u>, <u>dative</u>.

- Traditionally, the <u>nominative</u> was the case for the <u>subject</u> of the sentence. The subject 'drives' the action:

  The boy gave his mother's best shoes to Oxfam

- The accusative was for the direct object of the verb:
  The boy gave his mother's **best shoes** to Oxfam
- The genitive expresses possession or ownership:
  The boy gave **his mother's** best shoes to Oxfam
- The dative was the case for the indirect object, often marked by 'to'
  in English or '*da*', '*rish*' in Manx:
  The boy gave his mother's best shoes **to Oxfam**
- The vocative addresses someone directly:
  'Hey **Ealish**, did you know that wretched boy's gone and given
  your best shoes to Oxfam?'

Today, except in 'fixed' expressions, neither Manx nor English shows
the different cases as strongly as in the past, or as some languages still
do. In English, nouns no longer change their form when the case changes,
except for the genitive, which adds the morpheme 's' with an apostrophe:
Ealish's best shoes; **workers'** rights.

But pronouns in English still change to show case:

He (subject, nominative) sees **them** (direct object, accusative);
they (subject, nominative) see **him** (direct object, accusative)

In Manx, however, in the corresponding pair of sentences, the pronouns
do not change:

*T'***eh** *fakin* **ad**, *t'***ad** *fakin* **eh**

There are now only two cases in Manx, besides the vocative: the
nominative and the genitive, and the genitive is only shown in a small
number of nouns, mostly feminine, e.g. *blein*, year, gen. *bleeaney*.

Classical Manx
The language of the eighteenth-century Biblical and other religious
translations

Clause
A group of words containing a finite verb, i.e., a verb which is marked
for tense, number and person, and is not an infinitive or participle. A
sentence is made up of one or more clauses.

- A clause may be main or subordinate, introduced by a subordinating conjunction: a joining-word which links subordinate clauses
  to each other, or to main clauses: English examples of subordinating conjunctions include:
  because, while, so that, if, unless, when.

Manx subordinating conjunctions include:

er y fa, choud, dy, tra, mannagh, my.

Main clauses are linked together by a co-ordinating <u>conjunction</u>.
In Manx the co-ordinating <u>conjunctions</u> are *as, agh, ny*.
In English, these correspond to **and, but, or**.
Two main clauses linked by a co-ordinating conjunction:

Hug eh feoh da Peddyr *as* **hug eh graih da Breeshey**
He hated Peddyr and **he loved Breeshey**

- Main clause and subordinate clause linked by a subordinating conjunction (*er y fa*):
Hug eh feoh da Peddyr, *er y fa dy* **dug eh graih da Breeshey**
He hated Peddyr because **he loved Breeshey**

Collective noun
A collective noun is singular in form but plural in meaning, and takes a singular verb:

This furniture **is** really old-fashioned
A **gang** of yobs **has** been terrifying old ladies

When a collective noun means the individual members of the group, the verb is plural: consider the difference between:

The **audience** was enormous (a big crowd turned up)
The **audience** were enormous (two seats each required!)
My **family** is big (with many members)
My **family** are big (none of us is a sylph)

In Manx, a collective noun such as *mooinjer*, folk, requires a plural <u>adjective</u> which may <u>lenite</u>:

mooinjer veggey   little people

Comparative
The 'comparative' refers to <u>adjectives</u> and <u>adverbs</u>.
    Regular English <u>adjectives</u> and <u>adverbs</u> form the comparative either by adding -er or by using 'more'.

whiter than snow; **holier** than thou
more beautiful than an angel
Thomaase ran **faster**; he competed **more successfully** than Ealisaid did

Myr s'niessey da'n chraue s'miljey yn eill
The **nearer** the bone the **sweeter** the meat

Compound noun
A compound noun is a noun which is made up of two or more words, usually two nouns:

Glenney-feeyney	wine-glass
Thie-bee	restaurant

or a noun and an adjective:

pensyl gleashagh	propelling pencil
drogh-haghyrt	accident

Complement
The complements add information about the <u>subject</u> or the <u>object</u> of the sentence:

- subject complement:

  The girl is now **a student**
  His brother grew **crazier** day by day

- Object complement:

  Every year they make him **the chairman**
  They were made **redundant**

Complex sentence
A sentence with one main <u>clause</u> and one or more <u>subordinate clauses</u>. The sequence in the example is <u>main/subordinate/subordinate</u>:

John Betjeman wished/ that bombs would fall on Slough/ so that it would be flattened

Concessive comparison
The ordinary concessive comparison is so called because something is being conceded or admitted: there is an understood 'however' or 'although' in constructions like 'bad as she is, her mother was worse' ('I concede that she was bad; however, her mother was worse'; 'although she is bad, her mother was worse'). The Manx comparative/superlative is used in cases like this.

Note: In American English 'as' is used twice: 'As hard as I tried I could not get the key in the lock') Standard British English would have: 'Hard as/though I tried ...'

s'doo yn feeagh yiow eh sheshey
(As) black as the raven is, he'll find a mate

Conditional
A conditional sentence is one in which one thing depends upon another:

>I'll help you if I can
>I would kick you if I had the strength

A conditional sentence can refer to an imaginary situation, an unreal or hypothetical statement:

>**If I were you, I should keep quiet** (but then I'm not you)
>**I wish he would keep quiet** (but I fear he won't !)

The conditional tense is a special form of the Manx verb which expresses the sort of idea communicated by 'would' in English sentences like:

>I wish he **would** just shut up!
>If I'd had the money I **would** have helped you out
>If I were a cat **I would** snooze all day

>*dy **beagh** eh ayns shoh*
>if he were here (but he isn't)

See also subjunctive under mood.

Conjugation
Set of inflections, or changes in form, of a verb.
   For example, English verbs typically:

* add '-s' to express third person singular: I eat, the panda eat**s**

* add '-(e)d' to form past tense: I want, I want**ed**; I like, I like**d**

Conjunction
A joining word which links clauses and expresses the relationship between them:

>co-ordinating conjunctions: English: **and, but, or.**

Co-ordinating conjunctions link two main clauses:

>I did but see her passing by
>**And** yet I love her till I die
>Ealish stubbed her toe **and** cursed furiously
>You can eat that spaghetti **or** you can go hungry
>Taig looked for Eunys **but** she had left

* Manx: *as*, 'and'; *agh*, 'but'; *ny*, 'or', link main clauses together:

>*V'eh aeg agh **v'eh** daaney dy liooar*
>He was young **but** he was bold enough

*V'ee boght **agh** v'ee ynrick*
She was poor **but** she was honest

* subordinating conjunctions introduce <u>subordinate clauses</u>:

*V'eh cadjin, **er-yn-oyr** dy row eh coar*
He was popular, **because** he was kind

Consonant
In English and Manx, all sounds in speech are consonants, except for the five <u>vowels</u> -a-, -e-, -i-, -o-, -u-, either alone or combined to form <u>diphthongs</u>, and also final 'y' in words like 'silly', 'utterly', where -y sounds like -i.

Some consonants can be either 'broad' or 'slender' depending on their surroundings. These include -d-, -t-, -l-, -r-, -n- and -ng.

Copula
The copula is a 'linking verb' which means 'am, are, is, was, were'. It has but few forms and is only used in restricted circumstances. It is as if you were to write the symbol = without loss of meaning, e.g.

***She** thie eh*	**It's** a house (it = house)
***Nee** uss yn fer lhee?*	Are you the doctor?
She	**I am**
***She** Tarzan mish*	**Me** Tarzan
***Nee** uss Jinn?*	**You** Jane?

In the last two examples, you could omit the copula in Manx also: *Mish Tarzan, uss Jane*

Dative
The dative is typically the <u>case</u> of the <u>indirect object</u>:

Moses gave the Commandments to **the Israelites**
Jinnag gave **her poodle** a boiled sweet

Declension
The so-called 'declension' of a noun lists the various 'cases'. In some languages, such as Latin, German and Russian, nouns, pronouns and adjectives change their form according to the 'case' required by the **function** the word is performing in the sentence; case shows a word's relationship with other words in the sentence (nouns acting as subject, direct object, indirect object and so on). This is much easier than it sounds, because the only cases still used in modern Manx for most nouns are: <u>nominative</u>, <u>vocative</u> and <u>genitive</u>.

Defective verb
Defective verbs are verbs with an incomplete paradigm, i.e., one which does not exhibit all forms typical of regular verbal conjugation. Thus 'ought' is an example of a defective verb in English and *lhis*, ought, a Manx one, because they lack many forms possessed by full verbs – they may have no real present tense, infinitive or past participle.

For example, though 'to want', 'wanting' and 'wanted', etc., are acceptable forms of 'want', * to ought, *oughting, *oughted are impossible, because 'ought' simply lacks these forms. *Lhisagh* only has the endings of the conditional: *lhisin, lhisagh oo, eh, ee*, etc.

Demonstrative
The demonstratives, which belong to the class of determiners, point out exactly which person or thing is being referred to.

> English: **this, that, yon**
> Manx: *shen, shoh, shid*

> **Shoh** *jerrey yn çhiaghtoo vlein*
> **This** is the end of the seventh year
> > [Phil Gawne, *Dooraght* 28, December 2002]

Manx demonstratives combine with prepositions, especially *ayns*, to form 'here, there, over yonder':

> *Ta sleayd baa **ayns shoh** ayns y thalloo bog*
> There's a cow's trail here in the soft ground
> > [Brian Stowell, *Dhooraght* 36, December 2004]

Depalatalised consonant
Depalatalisation means that a consonant which was palatalised is so no longer. (The English word 'Canon' = 'canyon' with a depalatalised 'n'.) Depalatalisation of one consonant may affect other elements.

Dependent form of verb
The dependent is the name given to the form of the Manx verb which has to be used in questions and negatives, and after certain conjunctions and particles, especially *dy* and *nagh*:

> *Vel oo goll?*   Are you going?
> *Cha **nel** mee goll*   I'm not going.
> *Dooyrt mee **dy row** eh goll*   I said that he was going

Compare Independent form

Diminutive

Diminutives express smallness, often by means of a <u>suffix</u>, in English, typically, '-kin', '-ette' and '-let': mannikin, maisonette, twiglet, etc.

Manx has three sets of suffixes which form diminutives: -in/-een; -an/-ane; -ag/-age.

> *jallooeen*, statuette
> *rolteen*, starlet, asterisk

Diphthong

A diphthong is a complex <u>vowel</u> sound made by gliding continuously from one vowel to another within the same syllable: e.g. -ou- in 'house', '-oi-' in 'coil'

In Manx, *gaaue*, smith; *geayagh*, windy

Direct object

The direct object receives the action of the main verb and its <u>case</u> is <u>accusative</u>.

> *T'eh er chur **feysht***
> He has asked **a question**

> *Hooar mee **screeuyn** jea*
> I received a **letter** yesterday

In English sentences, the <u>case</u> and function of <u>nouns</u> is shown by word order: compare:

> 'man bites **dog**'
> 'dog bites **man**'

In the first, the dog gets bitten. In the second, the man gets bitten. This is because the direct object in a normal <u>active sentence</u> in English (i.e., where the order has not been changed for stylistic reasons in such cases as: 'A cloud saw Matilda in the azure sky') is <u>after</u> the main <u>verb</u>. (Normal order: Matilda saw **a cloud** ...)

In <u>pronouns</u>, change of <u>case</u> may be shown by a difference in form between the pronoun acting as <u>subject</u> and the pronoun acting as object:

He saw **me**: I saw **him**

Dual

daa, jees, mean 'two' in Manx. The noun remains singular after *daa*, but the adjective is plural, if it is the kind of adjective that has a different plural form

Elision
Elision is a slurring, blurring or running together with surrounding vowels, or omitting a sound, e.g. *laccal* becomes la:l

Emphasis
Emphasis is used to stress the importance of one particular word in a group. In both English and Manx this is done by word order, and sometimes by the addition of 'self', *-syn, -hene,* etc., e.g.:

Ren **mish** *eh*	I did it **myself**
Va seyrsnys oc **hene**	They **themselves** were free

Equative
Equatives 'equate' one thing with another:

as far as I can see; as good as new; as old as the hills

Final position, finally
A sound or letter occurring at the end of a word, e.g. *-y* in *moddey,* -l in thoughtful, is said to occupy 'final position', or to occur 'finally'.

Finite verb
The finite verb is 'marked' in English in three ways:

- Number: as singular/plural: she writes, they **write**

- Person: as first, second or third person: **I write**, **you write**, **she writes**

- Tense: as referring to future, present, or past actions, states or events, e.g. 'he will write', 'he **writes**', 'he **wrote**'. The English future is formed with auxiliary 'shall, will' + infinitive without 'to'.

- Because Manx operates with the verbnoun and auxiliary verbs, and cannot form the present tense in any other way, the situation is slightly different.

Future
The verbal tenses which refer to actions, states or events which have not yet happened and therefore lie in the future:

Hee'm *eh Jemayrt*	I **shall see** him on Tuesday

Gender
Grammatical gender is distinct from natural gender. Many languages, including those in the Celtic, Romance, Germanic and Slavic groups,

allocate a grammatical gender to every noun in the language, not just those which denote people or animals. So every noun in Manx is, in theory at any rate, assigned to either masculine or feminine gender, but in many cases it is not possible to do this. (Learned works have been written which seek to analyse why, in German, the word for 'moon' is masculine and the word for 'sun' feminine, while in French it is the other way round. No problems in Manx, where both are feminine!) In reality, the principles by which inanimate nouns are classified as either masculine or feminine appear fairly arbitrary and also unstable. In some languages you can guess by looking at the form of a noun whether it is more likely to be masculine or feminine, but this is not usually possible with Manx nouns. Also, some Manx nouns have switched their gender through time, and not even for such obvious reasons as *caillin*, girl, which clearly denotes a female person but was originally masculine in grammatical gender.

Genitive
The genitive expresses possession or 'belonging to'. English does this by adding 's or s', or by using 'of': The man's boots; Harral's trainers; the teachers' room; the Book of the Dead; the Workers' Charter; the pen of my aunt; Juan's money and Catreeney's sweet nature meant that the Wattersons' marriage was tranquil and the home of the Wattersons a haven of peace
  See case.

Gerund
The gerund is the name given to a noun formed from a verb. In English, the verb forms gerunds by adding the suffix '-ing' to the stem, or base form, of the verb: 'leave – leaving'. English has a habit of using '-ing' to form various words, but in this case the result ('leaving') is a noun. This can be confirmed because, like other nouns, this new noun can now:

- take an article (It's not **the leaving** of Liverpool that grieves me)

- take an adjective (Stop that **awful screaming!**)

- or form a plural (His **jottings** and **writings** were of no importance to anyone but himself).

  In Manx the verbnoun does not usually need to change its form, although verbnouns which begin with a vowel often add a prefixed *g-*:
(Gerund):

> *va mee currit da'n eeastagh*
> I was sent to **the fishing**   [Ned Maddrell (1877–1974)]

(Verb):

> *va shin* **geeastagh** *skeddan magh ass Purt ny hInshey*
> we **fished** for herring off Peel

Homographs
Words with different meanings and/or sounds written the same, e.g.
English 'bow' (bend) /'bow' (archery instrument, and other meanings),
'row' (row a boat, corn rows, etc./ 'row' (argument, loud noises)

Homophones
Words which sound the same but often have different spellings (compare
English 'four', 'for', 'fore')

Idiolect
Mannerisms and speech habits which make up an individual's unique
way of speaking.

Idiom
Special constructions in a language which often have a different meaning
from that of the individual words. English examples include 'flying off
the handle' (to fly into a rage); Manx examples include *'corree jiarg'*,
furious ('red anger'), etc.

Imperative
This is the <u>verb</u> form used to:

- give instructions:

  Cass *er dty heu yesh*
  Take the turning to your right

- issue commands:

  Gow *ayns shee*
  as ***ny jean*** *peccah reesht*
  Depart in peace/and **sin** no more
  > [Thomas Parnell, The Hermit, l.286]

- or invitations:

  My Vainsteryn ooilley ***gow boggey***
  So I pray you, my masters, **be merry**
  > ['Kione y Vuc' (Boar's Head Carol) tr. Paul Helps,
  > *Dhooraght* 36, December 2004]

- or pleas and entreaties:

  Cur *dooin nyn arran jiu as gagh laa as* **leih** *dooin nyn loghtyn ... as*
  ny leeid *shin ayns miolagh*

Give us this day our daily bread and **forgive** us our trespasses ...
and **lead** us **not** into temptation

[The Lord's Prayer]

Some Manx verbs have special forms for the Imperative. These forms may not look as if they belong to the same verb (just as, in English, 'went' does not appear to belong to 'go', or 'was' to 'be').

Tar! Come! (from *çheet*); ***Immee!*** Go! (from *goll*)

There is an alternative way of forming imperatives in Manx too. The imperative form of *jannoo* may be used to form the imperative of virtually every other Manx verb: *Jean cummal!* Hold! (This happens in English with 'do', where the effect is emphatic: Do be quiet! Do have some more pizza!)

Imperfect

The imperfect tense expresses actions which took place in the past, especially where the action is either:

- ongoing:

  He **was beating up** his wife when the police broke in

- or repeated:

  He **was** always **beating her up**

Inanimate

An inanimate object is something that is not living and has neither soul nor mind. Thus humans, animals, insects and fish are animates, but plant life, although from a biological point of view 'living', is thought of as inanimate.

Indefinite adverb

ennagh, *erbee*, English 'any-', '-ever' ('whatever', 'anyone', etc.), form 'indefinite' adverbs like wherever, anywhere, anyone, etc., with the meaning 'anywhere at all', and so on.

Independent form of verb

This is the name given to the form of the Manx verb used in affirmative statements:

Ta mee goll   I am going

Unlike English, Manx uses different forms of the verb according to whether the sentence is affirmative, interrogative, negative. Compare dependent form.

Indirect or dative object
The person or thing to whom something is given, said, passed, hinted, etc., is called the 'indirect' or 'dative' object:

> *As dooyrt ish **rish y vummig***
> She told **her mother**

> Jinnag's poodle gave **her** his paw
> The boss paid **the workers** a pittance

See case.

Indicative
A verb which is neither an interrogative (asking a question) nor an imperative (a command, instruction, invitation or plea) is said to be in the indicative mood.

> ***Huitt** eh sheese ayns y jeeig*
> He **fell** down into the ditch
>
> [Thomas Christian (1851–1930)]

> *V'ad **laccal** feeyn*
> **They lacked** wine   [John ii.3]

Indirect or reported speech
Where speech is reported indirectly (no quotation marks) it is called 'indirect' or 'reported' speech:

> He said: 'I will go.' (direct speech).
> He said **he would go** (indirect or reported speech)

> *T'ad gra **dy vel eh ry fakin foast***
> They say **that he is to be seen yet**
>
> [Thomas Christian (1851–1930)]

> *Dooyrt Einstein **dy vel traa lhoobagh bentyn rish foaynoo yn chymbyllaght mygeayrt y mysh***
> Einstein said **that time is variable depending on the state of its environment**
>
> [P. Gawne, *Dhooraght* 16, December 1999]

Infinitive
The base form of the verb, with (in English) no additional endings, and, unlike the finite form, unmarked for number, person or tense, but very often preceded by 'to':

> **To be** or **not to be**: that is the question
> 'Tis better **to have loved** and lost
> than never **to have loved**

To be born poor is **to have been born** free
I am going **to speak** about verbs

Sometimes in Manx the infinitive is preceded by *dy, ry, y,* or *gyn, dyn* in negatives:

(Ben) elley va jannoo oalys son **dy freill** *yn uill*
Another woman who was making a charm for **to stop** the blood
[Ned Maddrell (1877–1974)]

Abbyr rish Illiam **dyn traaue** *y magher*
Tell William **not to plough** the field

Inflected tense
The inflected tenses are one-word <u>tenses</u> constructed by changing the form of the verb itself, rather than by using <u>auxiliaries</u> such as *ve,* 'be'. For example:

coayl (lose): *chaill mee* (I lost); *chaillin* (I sh/would lose)

Inflection
The change of form by which a word indicates a change of grammatical relationship by means of adding different <u>morphemes</u>. Take the English verb walk:

- To form third sing. present of most English verbs, add the morpheme '-s' = walk**s**
- To form past <u>tense</u> and past <u>participle</u>, add the morpheme '-ed' = walk**ed**
- To form present <u>participle</u>, etc., add the <u>morpheme</u> '-ing' = walk**ing**

<u>Adjectives</u> and <u>adverbs</u> may inflect to form the <u>comparative</u> and <u>superlative</u>: **old**, <u>comparative</u> old-**er**, <u>superlative</u> old-**est**.

In Manx, <u>verb tenses</u> may be formed by inflection:

Cummym, I shall hold; *cummee eh*, he will hold; *chummin*, I sh/would hold (*cum* hold, keep)

Initial position, initially
A sound or letter which appears at the beginning of a word, e.g. *f-* in *fer; m-* in *moddey,* is said to occur 'in initial position', or 'initially'.

Intensifier
An adverb which heightens or lessens the meaning of the word it modifies:

feer vie   **very** good

Interrogative
Interrogatives are questions:

> *Quoi oo-hene?* Who are you?
> *Vel oo credjal?* Dost thou believe? [John i.50]

Intransitive verb
An intransitive verb is one which does not require an object:

> He is **sleeping**. She **laughed**. They **were arguing**.
> The fig tree **died**. Jesus **wept**.

These are complete statements, in the way that 'He **made** ...' is not, because we need to know WHAT he made in order for the statement to make sense.
   Many verbs can function as both transitive and intransitive: Juan ran. Juan ran a mile. Peddyr smelled. Peddyr smelled a rat.

Inversion
The expected word order within the sentence is changed. See Direct object, above.

Jussive
The 'jussive' gives an instruction for something to happen, or expresses an exhortation or encouragement:

> 'Let him be taken away to a place of execution'
> 'Let there be no argument about trivia'; 'Let us pray!'
> 'Let the hills rejoice!'

> *ny **lhig** da jymmoose ve ny mast'eu*
> **Let not** anger be amongst you   [John vi.43]

Lenition
Lenition is one of the main sound changes, or mutations, in Manx. Lenition, sometimes called 'aspiration', is a process whereby certain consonants appearing at the beginning of a word (in 'initial' position') are made 'softer' or 'weaker' in certain circumstances:

> *Ben*, woman or wife, changes to *ven* after *e*, his
> E *ven*, his wife (see 1)

Main clause
A main clause is a complete sentence or independent clause. It makes a statement which can stand alone if it has to, or be linked with other clauses:

> **The sun rose**   as it always did

Jole sulked	because he was unpopular
Paayl was hopeful	that he would win the prize
Voirrey sang,	although she'd been told to
	keep her mouth shut

↓	↓
Main <u>Clause</u>	<u>Subordinate</u>

Medial position, medially
A sound or letter found in the middle of a word, e.g -*dd*- in *moddey*; -*g*-
in *faagail*, -*d*- in 'subordinate', is said to occur 'in medial position' or
'medially'.

Modal verbs
Modals are auxiliary verbs which are used to express such ideas as
possibility, willingness, prediction, speculation, deduction, and necessity,
and in English are followed by an infinitive.

English modals include: shall/should, must/ought, can, will
Manx: *lhis, fod, shegin*, etc., used with a <u>verbnoun</u>.

> **Shegin** *dooin loayrt Gaelg, nagh* **nhegin** *dooin*?
> We **must** speak Manx, **mustn't** we?

> **Foddee** *shiu goll*   You **can** go

Mood of verbs
<u>Verbs</u> may have three moods:
* <u>Indicative</u>: the 'usual' mood: straightforward statement
  Ta *mee* **cosney**   I win, I am winning
* <u>Subjunctive</u>: expressing hypothesis, wishes, potentiality, uncertainty, obligation, desire, prediction, unreality
  Saillym **dy darragh** *oo*   I wish you **would come**
* <u>Imperative</u>: commands, etc.
  Irree *seose*! Get up!

Morpheme
The morpheme is the smallest unit of meaning. <u>Affixes</u> such as un-, -er,
-ness are morphemes in English.
Neu-, aa-, -agh are morphemes in Manx.
Words may consist of:
* one single morpheme (house) or more:
* (house/s, 2 morphemes)

- (house-keep/ing, 3 morphemes)
- (house-keep/er/s, 4 morphemes)

Mutation

Mutation is the name given to changes which occur in the sound and form of a Manx word, usually in accordance with rules:

- mutation affects the first letter(s) of the word. The three forms of change found in Manx are the two mutations:
- lenition (aspiration)
- nasalisation (eclipsis)
- Manx also sometimes calls for prefixed h- and n-, although this is not really a mutation

See 1, Initial sound change

Nasalisation

Nasalisation is one of the main forms of Mutation. It is sometimes called eclipsis. Typically, the effects of nasalisation are that unvoiced consonants (c, çh, f, k, p, t,) become voiced (g, j, v, g, b, d,) while voiced consonants (b, d, g, j,) become 'nasalised' to m, n, ng, n'gh, n'y. Like lenition, nasalisation affects the first element of a Manx word under certain circumstances: *beiyn*, animals; *nyn meiyn*, our/your/their animals. (See 1)

Nominal phrases

Nominal phrases, or noun phrases, are phrases or connected groups of elements in an ordered sequence which have a 'head noun' as their focus. This head noun may be preceded by an article, an adjective, or another noun. It may be followed by a prepositional phrase, a relative clause, an adjective, another noun, etc.

Jee ooilley-niartal   almighty God

Nominative

The case used for the grammatical subject of a sentence: **He** sees it. **The gods** defend us! **The cat** scratched Johnny-boy!

Noun

Nouns denote persons, things, states. Nouns can:

- take an adjective   **powerful** tornado
- or an article   **the** tornado
- a number   **one** tornado is enough
- a demonstrative   **this** tornado was the worst

- a <u>possessive</u>   **my** tornado was worse than yours
- (usually)* form <u>plurals</u>   tornado**s** are awesome
- act as the <u>subject</u>   **Tornados** ravaged America
- <u>object</u> (direct or indirect) I hate **tornados**

                            The Sheriff paid no mind to **the tornado**

- or <u>complement</u> of a verb   It was **a tornado**
- 'govern' a <u>preposition</u>   Florida was ravaged **by a tornado**

                            During the tornado, everyone was praying

* A few words (e.g. English 'sheep',) never show plural, or may have a slightly different meaning, such as 'varieties of', when they form plurals: 'fish'/ 'fishes', 'fruit', 'fruits')

Object
The object receives the action of the <u>verb</u>.

It may be direct: The dog bit **him**
or indirect: He said goodnight **to her**

See <u>direct</u> and <u>indirect object</u>, and <u>case</u>

Optative
The optative expresses a wish or desire:

Let the end come swiftly and peacefully!
Let me not be mad!

Ordinal numbers
The first, the second, the third, etc.
Yn chied, y nah, yn trass, a.m.s.

Palatalisation
Palatalisation involves the use of the blade of the tongue in the palatal region (the hard palate and the roof of the mouth) when pronouncing a sound. The Spanish 'ñ' is palatalised. For instance, in English 'piano' the 'p' is often palatalised so that you hear 'pyano' instead of 'pi-ano'. The 't' of English 'nature' is usually palatalised into 'ch'. The Spanish 'ñ' is palatalised: compare the pronunciation of 'n/ñ' in the girl's name 'Nina' and the Spanish 'El Niño'.

Paradigm

A paradigm is a structured set of forms with the same stem, one of which needs to be selected for each specific purpose. A major example of a paradigm is the verb paradigm.

The complete paradigm of a Manx regular verb is a combination of:

- inflected forms – imperative, future, conditional, preterite (simple past):

- periphrastic phrases utilising one of two auxiliaries, *ve*, be, or *jannoo*, do, which are marked to show the tense and person:

- *troggal*, lift(ing) (verbnoun) has inflected forms:

- *troggym*, I shall lift (inflected first person future tense)

  troggee, he, etc., will lift (most other persons, inflected future)

  hrog mee, I lifted (inflected past tense with first person singular pronoun)

  hroggin, I should lift (inflected first person conditional)

  hroggagh, would lift (inflected, all other persons, conditional)

  troggit, lifted (past participle)

Periphrastic tenses formed with auxiliary *jannoo*, *ve*, include: *ta mee troggal*, I lift/am lifting; *ren mee troggal*, I lifted; *va mee troggal*, I was lifting, used to lift

Participle

Present participle: in English, that '-ing' form which is used, not as a noun, like the gerund, (the **leaving** of Liverpool; the **Shining**; the **Greening** of America; the **Killing** of Sister George) but as either

- an adjective describing a noun:

  the **talking** mongoose; your **dancing** queen; the **thinking** woman's crumpet; the **mind-boggling** arrogance of Adolf and his henchmen

- or to form the 'continuous/progressive' tense of a verb:

  Don't you walk away when I'm **talking** to you; If you were **kicking** your sister you're in for trouble; the chimps were **rummaging** for fleas in each other's fur

Most Gaelic languages lack a present participle and use the verbnoun or a phrase instead:

*coraa fer **fockley-magh** ayns yn 'aasagh*
the voice of one **crying** in the wilderness

[John i.23]

Past participle: The English regular past participle ends in -ed:

I have **finished**; The house has been **painted**; The door is **closed** now

The Manx past participle usually ends in -*t*:

Ny buird nish **troggit**
The tables now (having been) set up

[Pargys Caillit: 247]

t'eh **soilshit** *magh dooin ec y cheayn …*
Ta'n slyst **aachummit** *lesh e phooar …*
Ta'n thalloo shoh **caghlaait** *dagh laa*

It's **demonstrated** to us by the sea …
The coastline is **reshaped** by its power …
This land is **changed** each day

[R. C. Carswell, 'Slyst ny marrey', Shelg yn Drane, 1994]

Particle

This minor part of speech often functions as

- place adjunct (he turned **down** the suggestion = rejected)

- intensifier (they closed **down** the factory = closed completely)

- perfective (drink **up** quickly = finish drinking), used to change the meaning of a verb.

One of the particles most frequently used in Manx is *dy* placed before an adjective, to form an adverb:

tappee, quick   *dy tappee*, quickly

Passive sentence

See active and passive sentences.

Active: The dog bit Joney

Passive: Joney was/got bitten by the dog
In a passive sentence, not only is the instigator of the action ('dog') less important, it could even be unstated, or unknown:

Poor Joney got badly bitten.
These cups **have been** inadequately **washed**
Another housing estate **is being built**
The window **has been broken** (by some vandal).

Manx has several ways of forming the passive (see 9).

Past tenses
<u>Verbs</u> or verbal constructions which refer to past events/states. Manx has a full range of options, both <u>inflected</u> and <u>periphrastic</u>:

Cheayll mee	I heard
Ren mee clashtyn	I heard
Va mee clashtyn	I heard, used to hear, was hearing
Ta mee er chlashtyn	I have heard
Va mee er chlashtyn	I had heard

Perfect tense
In English, the perfect <u>tense</u> is a <u>past tense</u> which is formed with <u>auxiliary</u> 'have'. It often implies a finished action rather than one which is ongoing:

He has forgotten Ealish; she **has been left** behind!

Future perfect, or future-in-the-past:

He **will have forgotten** Ealish by next week
I wonder how many people **will have been made** redundant by this time tomorrow

The situation in Manx is slightly different, because Manx does not have a verb 'to have', and for other reasons (see 9).

Periphrastic constructions
Periphrastic constructions are formed in English by using <u>auxiliary</u> <u>verbs</u> such as 'do,' 'be', 'have', Manx *'ve'*, *'jannoo'*, rather than by <u>inflections</u>.

- *Ren mee tilgey, va mee tilgey* = <u>periphrastic</u> past tenses in Manx. Both mean 'I threw', 'I was throwing'.

- *Hilg mee* = inflected past tense in Manx (*tilgey*, throw, has undergone initial mutation and lost the *-ey* ending to produce the equivalent of 'I threw'

- 'I threw' in English, *hilg mee* in Manx, are inflected past tenses, because the English verb 'throw' and the Manx verb *tilgey* have changed their base form

- whereas English 'I used to throw', 'I was throwing', Manx *ren mee tilgey, va mee tilgey*, are periphrastic constructions, because they use the <u>auxiliaries</u> 'used to' and 'was', *ren* and *va*, and the Manx verbnoun retains its base form, in this case, *tilgey* (see 9).

Person

First person refers to oneself (English I/we)

Second person refers to the person addressed (thou/you)

Third person refers to some thing or person other than the speaker and the person addressed (he, she, it, they, the bandersnatch, The Aussies, Tom, Dick and Harry, etc.)
In Manx the personal <u>pronouns</u> are:

		Singular		Plural
first person	*mee*	I, me	*shin*	we, us
second person	*oo, ou*	thou, you	*shiu*	you
third person (m)	*eh*	he, him (also usually 'it')		
third person (f)	*ee*	she, her both genders *ad*, they, them		

Note: As in some other languages, where the person addressed is an adult not on informal terms with the speaker, the second person plural (*shiu*) is used, for formality and courtesy, even when addressing one person only.

Phrasal prepositions

Phrasal prepositions are made up of several words, one of which is a preposition and one of which is often a possessive particle like 'my', 'dty':

> *er-my-hon*, for my sake; *er-dty-hon*, for your sake

Phrasal verbs

These are <u>verbs</u> which, by adding another element, take on a whole new meaning. Manx has many of these, and this is why a whole section has been devoted to them. (10, Phrasal Verbs).
In English, examples include:

> give + up = to renounce, surrender: he gave up easily

> fall + out = quarrel: they **fell out**

> find + out = discover; the police **found out** who was responsible

Manx:

> *cur + er bun* = to establish, found ('put' + 'on base')

> *goaill + arrane* = to sing ('take' + 'song')

> *geddyn + baase* = to die ('find' + 'death')

Phrasing
The sound-shape or pattern of spoken phrases and sentences, comparable to phrasing in music.

Pluperfect tense
The pluperfect refers to the distant past. In English, it is formed with 'had':

> He had forgotten Joney; she **had been left behind**

For the same reasons as those given under Perfect tense, see 9.

Plural
More than one of something. Opposite of singular.

child, **children**	bird, **birds**
paitçhey, ***paitçhyn/cloan***	*ushag,* ***ushagyn***

Possessive
The possessive marks ownership:
my, **your**, **his**, etc.   *my, dty, e, nyn*

Predicate
The rest of the sentence excluding the <u>subject</u>

Chalse	**then carefully searched the room**
↓	↓
Subject	**Predicate**

Predicative adjective
The predicative adjective is separated from its <u>noun</u> by a <u>verb</u> in English.

> The room was **empty**; the girl appeared **innocent**;
> We all felt **horrified**; his trainers smelled **repugnant**

Manx word order is different. See <u>adjective</u>, above

Prefix
A prefix is an <u>affix/morpheme</u> attached to the beginning of a word, with or without a hyphen, to alter its meaning, often making it mean just the opposite:

English in-: **in**correct;   un-: **un**grateful

Manx	*neu-:* ***neuchiart,***	incorrect
	mee-: ***meewooisal,***	ungrateful

Premodify
Adjectives are said to 'premodify' when they precede their noun. This is the normal word order in English for attributive adjectives (the old house, the dead beetle, the yellow brick road) whereas in Manx most attributive adjectives 'postmodify' or follow their noun (*y ven aalin*, the beautiful woman, literally, 'the woman beautiful'); Manx attributive adjectives like *drogh*, bad, and *shenn*, old, are therefore the exception, because they premodify or precede their nouns: *drogh earish*, bad weather; *shenn ven*, (an) old woman.

Preposition
Prepositions are small words like 'for', 'on', 'under', 'with', 'before', etc. (Manx: *son, er, fo, lesh, my, a.m.s.*) which indicate time, position, direction, instrument, etc.

Often, they are followed by a noun phrase:

Chymmylt *mysh dagh claare*
Round about each dish   [*Pargys Caillit*: 232]

Veih *çheer dy vel* **fo'n** *ghrian*
From any land **under** the sun   [*Pargys Caillit*: 238]

Agh **fo nyn gassyn** *hene ta mirrilyn dy liooar*
As markiagh **er y gheay** *ta feeagh braew mooar*
But **beneath our feet** there are miracles enough
And riding **on the wind** is a fine big raven
           [R. C. Carswell, 'Lomman', *Shelg yn Drane*, 1994]

ny **lurg shoh** *hee shiu niau foshlit*
after this you will see heaven opened   [John i.51]

lurg cliaghtey *ny Hewnyn*
following the custom of the Jews   [John ii.6]

Present tense
Refers to events/states going on **now**. Manx present tense is now always periphrastic, expressed with the present tense of *ve*, 'to be', + verbnoun:

Ta *mee* **fakin**   I see/I am seeing
Vel *oo* **goll?**   Are you going?
Cha nel *mee* **goll**   I'm not going

Preterite
Simple past tense formed without auxiliary verbs:

Hie *mee*   I **went**
The tyrant **died**   *Hooar yn tranlaasagh baase*

Pronoun
A word used instead of a <u>noun</u> or proper name, often to refer to some thing or person already mentioned:

> Juan counted his blessings: **they** were so few, **he** had soon finished
>
> Rome is the capital of Italy; **it** is a grand but noisy city
>
> I liked Status Quo; **they** were a good band
>
> Thobm tore off his hat and kicked **it**

- Personal pronouns are: **I, we, they**, etc.

  first person refers to the person or persons speaking (English I/we)

  second person refers to the person or persons being addressed (thou/you)

  third person refers to some thing(s) or person(s) other than the speaker and the person being addressed (he, she, it, they, the cat, the Babylonians, Liverpool supporters, the man in the moon, the river Jordan, etc.)

The pronouns *eh*, 'he, him', masculine, and *ee*, feminine, 'she, her', are used to refer to animate nouns, i.e. nouns denoting living beings such as people and animals, but for inanimate objects many people now use the masculine *eh* to mean 'it' for both genders.

- Indefinite pronouns are:

  someone, anybody, etc.:
  Anyone who had a heart
  You needed **someone**, but why did it have to be me?

- <u>Possessive</u> pronouns are:

  my, your, etc.
- <u>Interrogative</u> pronouns are:

  who? whose?, etc.
- <u>Reflexive</u> pronouns end in -**self**, -**selves**, in such sentences as:

  I hurt **myself**; you're getting above **yourself**; the cat washed **itself**

In Manx, -*hene* is added, see 3.4.2.

Pronoun-prepositions
Pronoun-prepositions are a main feature of the Celtic languages. They are special forms made up from prepositions combined with personal

pronouns, fused into a single word. This is all very different from what happens in English. The following simple prepositions combine with the seven personal pronouns to form single words:

> *ass*, out of; *ayns*, in; *da*, to; *ec*, at; *er*, on
> *fo*, under; *gys*, to; *jeh*, of; *harrish*, over;
> *mysh*, about; *liorish*, by; *rish*, to; *roish*, before;
> *veih*, *voish*, from; *lesh*, with (inanimates); *marish*, with (persons)

Pronoun-prepositions contribute to many idiomatic expressions in Manx.

Reflexive

A reflexive construction is one in which both the <u>subject</u> and the <u>object</u> (either direct or indirect) are identical: I saw **myself** in the mirror and screamed; I wash **myself sometimes**; he hurt **himself** badly; we saw **ourselves** as mighty warriors; I'm going to sit right down and write **myself** a letter; Why not treat **yourself** to a Mocca Chocca?

The pronouns in these examples, ending in -self, -selves, are 'reflexive' pronouns. In Manx these are usually formed by adding the suffix -*hene* to the pronoun.

Relative form

This is a special form of the Manx verb, required after certain <u>particles/conjunctions</u>:

> *my **ee-ys** dooinney erbee jeh'n arran shoh*
> if any man shall eat of this bread   [John vi.51]

The relative *vees* is used here after *my*, if, because the words refer to an indefinite time in the future, and also because possibly no man will eat the bread, bringing a hypothetical or subjunctive sense to the statement (see 9).

Relative clause

In English, a relative clause is introduced by a word such as **who, which, that**:

> Children **who eat too many sweets** get bad teeth
> The man **whose barn was burnt down** cursed Fate
> They fired the employee **who stole the money**
> Later a guest came **whom no-one knew**
> The horse **which won the National** had only three sound legs
> *This is the house **that Jack built**
> *This is the place **where I was born**
> *A man **whom I knew slightly** kept a tame giraffe
> *He confirmed a rumour **which I'd already heard**

* In the last four examples, the 'relatives' – the words **'that'**, **'where'**, **'whom'**, **'which'** – may be left out of the English sentences, and merely 'understood' without changing the meaning.

Manx usually does not need relative pronouns such as 'that', 'who', 'which':

> *Da'n Ayr ren y choyrt eh*
> To the Father **who** sent him   [John v.23]

> *'Yn dooinney mooar, va'n beaghey deyr 'ny hie ...'*
> 'The great, vain man, **who** fared on costly food ...'
> [Thomas Parnell, The Hermit, l.248]

> *... t'ad cur boirey*
> *Er liehbageyn – breck, kiare, jooigh – ta follit*
> ... they annoy
> the flatfish – plaice, sole, turbot – **that** are hidden
> [R. C. Carswell, 'Bun as Baare', *Shelg yn Drane*, 1994]

Stative
A stative verb refers to a state rather than to an action or event. Manx often has a special way of expressing this, by placing the possessive of the appropriate person (*my, dty, ny, nyn*) before the verbnoun, which is usually *shassoo*, stand; *soie*, sit; *cadley*, sleep; *lhie*, lie: *ta mee my hassoo*, I am standing; *ta fer ny hassoo*, one is standing amongst you.

Sometimes learners of Manx are told that this means something like: 'I am in-my-state-of' (see 9).

Stem
Basic form from which all other forms, especially <u>inflected forms</u> of <u>verbs</u>, are derived:

> Manx: *tilg-*, throw: stem or base form.
> Inflections include *hilg, tilgym, tilgey*, etc.

> English: throw-, stem or base form.
> Inflections include throw-ing, throw-s, threw

Subject
Within the sentence or <u>clause</u>, the subject is said to 'govern' the main verb and in English usually precedes it:

> <u>Active</u> sentence: **Jamys** left; **he**'d decided to leave Catreeney as soon as he could.

In the passive sentence, the person on the receiving end of the action is the subject, and appears first in the sentence in normal English syntax.

Passive sentence: **Catreeney** was abandoned; **she** was callously deserted by Jamys the moment he tired of her

Subjunctive
A mood of the verb used to express hypothesis, wishful thinking, indirect commands:

Saillym **dy darragh** *oo*   I wish you **would come**

Subordinate clause
A dependent, incomplete sentence, which needs a main clause with it in order to complete the message:

If you did that ...
Because you said that, ...
Although he is young, ...
As he was leaving the building ... etc. See clause.

Subordinate clauses are more frequent in English than in modern Manx, which appears to prefer a series of main clauses.

Suffix
A suffix is an affix or morpheme attached to the end of a word:

English: young, youth, youth**ful**
Manx: *aeg, aegid, aegoil*, young, youth, youngish

Superlative
The highest comparative form of an adjective or adverb:

Foddee yn moddey **s'jerree** *tayrtyn y mwaagh*
Maybe the **last** dog catches the hare

Tra **s'reaie** *yn cloie share faagail jeh*
When the play is **merriest**, 'tis better to leave off

(See 6)

Tense
Tense expresses the time an action, event or state is thought of as going on (present, future or past).
   Tense is shown either:
* by changes in the verb (inflections):
   hug mee, verym, I gave, I will give

- or by use of the auxiliary verbs (<u>periphrastic</u> construction):

  ren *mee cur,* **va** *mee cur,* **ta** *mee cur,* **nee** *eh cur*
  I gave, I was giving, I am giving, he will give

Note: In Manx the future is often expressed by an <u>inflected</u> tense, e.g.
verym, I shall give, whereas in English the future tense is always
formed with <u>auxiliary</u> verb 'shall, will'.

Transitive verb

<u>Verb</u> which can have a <u>direct</u>, or <u>accusative</u>, object:

We **beat them to a pulp**; They **guzzled all the ale**;
The wolf **gobbled up the infant**

Verbal phrase

The verbal phrase is a connected group of words with a finite verb as
its core. This verbal phrase may be either:

- a 'simple' verbal phrase centred around a simple verb:

  Nagh **dug** *oo ad?*   Didn't you send them?

- or a complex verbal phrase centred around a periphrastic
  construction comprising an auxiliary and a verbnoun:

  Ren *mee cur ad*   I did send them

Verbnoun

The verbnoun could be described as the cornerstone of Manx syntax.
The Manx verbnoun can function, without any change in its form, as a
noun rather than a verb in the sort of constructions traditionally known
as '<u>gerund</u>' constructions. These are constructions where English would
need to add the suffix '-ing' to a verb to form a gerund, or verbal noun,
which would then be able to perform all the functions within the
sentence that nouns perform, acting as:

subject: The lewd **dancing** appalled me;

object: I heard the insane incessant **ringing** of the bells: and so
on, and would also be able to form plurals by adding '-s', and to take
an article and adjectives if required:

After all **the savage beatings** his spirit was broken

In Manx, however, the verbnoun doesn't need to alter its form in order
to perform different functions:

giu, drink: *ta mee clashtyn dy vel eh* **coagyr**
I hear he **cooks**

Ta **coagyr** *taitnyssagh*   **Cooking** is enjoyable

The verbnoun is thus a versatile non-<u>finite</u> form (like English -ing forms such as 'doing', 'seeing', 'walking') which can be used with <u>auxiliaries</u> (*ve, jannoo*, <u>modals</u>) to form all <u>periphrastic tenses</u> in Manx, e.g.

- *Cha row mee rieau **eeastagh*** [sic] *aynshen*

  I never **fished** there

  [Ned Maddrell (1877–1974)]

- as well as being used as a noun

  *V'eh er goll er yn **eeastagh***
  He had gone to the **fishing**

  [Mrs Eleanor Karran (1870–1953)]

In reality, Manx often avoids using the verbnoun as a noun in 'nominal constructions', by introducing a finite verb or a prepositional phrase or some other device, or by omitting the verbnoun altogether:

*Agh veagh gaue ayn **dy beagh** rouyr sheshaghtyn ayn eisht.*
But then there would be a danger of [having] too many societies
                [Brian Stowell, *Dooraght* 16, December 1999]
(literally: 'but then there would be a danger that there would be too many societies')

*Va imnea imraait dy beagh Radio Vannin sluggey seose argid Ving Ymskeaylley Gaelgagh **lesh** y chlaare noa shoh.*
Concern was expressed that the Gaelic Broadcasting Committee's money would be swallowed up by Manx Radio **in putting on** this new programme.
(literally: '… Manx Radio would swallow up money with this new programme'). Same source.

- and even as a present <u>participle</u>. Most Gaelic languages lack a present <u>participle</u> and use the <u>verbnoun</u> or a phrase instead:

*coraa fer **fockley-magh** ayns yn 'aasagh*
the voice of one **crying** in the wilderness,

  [John i.23] (see 9)

Vocative
Manx, like Latin, uses the 'vocative case' when you speak directly to someone:

'Hey, Juan!' 'Oi, man!', 'Pass, friend!', 'Oh my honey!', and so on.

Many people remember Caesar's dying words in Shakespeare's play *Julius Caesar* and those who don't know Latin wonder why the great man exclaims 'Et tu, Brute?' Is he calling Brutus a brute? In fact, he's quite correctly using the vocative case of the name 'Brutus'. When addressing someone in Manx, the first letter of their name is lenited: so, someone called Moirrey becomes Voirrey when you speak to her directly; *Breeshey* becomes *Vreeshey!*

O God (*Jee*) becomes *O Yee!*
Friends! becomes *Chaarjyn!*

Voice
We speak of a verb being in the <u>active</u> or <u>passive</u> voice.
   Many verbs may be either <u>passive</u> or <u>active</u> in voice.
   The passive in English uses <u>auxiliary</u> 'be' + past <u>participle</u>.
   If the instigator (agent) of the action is known, it follows the <u>preposition</u> 'by'.

<u>Active</u>: Juan **ate** the cake.
<u>Passive</u>: The cake **was eaten by** Juan.

The agent may be omitted: The cake **was eaten**.
   There are several different options for forming the <u>passive</u> in Manx.

Voiced, voiceless
All vowels are 'voiced', i.e. the sound is made by vibrating the vocal chords. Consonants such as b, d, g, m, j, are voiced; p, t, k are unvoiced or voiceless. Some people recommend trying to hear the difference by pronouncing 't' and 'd' with your fingers in your ears, when only the 'd' can be heard.

Vowel
The vowels in English and Manx are: a, e, i, o, u.
   These vowels may combine to form <u>diphthongs</u>.
   In both languages, 'y' may be either a vowel or a <u>consonant</u>, depending on where in the word it occurs and the other sounds/letters it is combined with.

* Initially, 'y' in English is always consonantal:

   yellow: yawn; yob;

   <u>medially</u> and <u>finally</u> in English, 'y' is vocalic (vowel-like) though the sound it represents may differ:

   <u>medial</u>: babyish behaviour; psychotic;

   <u>final</u>: silly; serendipity; angry; horrify; fly; terrify

   <u>initially</u>, in Manx, 'y' followed by a vowel is consonantal, just as it would be in English: *yeean*, chick (young of bird);

   yiarn, iron; *yindys*, wonder

'y' followed by a consonant or consonants is vocalic (vowel-like):

ymmodee, many; *ynnyd*, place, site, location

- Medially and finally, combined with at least one vowel, 'y' is vocalic; it changes the length and quality of the other vowel or vowels:

  shiaulteyr, sailor; *shey*, six; *keyll*, forest
  jouyl, devil; *keayn*, ocean; *kayt*, cat
  moyrn, pride

- Medially (and finally too, although, in Manx words of more than one syllable, final 'y' is usually preceded by a vowel rather than a consonant) when it occurs after a consonant, or between two consonants, 'y' is vocalic.

  jymmoosagh, angry; *mwyllin*, mill; *dty*, your; *lommyrtagh*, sheep shearer; *tuarystal*, representation; *turrys taitnys*, pleasure trip

  Thus in the Manx word *yindyssyn*, wonders, 'y' is consonantal/vocalic/vocalic.

  In *ro yymmoosagh*, too angry, the lenited form of *jymmoosagh*, angry, 'y' is consonantal/vocalic.

Note: -i- and -e- are the 'slender' vowels:
-a-, -o, -u, and -y- are the 'broad' vowels.

Select bibliography

Note: YCG = The Manx Language Society

Broderick, G. 1984: *A Handbook of Late Spoken Manx*, Tübingen, Niemeyer Verlag

Clague, J. 1911: *Manx Reminiscences*, Oxford, Blackwell

Cregeen, A. 1835, repr. 1984: *Fockleyr ny Gaelgey*, Ilkley. YCG, Moxton Press

Fargher, D. 1979: *English–Manx Dictionary*, Douglas, Shearwater Press

Gell, J. 1954: *Conversational Manx*, Pt Erin, YCG

Gillies, William. 1993: 'Scottish Gaelic', in *The Celtic Languages*, ed. Martin J. Ball, London, Routledge, pp.145–227

Goodwin, E. 1901, repr. 1966: *First Lessons in Manx*, fourth edition, revised by R. L. Thomson, Ilkley, Scholar Press. YCG

Jackson, K. H. 1955: *Contributions to the Study of Manx Phonology*, Edinburgh, Nelson

Kelly, J. 1804: *A Practical Grammar of the Antient Gaelic, or Language of the Isle of Man, usually called Manks*, London, Nichols

Kelly, P. 1991: *Manx–English Dictionary*, Douglas, YCG

Kewley Draskau, J. 2006: *Account of the Isle of Man in Song: A New Translation*, Douglas, Centre for Manx Studies, Monograph, 5,

Kneen, J. 1970: *English–Manx Pronouncing Dictionary*, Isle of Man, YCG

— c 1938: *Manx Idioms and Phrases*, Ilkley, Scholar Press

— 1931: *A Grammar of the Manx Language*, Oxford, Oxford University Press

Mac Eoin, Gearóid. 1993: 'Irish', in Martin J. Ball, ed. *The Celtic Languages*, London, Routledge, pp. 101–44

Mackinnon, Roderick. 1971, repr. 1977: *Gaelic*, London, Hodder & Stoughton

Neddy Beg Hom Ruy. 1973: *Skeealyn 'sy Ghailck*, repr. Castletown Press, YCG (Printed in *Irish Folklore Society Journal*, 1948)

Pilgrim, Λ., and J. Kewley Draskau. 1991: 'Manx Gaelic: The Siege Continues. The Current State of Manx Gaelic, with especial reference to terminology', *International Journal for Terminology*, vol. 2 no. 2, pp. 76–81, Vienna

— forthcoming: *Oardagh Noa yn Erin*, Translation of the Latin Mass into Manx Gaelic for Use in Manx Catholic Churches

Pilgrim, A., and R. L. Thomson. 1988: *Outline of Manx Language and Literature*, St Jude's, YCG

Quirk, R., and S. Greenbaum. 1973: *A University Grammar of English*, London, Longman

Stowell, B. 2001: *Y Coorse Mooar*, Comprehensive Modern Manx Course, Douglas, YCG

Stowell, B., and D. O. Breaslain. 1996: *A Short History of the Manx Language*, first published May 1996 by An Clochán, Belfast

Stowell, B., and D. Fargher. 1986: *Abbyr shen*, tapes and text, Isle of Man, YCG

Thomson, R. L. 1960/1962–63: 'The Manx Traditionary Ballad', *Etudes celtiques*, IX, pp. 521–48; X, pp. 60–87

— 1969: 'The Study of Manx Gaelic', *Proceedings of the British Academy 55*, pp. 177–210

— 1979: 'Introduction' in G. Broderick, ed. *Five Stories from the Old Testament Apocrypha in Manx Gaelic*, Douglas, YCG

— 1981: *Lessoonyn Sodjey 'sy Ghailck Vanninagh*, Douglas, YCG

— 1984: 'The Manx Language', in P. Trudgill, ed. *Language in the British Isles*, Cambridge, Cambridge University Press